ON CUSTOM AND MYTH

ON CUSTOM AND MYTH

Andrew Lang

To E. B. Tylor,

author of 'Primitive Culture,'

these studies of the oldest stories are dedicated.

INTRODUCTION.

Though some of the essays in this volume have appeared in various serials, the majority of them were written expressly for their present purpose, and they are now arranged in a designed order. During some years of study of Greek, Indian, and savage mythologies, I have become more and more impressed with a sense of the inadequacy of the prevalent method of comparative mythology. That method is based on the belief that myths are the result of a disease of language, as the pearl is the result of a disease of the oyster. It is argued that men at some period, or periods, spoke in a singular style of coloured and concrete language, and that their children retained the phrases of this language after losing hold of the original meaning. The consequence was the growth of myths about supposed persons, whose names had originally been mere 'appellations.' In conformity with this hypothesis the method of comparative mythology examines the proper names which occur in myths. The notion is that these names contain a key to the meaning of the story, and that, in fact, of the story the names are the germs and the oldest surviving part.

The objections to this method are so numerous that it is difficult to state them briefly. The attempt, however, must be made. To desert the path opened by the most eminent scholars is in itself presumptuous; the least that an innovator can do is to give his reasons for advancing in a novel direction. If this were a question of scholarship merely, it would be simply foolhardy to differ from men like Max Müller, Adalbert Kuhn, Bréal, and many others. But a revolutionary mythologist is encouraged by finding that these scholars usually differ from each other. Examples will be found chiefly in the essays styled 'The Myth of Cronus,' 'A Far-travelled Tale,' and 'Cupid and Psyche.' Why, then, do distinguished scholars and mythologists reach such different goals? Clearly because their method is so precarious.

They all analyse the names in myths; but, where one scholar decides that the name is originally Sanskrit, another holds that it is purely Greek, and a third, perhaps, is all for an Accadian etymology, or a Semitic derivation. Again, even when scholars agree as to the original root from which a name springs, they differ as much as ever as to the meaning of the name in its present place. The inference is, that the analysis of names, on which the whole edifice of philological 'comparative mythology' rests, is a foundation of shifting sand. The method is called 'orthodox,' but, among those who practise it, there is none of the beautiful unanimity of orthodoxy.

These objections are not made by the unscholarly anthropologist alone. Curtius has especially remarked the difficulties which beset the 'etymological operation' in the case of proper names. 'Peculiarly dubious and perilous is mythological etymology. Are we to seek the sources of the divine names in aspects of nature, or in moral conceptions; in special Greek geographical conditions, or in natural circumstances which are everywhere the same: in dawn with her rays, or in clouds with their floods; are we to seek the origin of the names of heroes in things historical and human, or in physical phenomena?'[1] Professor Tiele, of Leyden, says much the same thing: 'The uncertainties are great, and there is a constant risk of taking mere *jeux d'esprit* for scientific results.'[2] Every name has, if we can discover or conjecture it, a meaning. That meaning—be it 'large' or 'small,' 'loud' or 'bright,' 'wise' or 'dark,' 'swift' or 'slow'—is always capable of being explained as an epithet of the sun, or of the cloud, or of both. Whatever, then, a name may signify, some scholars will find that it originally denoted the cloud, if they belong to one school, or the sun or dawn, if they belong to another faction. Obviously this process is a mere *jeu d'esprit*. This logic would be admitted in no other science, and, by similar arguments, any name whatever might be shown to be appropriate to a solar hero.

---

[1] Compare De Cara: *Essame Critico*, xx. i.
[2] *Revue de l'Hist. des Rel.* ii. 136.

The scholarly method has now been applied for many years, and what are the results? The ideas attained by the method have been so popularised that they are actually made to enter into the education of children, and are published in primers and catechisms of mythology. But what has a discreet scholar to say to the whole business? 'The difficult task of interpreting mythical names has, so far, produced few certain results'—so writes Otto Schrader. [3] Though Schrader still has hopes of better things, it is admitted that the present results are highly disputable. In England, where one set of these results has become an article of faith, readers chiefly accept the opinions of a single etymological school, and thus escape the difficulty of making up their minds when scholars differ. But differ scholars do, so widely and so often, that scarcely any solid advantages have been gained in mythology from the philological method.

The method of philological mythology is thus discredited by the disputes of its adherents. The system may be called orthodox, but it is an orthodoxy which alters with every new scholar who enters the sacred enclosure. Even were there more harmony, the analysis of names could throw little light on myths. In stories the names may well be, and often demonstrably are, the latest, not the original, feature. Tales, at first told of 'Somebody,' get new names attached to them, and obtain a new local habitation, wherever they wander. 'One of the leading personages to be met in the traditions of the world is really no more than—Somebody. There is nothing this wondrous creature cannot achieve; one only restriction binds him at all—that the name he assumes shall have some sort of congruity with the office he undertakes, *and even from this he oftentimes breaks loose.*'[4] We may be pretty sure that the adventures of Jason, Perseus, Œdipous, were originally told only of 'Somebody.' The names are later additions, and vary in various lands. A glance at the essay on 'Cupid and Psyche' will show that a history like theirs is known, where neither they nor

---

[3] *Sprachvergleichung und Urgeschichte*, p. 431.
[4] *Prim. Cult.* i. 394.

their counterparts in the Veda, Urvasi and Pururavas, were ever heard of; while the incidents of the Jason legend are familiar where no Greek word was ever spoken. Finally, the names in common use among savages are usually derived from natural phenomena, often from clouds, sky, sun, dawn. If, then, a name in a myth can be proved to mean cloud, sky, sun, or what not (and usually one set of scholars find clouds, where others see the dawn), we must not instantly infer that the myth is a nature-myth. Though, doubtless, the heroes in it were never real people, the names are as much common names of real people in the savage state, as Smith and Brown are names of civilised men.

For all these reasons, but chiefly because of the fact that stories are usually anonymous at first, that names are added later, and that stories naturally crystallise round any famous name, heroic, divine, or human, the process of analysis of names is most precarious and untrustworthy. A story is told of Zeus: Zeus means sky, and the story is interpreted by scholars as a sky myth. The modern interpreter forgets, first, that to the myth-maker sky did not at all mean the same thing as it means to him. Sky meant, not an airy, infinite, radiant vault, but a person, and, most likely, a savage person. Secondly, the interpreter forgets that the tale (say the tale of Zeus, Demeter, and the mutilated Ram) may have been originally anonymous, and only later attributed to Zeus, as unclaimed jests are attributed to Sheridan or Talleyrand. Consequently no heavenly phenomena will be the basis and explanation of the story. If one thing in mythology be certain, it is that myths are always changing masters, that the old tales are always being told with new names. Where, for example, is the value of a philological analysis of the name of Jason? As will be seen in the essay 'A Far-travelled Tale,' the analysis of the name of Jason is fanciful, precarious, disputed, while the essence of his myth is current in Samoa, Finland, North America, Madagascar, and other lands, where the name was never heard, and where the characters in the story have other names or are anonymous.

For these reasons, and others too many to be adduced here, I have ventured to differ from the current opinion that myths must be interpreted chiefly by philological analysis of names. The system adopted here is explained in the first essay, called 'The Method of Folklore.' The name, Folklore, is not a good one, but 'comparative mythology' is usually claimed exclusively by the philological interpreters.

The second essay, 'The Bull-Roarer,' is intended to show that certain peculiarities in the Greek mysteries occur also in the mysteries of savages, and that on Greek soil they are survivals of savagery.

'The Myth of Cronus' tries to prove that the first part of the legend is a savage nature-myth, surviving in Greek religion, while the sequel is a set of ideas common to savages.

'Cupid and Psyche' traces another Aryan myth among savage races, and attempts to show that the myth may have had its origin in a rule of barbarous etiquette.

'A Far-travelled Tale' examines a part of the Jason myth. This myth appears neither to be an explanation of natural phenomena (like part of the Myth of Cronus), nor based on a widespread custom (like Cupid and Psyche.) The question is asked whether the story may have been diffused by slow filtration from race to race all over the globe, as there seems no reason why it should have been invented separately (as a myth explanatory of natural phenomena or of customs might be) in many different places.

'Apollo and the Mouse' suggests hypothetically, as a possible explanation of the tie between the God and the Beast, that Apollo-worship superseded, but did not eradicate, Totemism. The suggestion is little more than a conjecture.

'Star Myths' points out that Greek myths of stars are a survival from the savage stage of fancy in which such stories are natural.

'Moly and Mandragora' is a study of the Greek, the modern, and the Hottentot folklore of magical herbs, with a criticism of a scholarly and philological hypothesis, according to which Moly is the dog-star, and Circe the moon.

'The Kalevala' is an account of the Finnish national poem; of all poems that in which the popular, as opposed to the artistic, spirit is strongest. The Kalevala is thus a link between *Märchen* and *Volkslieder* on one side, and epic poetry on the other.

'The Divining Rod' is a study of a European and civilised superstition, which is singular in its comparative lack of copious savage analogues.

'Hottentot Mythology' is a criticism of the philological method, applied to savage myth.

'Fetichism and the Infinite,' is a review of Mr. Max Müller's theory that a sense of the Infinite is the germ of religion, and that Fetichism is secondary, and a corruption. This essay also contains a defence of the *evidence* on which the anthropological method relies.

The remaining essays are studies of the 'History of the Family,' and of 'Savage Art.'

The essay on 'Savage Art' is reprinted, by the kind permission of Messrs. Cassell & Co., from two numbers (April and May, 1882) of the *Magazine of Art*. I have to thank the editors and publishers of the *Contemporary Review*, the *Cornhill Magazine*, and *Fraser's Magazine*, for leave to republish 'The Early History of the Family,' 'The Divining Rod,' and 'Star Myths,' and 'The Kalevala.' A few sentences in 'The Bull-Roarer,' and 'Hottentot Mythology,' appeared in essays in the *Saturday Review*, and some lines of 'The Method of Folklore' in the *Guardian*. To the editors of those journals also I owe thanks for their courteous permission to make this use of my old articles.

To Mr. E. B. Tylor and Mr. W. R. S. Ralston I must express my gratitude for the kindness with which they have always helped me in all difficulties.

I must apologise for the controversial matter in the volume. Controversy is always a thing to be avoided, but, in this particular case, when a system opposed to the prevalent method has to be advocated, controversy is unavoidable. My respect for the learning of my distinguished adversaries is none the less great because I am not convinced by their logic, and because my doubts are excited by their differences.

Perhaps, it should be added, that these essays are, so to speak, only flint-flakes from a neolithic workshop. This little book merely skirmishes (to change the metaphor) in front of a much more methodical attempt to vindicate the anthropological interpretation of myths. But lack of leisure and other causes make it probable that my 'Key to All Mythologies' will go the way of Mr. Casaubon's treatise.

THE METHOD OF FOLKLORE.

After the heavy rain of a thunderstorm has washed the soil, it sometimes happens that a child, or a rustic, finds a wedge-shaped piece of metal or a few triangular flints in a field or near a road. There was no such piece of metal, there were no such flints, lying there yesterday, and the finder is puzzled about the origin of the objects on which he has lighted. He carries them home, and the village wisdom determines that the wedge-shaped piece of metal is a 'thunderbolt,' or that the bits of flint are 'elf-shots,' the heads of fairy arrows. Such things are still treasured in remote nooks of England, and the 'thunderbolt' is applied to cure certain maladies by its touch.

As for the fairy arrows, we know that even in ancient Etruria they were looked on as magical, for we sometimes see their points set, as amulets, in the gold of Etruscan necklaces. In Perugia the arrowheads are still sold as charms. All educated people, of course, have long been aware that the metal wedge is a celt, or ancient bronze axe-head, and that it was not fairies, but the forgotten peoples of this island who used the arrows with the tips of flint. Thunder is only so far connected with them that the heavy rains loosen the surface soil, and lay bare its long hidden secrets.

There is a science, Archæology, which collects and compares the material relics of old races, the axes and arrow-heads. There is a form of study, Folklore, which collects and compares the similar but immaterial relics of old races, the surviving superstitions and stories, the ideas which are in our time but not of it. Properly speaking, folklore is only concerned with the legends, customs, beliefs, of the Folk, of the people, of the classes which have least been altered by education, which have shared least in progress. But the student of folklore soon finds that these unprogressive classes retain many of the beliefs and ways of savages, just as the Hebridean people use spindle-whorls of stone, and bake clay pots without the aid of the wheel, like modern South Sea Islanders, or like their own prehistoric ancestors.[5] The student of folklore is thus led to examine the usages, myths, and ideas of savages, which are still retained, in rude enough shape, by the European peasantry. Lastly, he observes that a few similar customs and ideas survive in the most conservative elements of the life of educated peoples, in ritual, ceremonial, and religious traditions and myths. Though such remains are rare in England, we may note the custom of leading the dead soldier's horse behind his master to the grave, a relic of days when the horse would have been sacrificed.[6] We may observe the persistence of the ceremony by which the monarch, at his coronation, takes his seat on the sacred stone of Scone, probably an ancient fetich stone. Not to speak, here, of our own religious traditions, the old vein of savage rite and belief is found very near the surface of ancient Greek religion. It needs but some stress of circumstance, something answering to the storm shower that reveals the flint arrow-heads, to bring savage ritual to the surface of classical religion. In sore need, a human victim was only too likely to be demanded; while a feast-day, or a mystery, set the Greeks dancing serpent-dances or bear-dances like Red Indians, or swimming with sacred pigs, or leaping about in imitation of wolves, or holding a dog-feast, and offering dog's flesh to the gods.[7] Thus the student of folklore soon finds that he must enlarge his field, and examine, not only popular European story and practice, but savage ways and ideas, and the myths and usages of the educated classes in civilised races. In this extended sense the term 'folklore' will frequently be used in the following essays. The idea of the

[5] A study of the contemporary stone age in Scotland will be found in Mitchell's *Past and Present*.

[6] About twenty years ago, the widow of an Irish farmer, in Derry, killed her deceased husband's horse. When remonstrated with by her landlord, she said, 'Would you have my man go about on foot in the next world?' She was quite in the savage intellectual stage.

[7] At the solemn festival suppers, ordained for the honour of the gods, they forget not to serve up certain dishes of young whelp's flesh. (Pliny, *H. N.* xxix. 4.)

writer is that mythology cannot fruitfully be studied apart from folklore, while some knowledge of anthropology is required in both sciences.

The science of Folklore, if we may call it a science, finds everywhere, close to the surface of civilised life, the remains of ideas as old as the stone elf-shots, older than the celt of bronze. In proverbs and riddles, and nursery tales and superstitions, we detect the relics of a stage of thought, which is dying out in Europe, but which still exists in many parts of the world. Now, just as the flint arrow-heads are scattered everywhere, in all the continents and isles, and everywhere are much alike, and bear no very definite marks of the special influence of race, so it is with the habits and legends investigated by the student of folklore. The stone arrow-head buried in a Scottish cairn is like those which were interred with Algonquin chiefs. The flints found in Egyptian soil, or beside the tumulus on the plain of Marathon, nearly resemble the stones which tip the reed arrow of the modern Samoyed. Perhaps only a skilled experience could discern, in a heap of such arrow-heads, the specimens which are found in America or Africa from those which are unearthed in Europe. Even in the products of more advanced industry, we see early pottery, for example, so closely alike everywhere that, in the British Museum, Mexican vases have, ere now, been mixed up on the same shelf with archaic vessels from Greece. In the same way, if a superstition or a riddle were offered to a student of folklore, he would have much difficulty in guessing its *provenance*, and naming the race from which it was brought. Suppose you tell a folklorist that, in a certain country, when anyone sneezes, people say 'Good luck to you,' the student cannot say *à priori* what country you refer to, what race you have in your thoughts. It may be Florida, as Florida was when first discovered; it may be Zululand, or West Africa, or ancient Rome, or Homeric Greece, or Palestine. In all these, and many other regions, the sneeze was welcomed as an auspicious omen. The little superstition is as widely distributed as the flint arrow-heads. Just as the object and use of the arrow-heads became intelligible when we found similar

16

weapons in actual use among savages, so the salutation to the sneezer becomes intelligible when we learn that the savage has a good reason for it. He thinks the sneeze expels an evil spirit. Proverbs, again, and riddles are as universally scattered, and the Wolufs puzzle over the same *devinettes* as the Scotch schoolboy or the Breton peasant. Thus, for instance, the Wolufs of Senegal ask each other, 'What flies for ever, and rests never?'—Answer, 'The Wind.' 'Who are the comrades that always fight, and never hurt each other?'—'The Teeth.' In France, as we read in the 'Recueil de Calembours,' the people ask, 'What runs faster than a horse, crosses water, and is not wet?'—Answer, 'The Sun.' The Samoans put the riddle, 'A man who stands between two ravenous fishes?'—Answer, 'The tongue between the teeth.' Again, 'There are twenty brothers, each with a hat on his head?'—Answer, 'Fingers and toes, with nails for hats.' This is like the French '*un père a douze fils?*'—'*l'an.*' A comparison of M. Rolland's 'Devinettes' with the Woluf conundrums of Boilat, the Samoan examples in Turner's' Samoa,' and the Scotch enigmas collected by Chambers, will show the identity of peasant and savage humour.

A few examples, less generally known, may be given to prove that the beliefs of folklore are not peculiar to any one race or stock of men. The first case is remarkable: it occurs in Mexico and Ceylon—nor are we aware that it is found elsewhere. In *Macmillan's Magazine* [8] is published a paper by Mrs. Edwards, called 'The Mystery of the Pezazi.' The events described in this narrative occurred on August 28, 1876, in a bungalow some thirty miles from Badiella. The narrator occupied a new house on an estate called Allagalla. Her native servants soon asserted that the place was haunted by a Pezazi. The English visitors saw and heard nothing extraordinary till a certain night: an abridged account of what happened then may be given in the words of Mrs. Edwards:—

---

[8] Nov. 1880.

Wrapped in dreams, I lay on the night in question tranquilly sleeping, but gradually roused to a perception that discordant sounds disturbed the serenity of my slumber. Loth to stir, I still dozed on, the sounds, however, becoming, as it seemed, more determined to make themselves heard; and I awoke to the consciousness that they proceeded from a belt of adjacent jungle, and resembled the noise that would be produced by some person felling timber.

Shutting my ears to the disturbance, I made no sign, until, with an expression of impatience, E--- suddenly started up, when I laid a detaining grasp upon his arm, murmuring that there was no need to think of rising at present—it must be quite early, and the kitchen cooly was doubtless cutting fire-wood in good time. E--- responded, in a tone of slight contempt, that no one could be cutting fire-wood at that hour, and the sounds were more suggestive of felling jungle; and he then inquired how long I had been listening to them. Now thoroughly aroused, I replied that I had heard the sounds for some time, at first confusing them with my dreams, but soon sufficiently awakening to the fact that they were no mere phantoms of my imagination, but a reality. During our conversation the noises became more distinct and loud; blow after blow resounded, as of the axe descending upon the tree, followed by the crash of the falling timber. Renewed blows announced the repetition of the operations on another tree, and continued till several were devastated.

It is unnecessary to tell more of the tale. In spite of minute examinations and close search, no solution of the mystery of the noises, on this or any other occasion, was ever found. The natives, of course, attributed the disturbance to the *Pezazi*, or goblin. No one, perhaps, has asserted that the Aztecs were connected by ties of race with the people of Ceylon. Yet, when the Spaniards conquered Mexico, and when Sahagun (one of the earliest missionaries) collected the legends of the people, he found them, like the Cingalese, strong believers in the mystic tree-felling. We translate Sahagun's account of the 'midnight axe':—

When so any man heareth the sound of strokes in the night, as if one were felling trees, he reckons it an evil boding. And this sound they call youaltepuztli (youalli, night; and tepuztli, copper), which signifies 'the midnight hatchet.' This noise cometh about the time of the first sleep, when all men slumber soundly, and the night is still. The sound of strokes smitten was first noted by the temple-servants, called tlamacazque, at the hour when they go in the night to make their offering of reeds or of boughs of pine, for so was their custom, and this penance they did on the neighbouring hills, and that when the night was far spent. Whenever they heard such a sound as one makes when he splits wood with an axe (a noise that may be heard afar off), they drew thence an omen of evil, and were afraid, and said that the sounds were part of the witchery of Tezeatlipoca, that often thus dismayeth men who journey in the night. Now, when tidings of these things came to a certain brave man, one exercised in war, he drew near, being guided by the sound, till he came to the very cause of the hubbub. And when he came upon it, with difficulty he caught it, for the thing was hard to catch: natheless at last he overtook that which ran before him; and behold, it was a man without a heart, and, on either side of the chest, two holes that opened and shut, and so made the noise. Then the man put his hand within the breast of the figure and grasped the breast and shook it hard, demanding some grace or gift.

As a rule, the grace demanded was power to make captives in war. The curious coincidence of the 'midnight axe,' occurring in lands so remote as Ceylon and Mexico, and the singular attestation by an English lady of the actual existence of the disturbance, makes this *youaltepuztli* one of the quaintest things in the province of the folklorist. But, whatever the cause of the noise, or of the beliefs connected with the noise, may be, no one would explain them as the result of community of *race* between Cingalese and Aztecs. Nor would this explanation be offered to account for the Aztec and English belief that the creaking of furniture is an omen of death in a house. Obviously, these opinions are the expression of a common state of superstitious fancy, not the signs of an original community of origin.

Let us take another piece of folklore. All North-country English folk know the *Kernababy*. The custom of the 'Kernababy' is commonly observed in England, or, at all events, in Scotland, where the writer has seen many a kernababy. The last gleanings of the last field are bound up in a rude imitation of the human shape, and dressed in some tag-rags of finery. The usage has fallen into the conservative hands of children, but of old 'the Maiden' was a regular image of the harvest goddess, which, with a sickle and sheaves in her arms, attended by a crowd of reapers, and accompanied with music, followed the last carts home to the farm.[9] It is odd enough that the 'Maiden' should exactly translate Κοπη, the old Sicilian name of the daughter of Demeter. 'The Maiden' has dwindled, then, among us to the rudimentary kernababy; but ancient Peru had her own Maiden, her Harvest Goddess. Here it is easy to trace the natural idea at the basis of the superstitious practice which links the shores of the Pacific with our own northern coast. Just as a portion of the yule-log and of the Christmas bread were kept all the year through, a kind of nest-egg of plenteous food and fire, so the kernababy, English or Peruvian, is an earnest that corn will not fail all through the year, till next harvest comes. For this reason the kernababy used to be treasured from autumn's end to autumn's end, though now it commonly disappears very soon after the harvest home. It is thus that Acosta describes, in Grimston's old translation (1604), the Peruvian kernababy and the Peruvian harvest home:—

This feast is made comming from the chacra or farme unto the house, saying certaine songs, and praying that the Mays (maize) may long continue, the which they call Mama cora.

What a chance this word offers to etymologists of the old school: how promptly they would recognise, in *mama* mother— μητηρ, and in *cora*—κοπη, the Mother and the Maiden, the

---

[9] 'Ah, once again may I plant the great fan on her corn-heap, while she stands smiling by, Demeter of the threshing floor, with sheaves and poppies in her hands' (Theocritus, vii. 155-157).

feast of Demeter and Persephone! However, the days of that old school of antiquarianism are numbered. To return to the Peruvian harvest home:—

They take a certaine portion of the most fruitefull of the Mays that growes in their farmes, the which they put in a certaine granary which they do calle Pirua, with certaine ceremonies, watching three nightes; they put this Mays in the richest garments they have, and, being thus wrapped and dressed, they worship this Pirua, and hold it in great veneration, saying it is the Mother of the Mays of their inheritances, and that by this means the Mays augments and is preserved. In this moneth they make a particular sacrifice, and the witches demand of this Pirua, 'if it hath strength sufficient to continue until the next yeare,' and if it answers 'no,' then they carry this Mays to the farme to burne, whence they brought it, according to every man's power, then they make another Pirua, with the same ceremonies, saying that they renue it, to the ende that the seede of the Mays may not perish.

The idea that the maize can speak need not surprise us; the Mexican held much the same belief, according to Sahagun:—

It was thought that if some grains of maize fell on the ground, he who saw them lying there was bound to lift them, wherein, if he failed, he harmed the maize, which plained itself of him to God, saying, 'Lord, punish this man, who saw me fallen and raised me not again; punish him with famine, that he may learn not to hold me in dishonour.'

Well, in all this affair of the Scotch kernababy, and the Peruvian *Mama cora*, we need no explanation beyond the common simple ideas of human nature. We are not obliged to hold, either that the Peruvians and Scotch are akin by blood, nor that, at some forgotten time, they met each other, and borrowed each other's superstitions. Again, when we find Odysseus sacrificing a black sheep to the dead, [10]and when we read that the Ovahereroes in South Africa also appease with a black sheep the spirits of the departed, we do not feel it necessary to hint that the

---

[10] *Odyssey*, xi. 32.

21

Ovahereroes are of Greek descent, or have borrowed their ritual from the Greeks. The connection between the colour black, and mourning for the dead, is natural and almost universal.

Examples like these might be adduced in any number. We might show how, in magic, negroes of Barbadoes make clay effigies of their enemies, and pierce them, just as Greeks did in Plato's time, or the men of Accad in remotest antiquity. We might remark the Australian black putting sharp bits of quartz in the tracks of an enemy who has gone by, that the enemy may be lamed; and we might point to Boris Godunof forbidding the same practice among the Russians. We might watch Scotch, and Australians, and Jews, and French, and Aztecs spreading dust round the body of a dead man, that the footprints of his ghost, or of other ghosts, may be detected next morning. We might point to a similar device in a modern novel, where the presence of a ghost is suspected, as proof of the similar workings of the Australian mind and of the mind of Mrs. Riddell. We shall later turn to ancient Greece, and show how the serpent-dances, the habit of smearing the body with clay, and other odd rites of the mysteries, were common to Hellenic religion, and to the religion of African, Australian, and American tribes.

Now, with regard to all these strange usages, what is the method of folklore? The method is, when an apparently irrational and anomalous custom is found in any country, to look for a country where a similar practice is found, and where the practice is no longer irrational and anomalous, but in harmony with the manners and ideas of the people among whom it prevails. That Greeks should dance about in their mysteries with harmless serpents in their hands looks quite unintelligible. When a wild tribe of Red Indians does the same thing, as a trial of courage, with real rattlesnakes, we understand the Red Man's motives, and may conjecture that similar motives once existed among the ancestors of the Greeks. Our method, then, is to compare the seemingly meaningless customs or manners of civilised races with the similar customs and manners which exist among the uncivilised and still retain their meaning. It is not necessary for comparison of this sort that the uncivilised and the civilised race should be of the same stock, nor need we prove that they were ever in contact with each other. Similar conditions of mind produce similar practices, apart from identity of race, or borrowing of ideas and manners.

Let us return to the example of the flint arrowheads. Everywhere neolithic arrow-heads are pretty much alike. The cause of the resemblance is no more than this, that men, with the same needs, the same materials, and the same rude instruments, everywhere produced the same kind of arrow-head. No hypothesis of interchange of ideas nor of community of race is needed to explain the resemblance of form in the missiles. Very early pottery in any region is, for the same causes, like very early pottery in any other region. The same sort of similarity was explained by the same resemblances in human nature, when we touched on the identity of magical practices and of superstitious beliefs. This method is fairly well established and orthodox when we deal with usages and superstitious beliefs; but may we apply the same method when we deal with myths?

Here a difficulty occurs. Mythologists, as a rule, are averse to the method of folklore. They think it scientific to compare only the myths of races which speak languages of the same family, and of races which have, in historic times, been actually in proved contact with each other. Thus, most mythologists hold it correct to compare Greek, Slavonic, Celtic, and Indian stories, because Greeks, Slavs, Celts, and Hindoos all speak languages of the same family. Again, they hold it correct to compare Chaldæan and Greek myths, because the Greeks and the Chaldæans were brought into contact through the Phœnicians, and by other intermediaries, such as the Hittites. But the same mythologists will vow that it is unscientific to compare a Maori or a Hottentot or an Eskimo myth with an Aryan story, because Maoris and Eskimo and Hottentots do not speak languages akin to that of Greece, nor can we show that the ancestors of Greeks, Maoris, Hottentots, and Eskimo were ever in contact with each other in historical times.

Now the peculiarity of the method of folklore is that it will venture to compare (with due caution and due examination of evidence) the myths of the most widely severed races. Holding that myth is a product of the early human fancy, working on the most rudimentary knowledge of the outer world, the student of folklore thinks that differences of race do not much affect the early mythopœic faculty. He will not be surprised if Greeks and Australian blacks are in the same tale.

In each case, he holds, all the circumstances of the case must be examined and considered. For instance, when the Australians tell a myth about the Pleiades very like the Greek myth of the Pleiades, we must ask a number of questions. Is the Australian version authentic? Can the people who told it have heard it from a European? If these questions are answered so as to make it apparent that the Australian Pleiad myth is of genuine native origin, we need not fly to the conclusion that the Australians are a lost and forlorn branch of the Aryan race. Two other hypotheses present themselves. First, the human species is of unknown antiquity. In the moderate allowance of 250,000 years, there is time for stories to have wandered all round the world, as the Aggry beads of Ashanti have probably crossed the continent from Egypt, as the Asiatic jade (if Asiatic it be) has arrived in Swiss lake-dwellings, as an African trade-cowry is said to have been found in a Cornish barrow, as an Indian Ocean shell has been discovered in a prehistoric bone-cave in Poland. This slow filtration of tales is not absolutely out of the question. Two causes would especially help to transmit myths. The first is slavery and slave-stealing, the second is the habit of capturing brides from alien stocks, and the law which forbids marriage with a woman of a man's own family. Slaves and captured brides would bring their native legends among alien peoples.

But there is another possible way of explaining the resemblance (granting that it is proved) of the Greek and Australian Pleiad myth. The object of both myths is to account for the grouping and other phenomena of the constellations. May not similar explanatory stories have occurred to the ancestors of the Australians, and to the ancestors of the Greeks, however remote their home, while they were still in the savage condition? The best way to investigate this point is to collect all known savage and civilised stellar myths, and see what points they have in common. If they all agree in character, though the Greek tales are full of grace, while those of the Australians or Brazilians are rude enough, we may plausibly account for the similarity of myths, as we accounted for the similarity of flint arrow-heads. The myths, like the arrow-heads, resemble each other because they were originally framed to meet the same needs out of the same material. In the case of the arrow-heads, the need was for something hard, heavy, and sharp—the material was flint. In the case of the myths, the need was to explain certain phenomena— the material (so to speak) was an early state of the human mind, to which all objects seemed equally endowed with human personality, and to which no metamorphosis appeared impossible.

In the following essays, then, the myths and customs of various peoples will be compared, even when these peoples talk languages of alien families, and have never (as far as history shows us) been in actual contact. Our method throughout will be to place the usage, or myth, which is unintelligible when found among a civilised race, beside the similar myth which is intelligible enough when it is found among savages. A mean term will be found in the folklore preserved by the non-progressive classes in a progressive people. This folklore represents, in the midst of a civilised race, the savage ideas out of which civilisation has been evolved. The conclusion will usually be that the fact which puzzles us by its presence in civilisation is a relic surviving from the time when the ancestors of a civilised race were in the state of savagery. By this method it is not necessary that 'some sort of genealogy should be established' between the Australian and the Greek narrators of a similar myth, nor between the Greek and Australian possessors of a similar usage. The hypothesis will be that the myth, or usage, is common to both races, not because of original community of stock, not because of contact and borrowing, but because the ancestors of the Greeks passed through the savage intellectual condition in which we find the Australians.

The questions may be asked, Has race nothing, then, to do with myth? Do peoples never consciously borrow myths from each other? The answer is, that race has a great deal to do with the development of myth, if it be race which confers on a people its national genius, and its capacity of becoming civilised. If race does this, then race affects, in the most powerful manner, the ultimate development of myth. No one is likely to confound a Homeric myth with a myth from the Edda, nor either with a myth from a Brahmana, though in all three cases the substance, the original set of ideas, may be much the same. In all three you have anthropomorphic gods, capable of assuming animal shapes, tricky, capricious, limited in many undivine ways, yet endowed with magical powers. So far the mythical gods of Homer, of the Edda, of any of the Brahmanas, are on a level with each other, and not much above the gods of savage mythology. This stuff of myth is *quod semper, quod ubique, quod ab omnibus*, and is the original gift of the savage intellect. But the final treatment, the ultimate literary form of the myth, varies in each race. Homeric gods, like Red Indian, Thlinkeet, or Australian gods, can assume the shapes of birds. But when we read, in Homer, of the arming of Athene, the hunting of Artemis, the vision of golden Aphrodite, the apparition of Hermes, like a young man when the flower of youth is loveliest, then we recognise the effect of race upon myth, the effect of the Greek genius at work on rude material. Between the Olympians and a Thlinkeet god there is all the difference that exists between the Demeter of Cnidos and an image from Easter Island. Again, the Scandinavian gods, when their tricks are laid aside, when Odin is neither assuming the shape of worm nor of raven, have a martial dignity, a noble enduring spirit of their own. Race comes out in that, as it does in the endless sacrifices, soma drinking, magical austerities, and puerile follies of Vedic and Brahmanic gods, the deities of a people fallen early into its sacerdotage and priestly second childhood. Thus race declares itself in the ultimate literary form

26

and character of mythology, while the common savage basis and stuff of myths may be clearly discerned in the horned, and cannibal, and shape-shifting, and adulterous gods of Greece, of India, of the North. They all show their common savage origin, when the poet neglects Freya's command and tells of what the gods did 'in the morning of Time.'

As to borrowing, we have already shown that in prehistoric times there must have been much transmission of myth. The migrations of peoples, the traffic in slaves, the law of exogamy, which always keeps bringing alien women into the families—all these things favoured the migration of myth. But the process lies behind history: we can only guess at it, we can seldom trace a popular legend on its travels. In the case of the cultivated ancient peoples, we know that they themselves believed they had borrowed their religions from each other. When the Greeks first found the Egyptians practising mysteries like their own, they leaped to the conclusion that their own rites had been imported from Egypt. We, who know that both Greek and Egyptian rites had many points in common with those of Mandans, Zunis, Bushmen, Australians—people quite unconnected with Egypt—feel less confident about the hypothesis of borrowing. We may, indeed, regard Adonis, and Zeus Bagæus, and Melicertes, as importations from Phœnicia. In later times, too, the Greeks, and still more the Romans, extended a free hospitality to alien gods and legends, to Serapis, Isis, the wilder Dionysiac revels, and so forth. But this habit of borrowing was regarded with disfavour by pious conservatives, and was probably, in the width of its hospitality at least, an innovation. As Tiele remarks, we cannot derive Dionysus from the Assyrian *Daian nisi,* 'judge of men,' a name of the solar god Samas, without ascertaining that the wine-god exercised judicial functions, and was a god of the sun. These derivations, 'shocking to common sense,' are to be distrusted as part of the intoxication of new learning. Some Assyrian scholars actually derive *Hades* from *Bit Edi* or *Bit Hadi*—'though, unluckily,' says Tiele, 'there is no such word in the Assyrian text.'

27

On the whole topic Tiele's essay [11] deserves to be consulted. Granting, then, that elements in the worship of Dionysus, Aphrodite, and other gods, may have been imported with the strange Ægypto-Assyrian vases and jewels of the Sidonians, we still find the same basis of rude savage ideas. We may push back a god from Greece to Phœnicia, from Phœnicia to Accadia, but, at the end of the end, we reach a legend full of myths like those which Bushmen tell by the camp-fire, Eskimo in their dark huts, and Australians in the shade of the *gunyeh*—myths cruel, puerile, obscene, like the fancies of the savage myth-makers from which they sprang.

[11] *Rev. de l'Hist. des Rel.*, vol. ii.

THE BULL-ROARER.
A Study of the Mysteries.

As the belated traveller makes his way through the monotonous plains of Australia, through the Bush, with its level expanses and clumps of grey-blue gum trees, he occasionally hears a singular sound. Beginning low, with a kind of sharp tone thrilling through a whirring noise, it grows louder and louder, till it becomes a sort of fluttering windy roar. If the traveller be a new comer, he is probably puzzled to the last degree. If he be an Englishman, country-bred, he says to himself, 'Why, that is the bull-roarer.' If he knows the colony and the ways of the natives, he knows that the blacks are celebrating their tribal mysteries. The roaring noise is made to warn all women to keep out of the way. Just as Pentheus was killed (with the approval of Theocritus) because he profaned the rites of the women-worshippers of Dionysus, so, among the Australian blacks, men must, at their peril, keep out of the way of female, and women out of the way of male, celebrations.

The instrument which produces the sounds that warn women to remain afar is a toy familiar to English country lads. They call it the bull-roarer. The common bull-roarer is an inexpensive toy which anyone can make. I do not, however, recommend it to families, for two reasons. In the first place, it produces a most horrible and unexampled din, which endears it to the very young, but renders it detested by persons of mature age. In the second place, the character of the toy is such that it will almost infallibly break all that is fragile in the house where it is used, and will probably put out the eyes of some of the inhabitants. Having thus, I trust, said enough to prevent all good boys from inflicting bull-roarers on their parents, pastors, and masters, I proceed (in the interests of science) to show how the toy is made. Nothing can be less elaborate. You take a piece of the commonest wooden board, say the lid of a packing-case, about a sixth of an inch in thickness, and about eight inches long and three broad, and you sharpen the ends. When finished, the toy may be about the shape of a large bay-leaf, or a 'fish' used as a counter (that is how the New Zealanders make it), or the sides may be left plain in the centre, and only sharpened towards the extremities, as in an Australian example lent me by Mr. Tylor. Then tie a strong piece of string, about thirty inches long, to one end of the piece of wood and the bull-roarer (the Australian natives call it *turndun*, and the Greeks called it ρομβος) is complete. Now twist the end of the string tightly about your finger, and whirl the bull-roarer rapidly round and round. For a few moments nothing will happen. In a very interesting lecture delivered at the Royal Institution, Mr. Tylor once exhibited a bull-roarer. At first it did nothing particular when it was whirled round, and the audience began to fear that the experiment was like those chemical ones often exhibited at institutes in the country, which contribute at most a disagreeable odour to the education of the populace. But when the bull-roarer warmed to its work, it justified its name, producing what may best be described as a mighty rushing noise, as if some supernatural being 'fluttered and buzzed his wings with fearful roar.' Grown-up people, of course, are satisfied with a very brief experience of this din, but boys have always known the bull-roarer in England as one of the most efficient modes of making the hideous and unearthly noises in which it is the privilege of youth to delight.

The bull-roarer has, of all toys, the widest diffusion, and the most extraordinary history. To study the bull-roarer is to take a lesson in folklore. The instrument is found among the most widely severed peoples, savage and civilised, and is used in the celebration of savage and civilised mysteries. There are students who would found on this a hypothesis that the various races that use the bull-roarer all descend from the same stock. But the bull roarer is introduced here for the very purpose of showing that similar minds, working with simple means towards similar ends, might evolve the bull-roarer and its mystic uses anywhere. There is no need for a hypothesis of common origin, or of borrowing, to account for this widely diffused sacred object.

The bull-roarer has been, and is, a sacred and magical instrument in many and widely separated lands. It is found, always as a sacred instrument, employed in religious mysteries, in New Mexico, in Australia, in New Zealand, in ancient Greece, and in Africa; while, as we have seen, it is a peasant-boy's plaything in England. A number of questions are naturally suggested by the bull-roarer. Is it a thing invented once for all, and carried abroad over the world by wandering races, or handed on from one people and tribe to another? Or is the bull-roarer a toy that might be accidentally hit on in any country where men can sharpen wood and twist the sinews of animals into string? Was the thing originally a toy, and is its religious and mystical nature later; or was it originally one of the properties of the priest, or medicine-man, which in England has dwindled to a plaything? Lastly, was this mystical instrument at first employed in the rites of a civilised people like the Greeks, and was it in some way borrowed or inherited by South Africans, Australians, and New Mexicans? Or is it a mere savage invention, surviving (like certain other features of the Greek mysteries) from a distant stage of savagery? Our answer to all these questions is that in all probability the presence of the ρομβος, or bull-roarer, in Greek mysteries was a survival from the time when Greeks were in the social condition of Australians.

In the first place, the bull-roarer is associated with mysteries and initiations. Now mysteries and initiations are things that tend to dwindle and to lose their characteristic features as civilisation advances. The rites of baptism and confirmation are not secret and hidden; they are common to both sexes, they are publicly performed, and religion and morality of the purest sort blend in these ceremonies. There are no other initiations or mysteries that civilised modern man is expected necessarily to pass through. On the other hand, looking widely at human history, we find mystic rites and initiations numerous, stringent, severe, and magical in character, in proportion to the lack of civilisation in those who practise them. The less the civilisation, the more mysterious and the more cruel are the rites. The more cruel the rites, the less is the civilisation. The red-hot poker with which Mr. Bouncer terrified Mr. Verdant Green at the sham masonic rites would have been quite in place, a natural instrument of probationary torture, in the Freemasonry of Australians, Mandans, or Hottentots. In the mysteries of Demeter or Bacchus, in the mysteries of a civilised people, the red-hot poker, or any other instrument of torture, would have been out of place. But in the Greek mysteries, just as in those of South Africans, Red Indians, and Australians, the disgusting practice of bedaubing the neophyte with dirt and clay was preserved. We have nothing quite like that in modern initiations. Except at Sparta, Greeks dropped the tortures inflicted on boys and girls in the initiations superintended by the cruel Artemis.[12] But Greek

---

[12] Pausanias, iii. 15. When the boys were being cruelly scourged, the priestess of Artemis Orthia held an ancient barbaric wooden image of the goddess in her hands. If the boys were spared, the image grew heavy; the more they were tortured, the lighter grew the image. In Samoa the image (shark's teeth) of the god Taema is consulted before battle. 'If it felt heavy, that was a bad omen; if light, the sign was good'—the god was pleased (Turner's *Samoa*, p. 55).

mysteries retained the daubing with mud and the use of the bull-roarer. On the whole, then, and on a general view of the subject, we prefer to think that the bull-roarer in Greece was a survival from savage mysteries, not that the bull-roarer in New Mexico, New Zealand, Australia, and South Africa is a relic of civilisation.

Let us next observe a remarkable peculiarity of the *turndun*, or Australian bull-roarer. The bull-roarer in England is a toy. In Australia, according to Howitt and Fison, [13] the bull-roarer is regarded with religious awe. 'When, on lately meeting with two of the surviving Kurnai, I spoke to them of the turndun, they first looked cautiously round them to see that no one else was looking, and then answered me in undertones.' The chief peculiarity in connection with the turndun is that women may never look upon it. The Chepara tribe, who call it *bribbun*, have a custom that, 'if seen by a woman, or shown by a man to a woman, the punishment to both is *death*.'

Among the Kurnai, the sacred mystery of the turndun is preserved by a legend, which gives a supernatural sanction to

[13] *Kamilaroi and Kurnai*, p. 268.

secrecy. When boys go through the mystic ceremony of initiation they are shown turnduns, or bull-roarers, and made to listen to their hideous din. They are then told that, if ever a woman is allowed to see a turndun, the earth will open, and water will cover the globe. The old men point spears at the boy's eyes, saying: 'If you tell this to any woman you will die, you will see the ground broken up and like the sea; if you tell this to any woman, or to any child, you will be killed!' As in Athens, in Syria, and among the Mandans, the deluge-tradition of Australia is connected with the mysteries. In Gippsland there is a tradition of the deluge. 'Some children of the Kurnai in playing about found a turndun, which they took home to the camp and showed the women. Immediately the earth crumbled away, and it was all water, and the Kurnai were drowned.'

In consequence of all this mummery the Australian women attach great sacredness to the very name of the turndun. They are much less instructed in their own theology than the men of the tribe. One woman believed she had heard Pundjel, the chief supernatural being, descend in a mighty rushing noise, that is, in the sound of the turndun, when boys were being 'made men,' or initiated.[14] On turnduns the Australian sorcerers can fly up to heaven. Turnduns carved with imitations of water-flowers are used by medicine-men in rain-making. New Zealand also has her bull-roarers; some of them, carved in relief, are in the Christy Museum, and one is engraved here. I have no direct evidence as to the use of these Maori bull-roarers in the Maori mysteries. Their employment, however, may perhaps be provisionally inferred.

One can readily believe that the New Zealand bull-roarer may be whirled by any man who is repeating a *Karakia*, or 'charm to raise the wind':—

> Loud wind,
> Lasting wind,
> Violent whistling wind,

---

[14] Fison, *Journal Anthrop. Soc.*, Nov. 1883.

Dig up the calm reposing sky,
Come, come.

In New Zealand [15] 'the natives regarded the wind as an indication of the presence of their god,' a superstition not peculiar to Maori religion. The 'cold wind' felt blowing over the hands at spiritualistic *séances* is also regarded (by psychical researchers) as an indication of the presence of supernatural beings. The windy roaring noise made by the bull-roarer might readily be considered by savages, either as an invitation to a god who should present himself in storm, or as a proof of his being at hand. We have seen that this view was actually taken by an Australian woman. The hymn called 'breath,' or *haha*, a hymn to the mystic wind, is pronounced by Maori priests at the moment of the initiation of young men in the tribal mysteries. It is a mere conjecture, and possibly enough capable of disproof, but we have a suspicion that the use of the *mystica vannus Iacchi* was a mode of raising a sacred wind analogous to that employed by whirlers of the turndun. [16]

Servius, the ancient commentator on Virgil, mentions, among other opinions, this—that the *vannus* was a sieve, and that it symbolised the purifying effect of the mysteries. But it is clear that Servius was only guessing; and he offers other explanations, among them that the *vannus* was a crate to hold offerings, *primitias frugum*.

We have studied the bull-roarer in Australia, we have caught a glimpse of it in England. Its existence on the American continent is proved by letters from New Mexico, and by a passage in Mr. Frank Cushing's 'Adventures in Zuni.'[17] In Zuni, too,

---

[15] Taylor's *New Zealand*, p. 181.

[16] This is not the view of le Père Lafitau, a learned Jesuit missionary in North America, who wrote (1724) a work on savage manners, compared with the manners of heathen antiquity. Lafitau, who was greatly struck with the resemblances between Greek and Iroquois or Carib initiations, takes Servius's other explanation of the *mystica vannus*, 'an osier vessel containing rural offerings of first fruits.' This exactly answers, says Lafitau, to the Carib *Matoutou*, on which they offer sacred cassava cakes.

[17] The Century Magazine, May 1883.

among a semi-civilised Indian tribe, or rather a tribe which has left the savage for the barbaric condition, we find the bull-roarer. Here, too, the instrument—a 'slat,' Mr. Gushing calls it—is used as a call to the ceremonial observance of the tribal ritual. The Zunis have various 'orders of a more or less sacred and sacerdotal character.' Mr. Cushing writes:—

These orders were engaged in their annual ceremonials, of which little was told or shown me; but, at the end of four days, I heard one morning a deep whirring noise. Running out, I saw a procession of three priests of the bow, in plumed helmets and closely-fitting cuirasses, both of thick buckskin—gorgeous and solemn with sacred embroideries and war-paint, begirt with bows, arrows, and war-clubs, and each distinguished by his badge of degree—coming down one of the narrow streets. The principal priest carried in his arms a wooden idol, ferocious in aspect, yet beautiful with its decorations of shell, turquoise, and brilliant paint. It was nearly hidden by symbolic slats and prayer-sticks most elaborately plumed. He was preceded by a guardian with drawn bow and arrows, while another followed, twirling the sounding slat, which had attracted alike my attention and that of hundreds of the Indians, who hurriedly flocked to the roofs of the adjacent houses, or lined the street, bowing their heads in adoration, and scattering sacred prayer-meal on the god and his attendant priests. Slowly they wound their way down the hill, across the river, and off toward the mountain of Thunder. Soon an identical procession followed and took its way toward the western hills. I watched them long until they disappeared, and a few hours afterward there arose from the top of 'Thunder Mountain' a dense column of smoke, simultaneously with another from the more distant western mesa of 'U-ha-na-mi,' or 'Mount of the Beloved.'

Then they told me that for four days I must neither touch nor eat flesh or oil of any kind, and for ten days neither throw any refuse from my doors, nor permit a spark to leave my house, for 'This was the season of the year when the "grandmother of men" (fire) was precious.'

Here then, in Zuni, we have the bull-roarer again, and once more we find it employed as a summons to the mysteries. We do not learn, however, that women in Zuni are forbidden to look upon the bull-roarer. Finally, the South African evidence, which is supplied by letters from a correspondent of Mr. Tylor's, proves that in South Africa, too, the bull-roarer is employed to call the men to the celebration of secret functions. A minute description of the instrument, and of its magical power to raise a wind, is given in Theal's 'Kaffir Folklore,' p. 209. The bull-roarer has not been made a subject of particular research; very probably later investigations will find it in other parts of the modern world besides America, Africa, New Zealand, and Australia. I have myself been fortunate enough to encounter the bull-roarer on the soil of ancient Greece and in connection with the Dionysiac mysteries. Clemens of Alexandria, and Arnobius, an early Christian father who follows Clemens, describe certain toys of the child Dionysus which were used in the mysteries. Among these are *turbines*, κωνοι, and ρομβοι. The ordinary dictionaries interpret all these as whipping-tops, adding that ρομβος is sometimes 'a magic wheel.' The ancient scholiast on Clemens, however, writes: 'The κωνος is a little piece of wood, to which a string is fastened, and in the mysteries it is whirled round to make a roaring noise.'[18] Here, in short, we have a brief but complete description of the bull-roarer of the Australian *turndun*. No single point is omitted. The κωνος, like the *turndun*, is a small object of wood, it is tied to a string, when whirled round it produces a roaring noise, and it is used at initiations. This is not the end of the matter.

In the part of the Dionysiac mysteries at which the toys of the child Dionysus were exhibited, and during which (as it seems) the κωνος, or bull-roarer, was whirred, the performers daubed themselves all over with clay. This we learn from a passage in which Demosthenes describes the youth of his hated adversary,

---

[18] Κωνος ξυλαριον ου εξηπται το σπαρτιον και εν ταις τελεταις εδονειτο ινα ροιζη. Lobeck, *Aglaophamus* (i. p. 700).

Æschines. The mother of Æschines, he says, was a kind of 'wise woman,' and dabbler in mysteries. Æschines used to aid her by bedaubing the initiate over with clay and bran.[19] The word αποματτων, here used by Demosthenes, is explained by Harpocration as the ritual term for daubing the initiated. A story was told, as usual, to explain this rite. It was said that, when the Titans attacked Dionysus and tore him to pieces, they painted themselves first with clay, or gypsum, that they might not be recognised. Nonnus shows, in several places, that down to his time the celebrants of the Bacchic mysteries retained this dirty trick. Precisely the same trick prevails in the mysteries of savage peoples. Mr. Winwood Reade [20] reports the evidence of Mongilomba. When initiated, Mongilomba was 'severely flogged in the Fetich House' (as young Spartans were flogged before the animated image of Artemis), and then he was 'plastered over with goat-dung.' Among the natives of Victoria, [21]the 'body of the initiated is bedaubed with clay, mud, charcoal powder, and filth of every kind.' The girls are plastered with charcoal powder and white clay, answering to the Greek gypsum. Similar daubings were performed at the mysteries by the Mandans, as described by Catlin; and the Zunis made raids on Mr. Cushing's black paint and Chinese ink for like purposes. On the Congo, Mr. Johnson found precisely the same ritual in the initiations. Here, then, not to multiply examples, we discover two singular features in common between Greek and savage mysteries. Both Greeks and savages employ the bull-roarer, both bedaub the initiated with dirt or with white paint or chalk. As to the meaning of the latter very un-Aryan practice, one has no idea. It is only certain that war parties of Australian blacks bedaub themselves with white clay to alarm their enemies in night attacks. The Phocians, according to Herodotus (viii. 27), adopted the same 'aisy

---

[19] *De Corona*, p. 313.

[20] *Savage Africa*. Captain Smith, the lover of Pocahontas, mentions the custom in his work on Virginia, pp. 245-248.

[21] Brough Smyth, i. 60, using evidence of Howitt, Taplin, Thomas, and Wilhelmi.

stratagem,' as Captain Costigan has it. Tellies, the medicine-man (μαντις), chalked some sixty Phocians, whom he sent to make a night attack on the Thessalians. The sentinels of the latter were seized with supernatural horror, and fled, 'and after the sentinels went the army.' In the same way, in a night attack among the Australian Kurnai, [22]'they all rapidly painted themselves with pipe-clay: red ochre is no use, it cannot frighten an enemy.' If, then, Greeks in the historic period kept up Australian tactics, it is probable that the ancient mysteries of Greece might retain the habit of daubing the initiated which occurs in savage rites.

'Come now,' as Herodotus would say, 'I will show once more that the mysteries of the Greeks resemble those of Bushmen.' In Lucian's Treatise on Dancing, [23]we read, 'I pass over the fact that you cannot find a single ancient mystery in which there is not dancing. . . . To prove this I will not mention the secret acts of worship, on account of the uninitiated. But this much all men know, that most people say of those who reveal the mysteries, that they "dance them out."' Here Liddell and Scott write, rather weakly, 'to dance out, let out, betray, probably of some dance which burlesqued these ceremonies.' It is extremely improbable that, in an age when it was still forbidden to reveal the οργια, or secret rites, those rites would be mocked in popular burlesques. Lucian obviously intends to say that the matter of the mysteries was set forth in *ballets d'action.* Now this is exactly the case in the surviving mysteries of the Bushmen. Shortly after the rebellion of Langalibalele's tribe, Mr. Orpen, the chief magistrate in St. John's Territory, made the acquaintance of Qing, one of the last of an all but exterminated tribe. Qing 'had never seen a white man, except fighting,' when he became Mr. Orpen's guide. He gave a good deal of information about the myths of his people, but refused to answer certain questions. 'You are now asking the secrets that are not spoken of.' Mr. Orpen asked, 'Do you know the secrets?' Qing replied, 'No, only the initiated men of that

---

[22] Kamilaroi and Kurnai, p. 214.
[23] Περι ορχησεως, c. 15.

dance know these things.' To 'dance' this or that means, 'to be acquainted with this or that mystery;' the dances were originally taught by Cagn, the mantis, or grasshopper god. In many mysteries, Qing, as a young man, was not initiated. He could not 'dance them out.' [24]

There are thus undeniably close resemblances between the Greek mysteries and those of the lowest contemporary races.

As to the bull-roarer, its recurrence among Greeks, Zunis, Kamilaroi, Maoris, and South African races, would be regarded, by some students, as a proof that all these tribes had a common origin, or had borrowed the instrument from each other. But this theory is quite unnecessary. The bull-roarer is a very simple invention. Anyone might find out that a bit of sharpened wood, tied to a string, makes, when whirred, a roaring noise. Supposing that discovery made, it is soon turned to practical use. All tribes have their mysteries. All want a signal to summon the right persons together and warn the wrong persons to keep out of the way. The church bell does as much for us, so did the shaken *seistron* for the Egyptians. People with neither bells nor *seistra* find the bull-roarer, with its mysterious sound, serve their turn. The hiding of the instrument from women is natural enough. It merely makes the alarm and absence of the curious sex doubly sure. The stories of supernatural consequences to follow if a woman sees the turndun lend a sanction. This is not a random theory, without basis. In Brazil, the natives have no bull-roarer, but they have mysteries, and the presence of the women at the mysteries of the men is a terrible impiety. To warn away the women, the Brazilians make loud 'devil-music' on what are called 'jurupari pipes.' Now, just as in Australia, *the women may not see the jurupari pipes on pain of death.* When the sound of the jurupari pipes is heard, as when the turndun is heard in Australia, every woman flees and hides herself. The women are always executed if they see the pipes. Mr. Alfred Wallace bought a pair of these pipes, but he had to embark them at a distance from the

---

[24] Cape Monthly Magazine, July 1874.

village where they were procured. The seller was afraid that some unknown misfortune would occur if the women of his village set eyes on the juruparis. [25]

The conclusion from all these facts seems obvious. The bull-roarer is an instrument easily invented by savages, and easily adopted into the ritual of savage mysteries. If we find the bull-roarer used in the mysteries of the most civilised of ancient peoples, the most probable explanation is, that the Greeks retained both the mysteries, the bull-roarer, the habit of bedaubing the initiate, the torturing of boys, the sacred obscenities, the antics with serpents, the dances, and the like, from the time when their ancestors were in the savage condition. That more refined and religious ideas were afterwards introduced into the mysteries seems certain, but the rites were, in many cases, simply savage. Unintelligible (except as survivals) when found among Hellenes, they become intelligible enough among savages, because they correspond to the intellectual condition and magical fancies of the lower barbarism. The same sort of comparison, the same kind of explanation, will account, as we shall see, for the savage myths as well as for the savage customs which survived among the Greeks.

---

[25] Wallace, *Travels on the Amazon*, p. 349.

THE MYTH OF CRONUS.

In a Maori pah, when a little boy behaves rudely to his parents, he is sometimes warned that he is 'as bad as cruel Tutenganahau.' If he asks who Tutenganahau was, he is told the following story:—

'In the beginning, the Heaven, Rangi, and the Earth, Papa, were the father and mother of all things. "In these days the Heaven lay upon the Earth, and all was darkness. They had never been separated." Heaven and Earth had children, who grew up and lived in this thick night, and they were unhappy because they could not see. Between the bodies of their parents they were imprisoned, and there was no light. The names of the children were Tumatuenga, Tane Mahuta, Tutenganahau, and some others. So they all consulted as to what should be done with their parents, Rangi and Papa. "Shall we slay them, or shall we separate them?" "Go to," said Tumatuenga, "let us slay them." "No," cried Tane Mahuta, "let us rather separate them. Let one go upwards, and become a stranger to us; let the other remain below, and be a parent to us." Only Tawhiri Matea (the wind) had pity on his own father and mother. Then the fruit-gods, and the war-god, and the sea-god (for all the children of Papa and Rangi were gods) tried to rend their parents asunder. Last rose the forest-god, cruel Tutenganahau. He severed the sinews which united Heaven and Earth, Rangi and Papa. Then he pushed hard with his head and feet. Then wailed Heaven and exclaimed Earth, "Wherefore this murder? Why this great sin? Why destroy us? Why separate us?" But Tane pushed and pushed: Rangi was driven far away into the air. "*They became visible, who had hitherto been concealed between the hollows of their parents' breasts.*" Only the storm-god differed from his brethren: he arose and followed his father, Rangi, and abode with him in the open spaces of the sky.'

This is the Maori story of the severing of the wedded Heaven and Earth. The cutting of them asunder was the work of Tutenganahau and his brethren, and the conduct of Tutenganahau is still held up as an example of filial impiety.[26] The story is preserved in sacred hymns of very great antiquity, and many of the myths are common to the other peoples of the Pacific. [27]

Now let us turn from New Zealand to Athens, as she was in the days of Pericles. Socrates is sitting in the porch of the King Archon, when Euthyphro comes up and enters into conversation with the philosopher. After some talk, Euthyphro says, 'You will think me mad when I tell you whom I am prosecuting and pursuing!' 'Why, has the fugitive wings?' asks Socrates. 'Nay, he is not very volatile at his time of life!' 'Who is he?' 'My father.' 'Good heavens! you don't mean that. What is he accused of?' 'Murder, Socrates.' Then Euthyphro explains the case, which quaintly illustrates Greek civilisation. Euthyphro's father had an agricultural labourer at Naxos. One day this man, in a drunken passion, killed a slave. Euthyphro's father seized the labourer, bound him, threw him into a ditch, 'and then sent to Athens to ask a diviner what should be done with him.' Before the answer of the diviner arrived, the labourer literally 'died in a ditch' of hunger and cold. For this offence, Euthyphro was prosecuting his own father. Socrates shows that he disapproves, and Euthyphro thus defends the piety of his own conduct: 'The impious, whoever he may be, ought not to go unpunished. For do not men regard Zeus as the best and most righteous of gods? Yet even they admit that Zeus bound his own father Cronus, because he wickedly devoured his sons; and that Cronus, too, had punished his own father, Uranus, for a similar reason, in a nameless manner. And yet when *I* proceed against *my* father, people are angry with me.

---

[26] *New Zealand*, Taylor, pp. 119-121. *Die heilige Sage der Polynesier*, Bastian, pp. 36-39.
[27] A crowd of similar myths, in one of which a serpent severs Heaven and Earth, are printed in Turner's *Samoa*.

This is their inconsistent way of talking, when the gods are concerned, and when I am concerned.'

Here Socrates breaks in. He 'cannot away with these stories about the gods,' and so he has just been accused of impiety, the charge for which he died. Socrates cannot believe that a god, Cronus, mutilated his father Uranus, but Euthyphro believes the whole affair: 'I can tell you many other things about the gods which would quite amaze you.' [28]

✳ ✳ ✳ ✳ ✳

We have here a typical example of the way in which mythology puzzled the early philosophers of Greece. Socrates was anxious to be pious, and to respect the most ancient traditions of the gods. Yet at the very outset of sacred history he was met by tales of gods who mutilated and bound their own parents. Not only were such tales hateful to him, but they were of positively evil example to people like Euthyphro. The problem remained, how did the fathers of the Athenians ever come to tell such myths?

✳ ✳ ✳ ✳ ✳

Let us now examine the myth of Cronus, and the explanations which have been given by scholars. Near the beginning of things, according to Hesiod (whose cosmogony was accepted in Greece), Earth gave birth to Heaven. Later, Heaven, Uranus, became the husband of Gæa, Earth. Just as Rangi and Papa, in New Zealand, had many children, so had Uranus and Gæa. As in New Zealand, some of these children were gods of the various elements. Among them were Oceanus, the deep, and Hyperion, the sun—as among the children of Earth and Heaven, in New Zealand, were the Wind and the Sea. The youngest child of the Greek Heaven and Earth was 'Cronus of crooked counsel, who ever hated his mighty sire.' Now even as the children of the Maori Heaven and Earth were 'concealed between the hollows of their parents' breasts,' so the Greek Heaven used to 'hide his

---

[28] The translation used is Jowett's.

44

children from the light in the hollows of Earth.' Both Earth and her children resented this, and, as in New Zealand, the children conspired against Heaven, taking Earth, however, into their counsels. Thereupon Earth produced iron, and bade her children avenge their wrongs.[29] Now fear fell on all of them, except Cronus, who, like Tutenganahau, was all for action. Cronus determined to end the embraces of Heaven and Earth. But, while the Maori myth conceives of Heaven and Earth as of two beings which have never been separated before, Hesiod makes Heaven amorously approach his wife from a distance. Then Cronus stretched out his hand, armed with a sickle of iron, or steel, and mutilated Uranus. Thus were Heaven and Earth practically divorced. But as in the Maori myth one of the children of Heaven clave to his sire, so, in Greek, Oceanus remained faithful to his father. [30]

This is the first portion of the Myth of Cronus. Can it be denied that the story is well illustrated and explained by the New Zealand parallel, the myth of the cruelty of Tutenganahau? By means of this comparison, the meaning of the myth is made clear enough. Just as the New Zealanders had conceived of Heaven and Earth as at one time united, to the prejudice of their children, so the ancestors of the Greeks had believed in an ancient union of Heaven and Earth. Both by Greeks and Maoris, Heaven and Earth were thought of as living persons, with human parts and passions. Their union was prejudicial to their children, and so the children violently separated the parents. This conduct is regarded as impious, and as an awful example to be avoided, in Maori pahs. In Naxos, on the other hand, Euthyphro deemed that the conduct of Cronus deserved imitation. If ever the Maoris had reached a high civilisation, they would probably have been revolted, like Socrates, by the myth which survived from their period of savagery. Mr. Tylor well says, [31]"Just as the adzes of polished jade, and the cloaks of tied flax-fibre, which these New

---

[29] *Theog.*, 166.
[30] Apollodorus, i. 15.
[31] *Primitive Culture*, i. 325.

Zealanders were using but yesterday, are older in their place in history than the bronze battle-axes and linen mummy-cloths of ancient Egypt, so the Maori poet's shaping of nature into nature-myth belongs to a stage of intellectual history which was passing away in Greece five-and-twenty centuries ago. The myth-maker's fancy of Heaven and Earth as father and mother of all things naturally suggested the legend that they in old days abode together, but have since been torn asunder.'

* * * * *

That this view of Heaven and Earth is natural to early minds, Mr. Tylor proves by the presence of the myth of the union and violent divorce of the pair in China.[32] Puang-ku is the Chinese Cronus, or Tutenganahau. In India, [33]Dyaus and Prithivi, Heaven and Earth, were once united, and were severed by Indra, their own child.

This, then, is our interpretation of the exploit of Cronus. It is an old surviving nature-myth of the severance of Heaven and Earth, a myth found in China, India, New Zealand, as well as in Greece. Of course it is not pretended that Chinese and Maoris borrowed from Indians and Greeks, or came originally of the same stock. Similar phenomena, presenting themselves to be explained by human minds in a similar stage of fancy and of ignorance, will account for the parallel myths.

The second part of the myth of Cronus was, like the first, a stumbling-block to the orthodox in Greece. Of the second part we offer no explanation beyond the fact that the incidents in the myth are almost universally found among savages, and that, therefore, in Greece they are probably survivals from savagery. The sequel of the myth appears to account for nothing, as the first part accounts for the severance of Heaven and Earth. In the sequel a world-wide *Märchen*, or tale, seems to have been attached to Cronus, or attracted into the cycle of which he is

---

[32] Pauthier, *Livres sacrés de l'Orient*, p. 19.
[33] Muir's *Sanskrit Texts*, v. 23. Aitareya Brahmana.

centre, without any particular reason, beyond the law which makes detached myths crystallise round any celebrated name. To look further is, perhaps, *chercher raison où il n'y en a pas.*

The conclusion of the story of Cronus runs thus:—He wedded his sister, Rhea, and begat children—Demeter, Hera, Hades, Poseidon, and, lastly, Zeus. 'And mighty Cronus swallowed down each of them, each that came to their mother's knees from her holy womb, with this intent, that none other of the proud children of Uranus should hold kingly sway among the Immortals.' Cronus showed a ruling father's usual jealousy of his heirs. It was a case of Friedrich Wilhelm and Friedrich. But Cronus (acting in a way natural in a story perhaps first invented by cannibals) swallowed his children instead of merely imprisoning them. Heaven and Earth had warned him to beware of his heirs, and he could think of no safer plan than that which he adopted. When Rhea was about to become the mother of Zeus, she fled to Crete. Here Zeus was born, and when Cronus (in pursuit of his usual policy) asked for the baby, he was presented with a stone wrapped up in swaddling bands. After swallowing the stone, Cronus was easy in his mind; but Zeus grew up, administered a dose to his father, and compelled him to disgorge. 'The stone came forth first, as he had swallowed it last.'[34] The other children also emerged, all alive and well. Zeus fixed the stone at Delphi, where, long after the Christian era, Pausanias saw it.[35] It was not a large stone, Pausanias tells us, and the Delphians used to anoint it with oil and wrap it up in wool on feast-days. All Greek temples had their fetich-stones, and each stone had its legend. This was the story of the Delphian stone, and of the fetichism which survived the early years of Christianity. A very pretty story it is. Savages more frequently smear their fetich-stones with red paint than daub them with oil, but the latter, as we learn from Theophrastus's account of the 'superstitious man,' was the Greek ritual.

---

[34] Hesiod, *Theog.*, 497.
[35] Paus. x. 24.

* * * * *

This anecdote about Cronus was the stumbling-block of the orthodox Greek, the jest of the sceptic, and the butt of the early Christian controversialists. Found among Bushmen or Australians the narrative might seem rather wild, but it astonishes us still more when it occurs in the holy legends of Greece. Our explanation of its presence there is simple enough. Like the erratic blocks in a modern plain, like the flint-heads in a meadow, the story is a relic of a very distant past. The glacial age left the boulders on the plain, the savage tribes of long ago left the arrowheads, the period of savage fancy left the story of Cronus and the rites of the fetich-stone. Similar rites are still notoriously practised in the South Sea Islands, in Siberia, in India and Africa and Melanesia, by savages. And by savages similar tales are still told.

* * * * *

We cannot go much lower than the Bushmen, and among Bushman divine myths is room for the 'swallowing trick' attributed to Cronus by Hesiod. The chief divine character in Bushman myth is the Mantis insect. His adopted daughter is the child of Kwai Hemm, a supernatural character, 'the all-devourer.' The Mantis gets his adopted daughter to call the swallower to his aid; but Kwai Hemm swallows the Mantis, the god-insect. As Zeus made his own wife change herself into an insect, for the convenience of swallowing her, there is not much difference between Bushman and early Greek mythology. Kwai Hemm is killed by a stratagem, and all the animals whom he has got outside of, in a long and voracious career, troop forth from him alive and well, like the swallowed gods from the maw of Cronus. [36]Now, story for story, the Bushman version is much less offensive than that of Hesiod. But the Bushman story is just the sort of story we expect from Bushmen, whereas the Hesiodic story is not at all the kind of tale we look for from Greeks. The explanation is, that

---

[36] Bleek, *Bushman Folklore*, pp. 6-8.

the Greeks had advanced out of a savage state of mind and society, but had retained their old myths, myths evolved in the savage stage, and in harmony with that condition of fancy. Among the Kaffirs [37] we find the same 'swallow-myth.' The Igongqongqo swallows all and sundry; a woman cuts the swallower with a knife, and 'people came out, and cattle, and dogs.' In Australia, a god is swallowed. As in the myth preserved by Aristophanes in the 'Birds,' the Australians believe that birds were the original gods, and the eagle, especially, is a great creative power. The Moon was a mischievous being, who walked about the world, doing what evil he could. One day he swallowed the eagle-god. The wives of the eagle came up, and the Moon asked them where he might find a well. They pointed out a well, and, as he drank, they hit the Moon with a stone tomahawk, and out flew the eagle.[38] This is oddly like Grimm's tale of 'The Wolf and the Kids.' The wolf swallowed the kids, their mother cut a hole in the wolf, let out the kids, stuffed the wolf with stones, and sewed him up again. The wolf went to the well to drink, the weight of the stones pulled him in, and he was drowned. Similar stories are common among the Red Indians, and Mr. Im Thurn has found them in Guiana. How savages all over the world got the idea that men and beasts could be swallowed and disgorged alive, and why they fashioned the idea into a divine myth, it is hard to say. Mr. Tylor, in 'Primitive Culture,' [39]adds many examples of the narrative. The Basutos have it; it occurs some five times in Callaway's 'Zulu Nursery Tales.' In Greenland the Eskimo have a shape of the incident, and we have all heard of the escape of Jonah.

It has been suggested that night, covering up the world, gave the first idea of the swallowing myth. Now in some of the stories the night is obviously conceived of as a big beast which swallows all things. The notion that night is an animal is entirely in harmony with savage metaphysics. In the opinion of the savage

---

[37] Theal, *Kaffir Folklore*, pp. 161-167.
[38] Brough Smith, i. 432-433.
[39] i. 338.

speculator, all things are men and animals. 'Ils se persuadent que non seulement les hommes et les autres animaux, mais aussi que toutes les autres choses sont animées,' says one of the old Jesuit missionaries in Canada.[40] 'The wind was formerly a person; he became a bird,' say the Bushmen.

G' oö ka! Kui (a very respectable Bushman, whose name seems a little hard to pronounce), once saw the wind-person at Haarfontein. Savages, then, are persuaded that night, sky, cloud, fire, and so forth, are only the *schein*, or sensuous appearance, of things that, in essence, are men or animals. A good example is the bringing of Night to Vanua Lava, by Qat, the 'culture-hero' of Melanesia. At first it was always day, and people tired of it. Qat heard that Night was at the Torres Islands, and he set forth to get some. Qong (Night) received Qat well, blackened his eyebrows, showed him Sleep, and sent him off with fowls to bring Dawn after the arrival of Night should make Dawn a necessary. Next day Qat's brothers saw the sun crawl away west, and presently Night came creeping up from the sea. 'What is this?' cried the brothers. 'It is Night,' said Qat; 'sit down, and when you feel something in your eyes, lie down and keep quiet.' So they went to sleep. 'When Night had lasted long enough, Qat took a piece of red obsidian, and cut the darkness, and the Dawn came out.' [41]

Night is more or less personal in this tale, and solid enough to be cut, so as to let the Dawn out. This savage conception of night, as the swallower and disgorger, might start the notion of other swallowing and disgorging beings. Again the Bushmen, and other savage peoples, account for certain celestial phenomena by saying that 'a big star has swallowed his daughter, and spit her out again.' While natural phenomena, explained on savage principles,

---

[40] *Rel. de la Nouvelle-France* (1636), p. 114.

[41] Codrington, in *Journal Anthrop. Inst.* Feb. 1881. There is a Breton *Märchen* of a land where people had to 'bring the Dawn' daily with carts and horses. A boy, whose sole property was a cock, sold it to the people of this country for a large sum, and now the cock brings the dawn, with a great saving of trouble and expense. The *Märchen* is a survival of the state of mind of the Solomon Islanders.

might give the data of the swallow-myth, we must not conclude that all beings to whom the story is attached are, therefore, the Night. On this principle Cronus would be the Night, and so would the wolf in Grimm. For our purposes it is enough that the feat of Cronus is a feat congenial to the savage fancy and repugnant to the civilised Greeks who found themselves in possession of the myth. Beyond this, and beyond the inference that the Cronus myth was first evolved by people to whom it seemed quite natural, that is, by savages, we do not pretend to go in our interpretation.

* * * * *

To end our examination of the Myth of Cronus, we may compare the solutions offered by scholars. As a rule, these solutions are based on the philological analysis of the names in the story. It will be seen that very various and absolutely inconsistent etymologies and meanings of Cronus are suggested by philologists of the highest authority. These contradictions are, unfortunately, rather the rule than the exception in the etymological interpretation of myths.

* * * * *

The opinion of Mr. Max Müller has always a right to the first hearing from English inquirers. Mr. Müller, naturally, examines first the name of the god whose legend he is investigating. He writes: 'There is no such being as Kronos in Sanskrit. Kronos did not exist till long after Zeus in Greece. Zeus was called by the Greeks the son of Time (Κρονος). This is a very simple and very common form of mythological expression. It meant originally, not that time was the origin or source of Zeus, but Κρονιων or Κρονιδης was used in the sense of "connected with time, representing time, existing through all time." Derivatives in -ιων and -ιδης took, in later times, the more exclusive meaning of patronymics. . . . When this (the meaning of Κρονιδης as equivalent to Ancient of Days) ceased

51

to be understood, . . . people asked themselves the question, Why is Ζευς called Κρονιδης? And the natural and almost inevitable answer was, Because he is the son, the offspring of a more ancient god, Κρονος. This may be a very old myth in Greece; but the misunderstanding which gave rise to it could have happened in Greece only. We cannot expect, therefore, a god Κρονος in the Veda.' To expect Greek in the Veda would certainly be sanguine. 'When this myth of Κρονος had once been started, it would roll on irresistibly. If Ζευς had once a father called Κρονος, Κρονος must have a wife.' It is added, as confirmation, that 'the name of Κρονιδης belongs originally to Zeus only, and not to his later' (in Hesiod elder) 'brothers, Poseidon and Hades.'
[42]

Mr. Müller says, in his famous essay on 'Comparative Mythology'[43]: 'How can we imagine that a few generations before that time' (the age of Solon) 'the highest notions of the Godhead among the Greeks were adequately expressed by the story of Uranos maimed by Kronos,—of Kronos eating his children, swallowing a stone, and vomiting out alive his whole progeny. Among the lowest tribes of Africa and America, we hardly find anything more hideous and revolting.' We have found a good deal of the sort in Africa and America, where it seems not out of place.

One objection to Mr. Müller's theory is, that it makes the mystery no clearer. When Greeks were so advanced in Hellenism that their own early language had become obsolete and obscure, they invented the god Κρονος, to account for the patronymic (as they deemed it) Κρονιδης, son of Κρονος. But why did they tell such savage and revolting stories about the god they had invented? Mr. Müller only says the myth 'would roll on irresistibly.' But why did the rolling myth gather such very strange moss? That is the problem; and, while Mr. Müller's

---

[42] *Selected Essays,* i. 460.
[43] *Ibid.* i. 311.

hypothesis accounts for the existence of a god called Κρονος, it does not even attempt to show how full-blown Greeks came to believe such hideous stories about the god.

* * * * *

This theory, therefore, is of no practical service. The theory of Adalbert Kuhn, one of the most famous of Sanskrit scholars, and author of 'Die Herabkunft des Feuers,' is directly opposed to the ideas of Mr. Müller. In Cronus, Mr. Müller recognises a god who could only have come into being among Greeks, when the Greeks had begun to forget the original meaning of 'derivatives in -ιων and -ιδης.' Kuhn, on the other hand, derives Κρονος from the same root as the Sanskrit *Krāna*.[44] *Krāna* means, it appears, *der für sich schaffende*, he who creates for himself, and Cronus is compared to the Indian Pragapati, about whom even more abominable stories are told than the myths which circulate to the prejudice of Cronus. According to Kuhn, the 'swallow-myth' means that Cronus, the lord of light and dark powers, swallows the divinities of light. But in place of Zeus (that is, according to Kuhn, of the daylight sky) he swallows a stone, that is, the sun. When he disgorges the stone (the sun), he also disgorges the gods of light whom he had swallowed.

I confess that I cannot understand these distinctions between the father and lord of light and dark (Cronus) and the beings he swallowed. Nor do I find it easy to believe that myth-making man took all those distinctions, or held those views of the Creator. However, the chief thing to note is that Mr. Müller's etymology and Kuhn's etymology of Cronus can hardly both be true, which, as their systems both depend on etymological analysis, is somewhat discomfiting.

The next etymological theory is the daring speculation of Mr. Brown. In 'The Great Dionysiak Myth' [45] Mr. Brown writes: 'I regard Kronos as the equivalent of Karnos, Karnaios, Karnaivis,

---

[44] *Ueber Entwicklungsstufen der Mythenbildung* (1874), p. 148.
[45] ii. 127.

53

the Horned God; Assyrian, KaRNu; Hebrew, KeReN, horn; Hellenic, KRoNos, or KaRNos.' Mr. Brown seems to think that Cronus is 'the ripening power of harvest,' and also 'a wily savage god,' in which opinion one quite agrees with him. Why the name of Cronus should mean 'horned,' when he is never represented with horns, it is hard to say. But among the various foreign gods in whom the Greeks recognised their own Cronus, one Hea, 'regarded by Berosos as Kronos,' seems to have been 'horn-wearing.'[46] Horns are lacking in Seb and Il, if not in Baal Hamon, though Mr. Brown would like to behorn them.

Let us now turn to Preller.[47] According to Preller, Κρονος is connected with κραινω, to fulfil, to bring to completion. The harvest month, the month of ripening and fulfilment, was called *κρονιων* in some parts of Greece, and the jolly harvest-feast, with its memory of Saturn's golden days, was named κρονια. The sickle of Cronus, the sickle of harvest-time, works in well with this explanation, and we have a kind of pun in Homer which points in the direction of Preller's derivation from κραινω:—

ουδ αρα πω οι επεκραιαινε Κρονιων

and in Sophocles ('Tr.' 126)—

ο παντα κραινων βασιλευς Κρονιδας.

Preller illustrates the mutilation of Uranus by the Maori tale of Tutenganahau. The child-swallowing he connects with Punic and Phœnician influence, and Semitic sacrifices of men and children. Porphyry [48] speaks of human sacrifices to Cronus in Rhodes, and the Greeks recognised Cronus in the Carthaginian god to whom children were offered up.

Hartung [49] takes Cronus, when he mutilates Uranus, to be the fire of the sun, scorching the sky of spring. This, again, is somewhat out of accord with Schwartz's idea, that Cronus is the storm-god, the cloud-swallowing deity, his sickle the rainbow,

---

[46] *G. D. M.*, ii. 127, 129.
[47] *Gr. My.*, i. 144.
[48] *De Abst.*, ii. 202, 197.
[49] *Rel. und Myth.*, ii. 3.

and the blood of Uranus the lightning. [50]According to Prof. Sayce, again, [51]the blood-drops of Uranus are rain-drops. Cronus is the sun-god, piercing the dark cloud, which is just the reverse of Schwartz's idea. Prof. Sayce sees points in common between the legend of Moloch, or of Baal under the name of Moloch, and the myth of Cronus. But Moloch, he thinks, is not a god of Phœnician origin, but a deity borrowed from 'the primitive Accadian population of Babylonia.' Mr. Isaac Taylor, again, explains Cronus as the sky which swallows and reproduces the stars. The story of the sickle may be derived from the crescent moon, the 'silver sickle,' or from a crescent-shaped piece of meteoric iron—for, in this theory, the fetich-stone of Delphi is a piece of that substance.

* * * * *

It will be observed that any one of these theories, if accepted, is much more 'minute in detail' than our humble suggestion. He who adopts any one of them, knows all about it. He knows that Cronus is a purely Greek god, or that he is connected with the Sanskrit *Krāna*, which Tiele, [52]unhappily, says is 'a very dubious word.' Or the mythologist may be quite confident that Cronus is neither Greek nor, in any sense, Sanskrit, but Phœnician. A not less adequate interpretation assigns him ultimately to Accadia. While the inquirer who can choose a system and stick to it knows the exact nationality of Cronus, he is also well acquainted with his character as a nature-god. He may be Time, or perhaps he is the Summer Heat, and a horned god; or he is the harvest-god, or the god of storm and darkness, or the midnight sky,—the choice is wide; or he is the lord of dark and light, and his children are the stars, the clouds, the summer months, the light-powers, or what you will. The mythologist has only to make his selection.

---

[50] *Ursprung der Myth.*, pp. 133, 135, 139, 149.
[51] *Contemporary Review*, Sept. 1883.
[52] *Rev. de l'Hist. rel.* i. 179.

The system according to which we tried to interpret the myth is less *ondoyant et divers*. We do not even pretend to explain everything. We do not guess at the meaning and root of the word Cronus. We only find parallels to the myth among savages, whose mental condition is fertile in such legends. And we only infer that the myth of Cronus was originally evolved by persons also in the savage intellectual condition. The survival we explain as, in a previous essay, we explained the survival of the bull-roarer by the conservatism of the religious instinct.

CUPID, PSYCHE, AND THE 'SUN-FROG.'

'Once upon a time there lived a king and a queen,' says the old woman in Apuleius, beginning the tale of Cupid and Psyche with that ancient formula which has been dear to so many generations of children. In one shape or other the tale of Cupid and Psyche, of the woman who is forbidden to see or to name her husband, of the man with the vanished fairy bride, is known in most lands, 'even among barbarians.' According to the story the mystic prohibition is always broken: the hidden face is beheld; light is brought into the darkness; the forbidden name is uttered; the bride is touched with the tabooed metal, iron, and the union is ended. Sometimes the pair are re-united, after long searchings and wanderings; sometimes they are severed for ever. Such are the central situations in tales like that of Cupid and Psyche.

In the attempt to discover how the ideas on which this myth is based came into existence, we may choose one of two methods. We may confine our investigations to the Aryan peoples, among whom the story occurs both in the form of myth and of household tale. Again, we may look for the shapes of the legend which hide, like Peau d'Ane in disguise, among the rude kraals and wigwams, and in the strange and scanty garb of savages. If among savages we find both narratives like Cupid and Psyche, and also customs and laws out of which the myth might have arisen, we may provisionally conclude that similar customs once existed among the civilised races who possess the tale, and that from these sprang the early forms of the myth.

In accordance with the method hitherto adopted, we shall prefer the second plan, and pursue our quest beyond the limits of the Aryan peoples.

The oldest literary shape of the tale of Psyche and her lover is found in the Rig Veda (x. 95). The characters of a singular and cynical dialogue in that poem are named Urvasi and Pururavas. The former is an Apsaras, a kind of fairy or sylph, the mistress (and a *folle maîtresse,* too) of Pururavas, a mortal man.[53] In the poem Urvasi remarks that when she dwelt among men she 'ate once a day a small piece of butter, and therewith well satisfied went away.' This slightly reminds one of the common idea that the living may not eat in the land of the dead, and of Persephone's tasting the pomegranate in Hades.

Of the dialogue in the Rig Veda it may be said, in the words of Mr. Toots, that 'the language is coarse and the meaning is obscure.' We only gather that Urvasi, though she admits her sensual content in the society of Pururavas, is leaving him 'like the first of the dawns'; that she 'goes home again, hard to be caught, like the winds.' She gives her lover some hope, however—that the gods promise immortality even to him, 'the kinsman of Death' as he is. 'Let thine offspring worship the gods with an oblation; in Heaven shalt thou too have joy of the festival.'

In the Rig Veda, then, we dimly discern a parting between a mortal man and an immortal bride, and a promise of reconciliation.

The story, of which this Vedic poem is a partial dramatisation, is given in the Brahmana of the Yajur Veda. Mr. Max Müller has translated the passage.[54] According to the Brahmana, 'Urvasi, a kind of fairy, fell in love with Pururavas, and when she met him she said: Embrace me three times a day, but never against my will, and let me never see you without your royal garments, *for this is the manner of women.*'[55] The Gandharvas, a spiritual race, kinsmen of Urvasi, thought she had lingered too long among men. They therefore plotted some way of parting her from Pururavas. Her covenant with her lord declared that she

---

[53] That Pururavas is regarded as a mortal man, in relations with some sort of spiritual mistress, appears from the poem itself (v. 8, 9, 18). The human character of Pururavas also appears in R. V. i. 31, 4.

[54] *Selected Essays,* i. 408.

[55] The Apsaras is an ideally beautiful fairy woman, something 'between the high gods and the lower grotesque beings,' with 'lotus eyes' and other agreeable characteristics. A list of Apsaras known by name is given in Meyer's *Gandharven-Kentauren,* p. 28. They are often regarded as cloud-maidens by mythologists.

was never to see him naked. If that compact were broken she would be compelled to leave him. To make Pururavas break this compact the Gandharvas stole a lamb from beside Urvasi's bed: Pururavas sprang up to rescue the lamb, and, in a flash of lightning, Urvasi saw him naked, contrary to the *manner of women*. She vanished. He sought her long, and at last came to a lake where she and her fairy friends were playing *in the shape of birds*. Urvasi saw Pururavas, revealed herself to him, and, according to the Brahmana, part of the strange Vedic dialogue was now spoken. Urvasi promised to meet him on the last night of the year: a son was to be the result of the interview. Next day, her kinsfolk, the Gandharvas, offered Pururavas the wish of his heart. He wished to be one of them. They then initiated him into the mode of kindling a certain sacred fire, after which he became immortal and dwelt among the Gandharvas.

It is highly characteristic of the Indian mind that the story should be thus worked into connection with ritual. In the same way the Bhagavata Purana has a long, silly, and rather obscene narrative about the sacrifice offered by Pururavas, and the new kind of sacred fire. Much the same ritual tale is found in the Vishnu Purana (iv. 6, 19).

Before attempting to offer our own theory of the legend, we must examine the explanations presented by scholars. The philological method of dealing with myths is well known. The hypothesis is that the names in a myth are 'stubborn things,' and that, as the whole narrative has probably arisen from forgetfulness of the meaning of language, the secret of a myth must be sought in analysis of the proper names of the persons. On this principle Mr. Max Müller interprets the myth of Urvasi and Pururavas, their loves, separation, and reunion. Mr. Müller says that the story 'expresses the identity of the morning dawn and the evening twilight.'[56] To prove this, the names are analysed. It is Mr. Müller's object to show that though, even in the Veda, Urvasi and Pururavas are names of persons, they were originally

---

[56] *Selected Essays*, i. p. 405.

'appellations'; and that Urvasi meant 'dawn,' and Pururavas 'sun.' Mr. Müller's opinion as to the etymological sense of the names would be thought decisive, naturally, by lay readers, if an opposite opinion were not held by that other great philologist and comparative mythologist, Adalbert Kuhn. Admitting that 'the etymology of Urvasi is difficult,' Mr. Müller derives it from '*uru*, wide (ευρυ), and a root *as* = to pervade.' Now the dawn is 'widely pervading,' and has, in Sanskrit, the epithet urûkî, 'far-going.' Mr. Müller next assumes that 'Eurykyde,' 'Eurynome,' 'Eurydike,' and other heroic Greek female names, are 'names of the dawn'; but this, it must be said, is merely an assumption of his school. The main point of the argument is that Urvasi means 'far-going,' and that 'the far and wide splendour of dawn' is often spoken of in the Veda. 'However, the best proof that Urvasi was the dawn is the legend told of her and of her love to Pururavas, a story that is true only of the sun and the dawn' (i. 407).

We shall presently see that a similar story is told of persons in whom the dawn can scarcely be recognised, so that 'the best proof' is not very good.

The name of Pururavas, again, is 'an appropriate name for a solar hero.' . . . Pururavas meant the same as Πολυδευκης, 'endowed with much light,' for, though *rava* is generally used of sound, yet the root *ru*, which means originally 'to cry,' is also applied to colour, in the sense of a loud or crying colour, that is, red.[57] Violet also, according to Sir G. W. Cox, [58]is a loud or crying colour. 'The word (ιος), as applied to colour, is traced by Professor Max Müller to the root *i*, as denoting a "crying hue," that is, a loud colour.' It is interesting to learn that our Aryan fathers spoke of 'loud colours,' and were so sensitive as to think violet 'loud.' Besides, Pururavas calls himself Vasistha, which, as we know, is a name of the sun; and if he is called Aido, the son of Ida, the same name is elsewhere given [59] to Agni, the fire. 'The conclusion of the argument is that antiquity spoke of the naked

---

[57] Cf. *ruber*, *rufus*, O. H. G. *rôt*, *rudhira*, ερυθρος; also Sanskrit, *ravi*, sun.
[58] *Myth. Ar. Nat.*, ii. 81.
[59] R. V. iii. 29, 3.

sun, and of the chaste dawn hiding her face when she had seen her husband. Yet she says she will come again. And after the sun has travelled through the world in search of his beloved, when he comes to the threshold of Death and is going to end his solitary life, she appears again, in the gloaming, the same as the dawn, as Eos in Homer, begins and ends the day, and she carries him away to the golden seats of the Immortals.' [60]

Kuhn objects to all this explanation, partly on what we think the inadequate ground that there is no necessary connection between the story of Urvasi (thus interpreted) and the ritual of sacred fire-lighting. Connections of that sort were easily invented at random by the compilers of the Brahmanas in their existing form. Coming to the analysis of names, Kuhn finds in Urvasi 'a weakening of Urvankî (*uru* + *anc*), like *yuvaça* from *yuvanka*, Latin *juvencus* . . . the accent is of no decisive weight.' Kuhn will not be convinced that Pururavas is the sun, and is unmoved by the ingenious theory of 'a crying colour,' denoted by his name, and the inference, supported by such words as *rufus*, that crying colours are red, and therefore appropriate names of the red sun. The connection between Pururavas and Agni, fire, is what appeals to Kuhn—and, in short, where Mr. Müller sees a myth of sun and dawn, Kuhn recognises a fire-myth. Roth, again (whose own name means *red*), far from thinking that Urvasi is 'the chaste dawn,' interprets her name as *die geile*, that is, 'lecherous, lascivious, lewd, wanton, obscene'; while Pururavas, as 'the Roarer,' suggests 'the Bull in rut.' In accordance with these views Roth explains the myth in a fashion of his own. [61]

Here, then, as Kuhn says, 'we have three essentially different modes of interpreting the myth,' [62]all three founded on philological analysis of the names in the story. No better example

---

[60] The passage alluded to in Homer does not mean that dawn 'ends' the day, but 'when the fair-tressed Dawn brought the full light of the third day' (*Od.*, v. 390).

[61] Liebrecht (*Zur Volkskunde*, 241) is reminded by Pururavas (in Roth's sense of *der Brüller*) of loud-thundering Zeus, ἐριγδουπος.

[62] *Herabkunft des Fetters*, p. 86-89.

could be given to illustrate the weakness of the philological method. In the first place, that method relies on names as the primitive relics and germs of the tale, although the tale may occur where the names have never been heard, and though the names are, presumably, late additions to a story in which the characters were originally anonymous. Again, the most illustrious etymologists differ absolutely about the true sense of the names. Kuhn sees fire everywhere, and fire-myths; Mr. Müller sees dawn and dawn-myths; Schwartz sees storm and storm-myths, and so on. As the orthodox teachers are thus at variance, so that there is no safety in orthodoxy, we may attempt to use our heterodox method.

None of the three scholars whose views we have glanced at— neither Roth, Kuhn, nor Mr. Müller—lays stress on the saying of Urvasi, 'never let me see you without your royal garments, *for this is the custom of women.*'[63] To our mind, these words contain the gist of the myth. There must have been, at some time, a custom which forbade women to see their husbands without their garments, or the words have no meaning. If any custom of this kind existed, a story might well be evolved to give a sanction to the law. 'You must never see your husband naked: think what happened to Urvasi—she vanished clean away!' This is the kind of warning which might be given. If the customary prohibition had grown obsolete, the punishment might well be assigned to a being of another, a spiritual, race, in which old human ideas lingered, as the neolithic dread of iron lingers in the Welsh fairies.

Our method will be, to prove the existence of singular rules of etiquette, corresponding to the etiquette accidentally infringed by Pururavas. We shall then investigate stories of the same character as that of Urvasi and Pururavas, in which the infringement of the etiquette is chastised. It will be seen that, in

---

[63] Liebrecht (*Zur Volkskunde*, p. 241) notices the reference to the 'custom of women.' But he thinks the clause a mere makeshift, introduced late to account for a prohibition of which the real meaning had been forgotten. The improbability of this view is indicated by the frequency of similar prohibitions in actual custom.

most cases, the bride is of a peculiar and perhaps supernatural race. Finally, the tale of Urvasi will be taken up again, will be shown to conform in character to the other stories examined, and will be explained as a myth told to illustrate, or sanction, a nuptial etiquette.

The lives of savages are bound by the most closely-woven fetters of custom. The simplest acts are 'tabooed,' a strict code regulates all intercourse. Married life, especially, moves in the strangest fetters. There will be nothing remarkable in the wide distribution of a myth turning on nuptial etiquette, if this law of nuptial etiquette proves to be also widely distributed. That it is widely distributed we now propose to demonstrate by examples.

The custom of the African people of the kingdom of Futa is, or was, even stricter than the Vedic *custom of women*—'wives never permit their husbands to see them unveiled for three years after their marriage.' [64]

In his 'Travels to Timbuctoo' (i. 94), Caillié says that the bridegroom 'is not allowed to see his intended during the day.' He has a tabooed hut apart, and 'if he is obliged to come out he covers his face.' He 'remains with his wife only till daybreak'— like Cupid—and flees, like Cupid, before the light. Among the Australians the chief deity, if deity such a being can be called, Pundjel, 'has a wife whose face he has never seen,' probably in compliance with some primæval etiquette or taboo. [65]

Among the Yorubas 'conventional modesty forbids a woman to speak to her husband, or even to see him, if it can be avoided.'[66] Of the Iroquois Lafitau says: 'Ils n'osent aller dans les cabanes particulières où habitent leurs épouses que durant l'obscurité de la nuit.' [67]The Circassian women live on distant

---

[64] Astley, *Collection of Voyages*, ii. 24. This is given by Bluet and Moore on the evidence of one Job Ben Solomon, a native of Bunda in Futa. 'Though Job had a daughter by his last wife, yet he never saw her without her veil, as having been married to her only two years.' Excellently as this prohibition suits my theory, yet I confess I do not like Job's security.

[65] Brough Smyth, i. 423.

[66] Bowen, *Central Africa*, p. 303.

[67] Lafitau, i. 576.

terms with their lords till they become mothers. [68]Similar examples of reserve are reported to be customary among the Fijians.

In backward parts of Europe a strange custom forbids the bride to speak to her lord, as if in memory of a time when husband and wife were always of alien tribes, and, as among the Caribs, spoke different languages.

In the Bulgarian 'Volkslied,' the Sun marries Grozdanka, a mortal girl. Her mother addresses her thus:—

Grozdanka, mother's treasure mine,
For nine long years I nourished thee,
For nine months see thou do not speak
To thy first love that marries thee.

M. Dozon, who has collected the Bulgarian songs, says that this custom of prolonged silence on the part of the bride is very common in Bulgaria, though it is beginning to yield to a sense of the ludicrous.[69] In Sparta and in Crete, as is well known, the bridegroom was long the victim of a somewhat similar taboo, and was only permitted to seek the company of his wife secretly, and in the dark, like the Iroquois described by Lafitau.

Herodotus tells us (i. 146) that some of the old Ionian colonists 'brought no women with them, but took wives of the women of the Carians, whose fathers they had slain. Therefore the women made a law for themselves, and handed it down to their daughters, that they should never sit at meat with their husbands, and *that none should ever call her husband by his name.*' In precisely the same way, in Zululand the wife may not mention her husband's name, just as in the Welsh fairy tale the husband may not even know the name of his fairy bride, on pain of losing her for ever. These ideas about names, and freakish ways of avoiding the use of names, mark the childhood of languages, according to Mr. Max Müller, [70]and, therefore, the childhood of Society. The Kaffirs call this etiquette 'Hlonipa.' It

---

[68] Lubbock, *Origin of Civilisation* (1875), p. 75.
[69] *Chansons Pop. Bulg.*, p. 172.
[70] *Lectures on Language*, Second Series, p. 41.

applies to women as well as men. A Kaffir bride is not called by her own name in her husband's village, but is spoken of as 'mother of so and so,' even before she has borne a child. The universal superstition about names is at the bottom of this custom. The Aleutian Islanders, according to Dall, are quite distressed when obliged to speak to their wives in the presence of others. The Fijians did not know where to look when missionaries hinted that a man might live under the same roof as his wife.[71] Among the Turkomans, for six months, a year, or two years, a husband is only allowed to visit his wife by stealth.

The number of these instances could probably be increased by a little research. Our argument is that the widely distributed myths in which a husband or a wife transgresses some 'custom'— sees the other's face or body, or utters the forbidden name— might well have arisen as tales illustrating the punishment of breaking the rule. By a very curious coincidence, a Breton sailor's tale of the 'Cupid and Psyche' class is confessedly founded on the existence of the rule of nuptial etiquette. [72]

In this story the son of a Boulogne pilot marries the daughter of the King of Naz—wherever that may be. In Naz a man is never allowed to see the face of his wife till she has borne him a child—a modification of the Futa rule. The inquisitive French husband unveils his wife, and, like Psyche in Apuleius, drops wax from a candle on her cheek. When the pair return to Naz, the king of that country discovers the offence of the husband, and, by the aid of his magicians, transforms the Frenchman into a monster. Here we have the old formula—the infringement of a 'taboo,' and the magical punishment—adapted to the ideas of Breton peasantry. The essential point of the story, for our purpose, is that the veiling of the bride is 'the custom of women,' in the mysterious land of Naz. 'C'est l'usage du pays: les maris ne voient leurs femmes sans voile que lorsqu'elles sont devenues mères.' Now our theory of the myth of Urvasi is simply this: 'the custom of women,' which Pururavas transgresses, is probably a

---

[71] J. A. Farrer, *Primitive Manners*, p. 202, quoting Seemann.
[72] Sébillot, *Contes Pop. de la Haute-Bretagne*, p. 183.

traditional Aryan law of nuptial etiquette, *l'usage du pays*, once prevalent among the people of India.

If our view be correct, then several rules of etiquette, and not one alone, will be illustrated in the stories which we suppose the rules to have suggested. In the case of Urvasi and Pururavas, the rule was, not to see the husband naked. In 'Cupid and Psyche,' the husband was not to be looked upon at all. In the well-known myth of Mélusine, the bride is not to be seen naked. Mélusine tells her lover that she will only abide with him *dum ipsam nudam non viderit*.[73] The same taboo occurs in a Dutch *Märchen.*[74]

We have now to examine a singular form of the myth, in which the strange bride is not a fairy, or spiritual being, but an animal. In this class of story the husband is usually forbidden to perform some act which will recall to the bride the associations of her old animal existence. The converse of the tale is the well-known legend of the Forsaken Merman. The king of the sea permits his human wife to go to church. The ancient sacred associations are revived, and the woman returns no more.

She will not come though you call all day
Come away, come away.

Now, in the tales of the animal bride, it is her associations with her former life among the beasts that are not to be revived, and when they are reawakened by the commission of some act which she has forbidden, or the neglect of some precaution which she has enjoined, she, like Urvasi, disappears.

＊ ＊ ＊ ＊ ＊

·   The best known example of this variant of the tale is the story of Bheki, in Sanskrit. Mr. Max Müller has interpreted the myth in accordance with his own method.[75] His difficulty is to account for the belief that a king might marry a frog. Our

---

[73] Gervase of Tilbury.
[74] Kuhn, *Herabkunft*, p. 92.
[75] *Chips*, ii. 251.

ancestors, he remarks, 'were not idiots,' how then could they tell such a story? We might reply that our ancestors, if we go far enough back, were savages, and that such stories are the staple of savage myth. Mr. Müller, however, holds that an accidental corruption of language reduced Aryan fancy to the savage level. He explains the corruption thus: 'We find, in Sanskrit, that Bheki, the frog, was a beautiful girl, and that one day, when sitting near a well, she was discovered by a king, who asked her to be his wife. She consented, *on condition that he should never show her a drop of water*. One day, being tired, she asked the king for water; the king forgot his promise, brought water, and Bheki disappeared.' This myth, Mr. Müller holds, 'began with a short saying, such as that "Bheki, the sun, will die at the sight of water," as we should say that the sun will set, when it approaches the water from which it rose in the morning.' But how did the sun come to be called Bheki, 'the frog'? Mr. Müller supposes that this name was given to the sun by some poet or fisherman. He gives no evidence for the following statement: 'It can be shown that "frog" was used as a name for the sun. Now at sunrise and sunset, when the sun was squatting on the water, it was called the "frog."' At what historical period the Sanskrit-speaking race was settled in seats where the sun rose and set in water, we do not know, and 'chapter and verse' are needed for the statement that 'frog' was actually a name of the sun. Mr. Müller's argument, however, is that the sun was called 'the frog,' that people forgot that the frog and sun were identical, and that Frog, or Bheki, was mistaken for the name of a girl to whom was applied the old saw about dying at sight of water. 'And so,' says Mr. Müller, 'the change from sun to frog, and from frog to man, which was at first due to the mere spell of language, would in our nursery tales be ascribed to miraculous charms more familiar to a later age.' As a matter of fact, magical metamorphoses are infinitely more familiar to the lowest savages than to people in a 'later age.' Magic, as Castren observes, 'belongs to the lowest known stages of civilisation.' Mr. Müller's theory, however, is this—that a Sanskrit-speaking people, living where the sun rose out of and set in some ocean, called the sun, as he touched the water, Bheki, the frog, and said he would die at the sight of water. They ceased to call the sun the frog, or Bheki, but kept the saying, 'Bheki will die at sight of water.' Not knowing who or what Bheki might be, they took her for a frog, who also was a pretty wench. Lastly, they made the story of Bheki's distinguished wedding and mysterious disappearance. For this interpretation, historical and linguistic evidence is not offered. When did a Sanskrit-speaking race live beside a great sea? How do we know that 'frog' was used as a name for 'sun'?

* * * * *

We have already given our explanation. To the savage intellect, man and beast are on a level, and all savage myth makes men descended from beasts; while stories of the loves of gods in bestial shape, or the unions of men and animals, incessantly occur. 'Unnatural' as these notions seem to us, no ideas are more familiar to savages, and none recur more frequently in Indo-Aryan, Scandinavian, and Greek mythology. An extant tribe in North-West America still claims descent from a frog. The wedding of Bheki and the king is a survival, in Sanskrit, of a tale of this kind. Lastly, Bheki disappears, when her associations with her old amphibious life are revived in the manner she had expressly forbidden.

* * * * *

Our interpretation may be supported by an Ojibway parallel. A hunter named Otter-heart, camping near a beaver lodge, found a pretty girl loitering round his fire. She keeps his wigwam in order, and 'lays his blanket near the deerskin she had laid for herself. "Good," he muttered, "this is my wife."' She refuses to eat the beavers he has shot, but at night he hears a noise, '*krch, krch*, as if beavers were gnawing wood.' He sees, by the glimmer of the fire, his wife nibbling birch twigs. In fact, the good little wife is a beaver, as the pretty Indian girl was a frog. The pair

68

lived happily till spring came and the snow melted and the streams ran full. Then his wife implored the hunter to build her a bridge over every stream and river, that she might cross dry-footed. 'For,' she said, 'if my feet touch water, this would at once cause thee great sorrow.' The hunter did as she bade him, but left unbridged one tiny runnel. The wife stumbled into the water, and, as soon as her foot was wet, she immediately resumed her old shape as a beaver, her son became a beaverling, and the brooklet, changing to a roaring river, bore them to the lake. Once the hunter saw his wife again among her beast kin. 'To thee I sacrificed all,' she said, 'and I only asked thee to help me dry-footed over the waters. Thou didst cruelly neglect this. Now I must remain for ever with my people.'

* * * * *

This tale was told to Kohl by 'an old insignificant squaw among the Ojibways.'[76] Here we have a precise parallel to the tale of Bheki, the frog-bride, and here the reason of the prohibition to touch water is made perfectly unmistakable. The touch magically revived the bride's old animal life with the beavers. Or was the Indian name for beaver (*temaksé*) once a name for the sun? [77]

A curious variant of this widely distributed *Märchen* of the animal bride is found in the mythical genealogy of the Raja of Chutia Nagpur, a chief of the Naga, or snake race. It is said that Raja Janameja prepared a *yajnya*, or great malevolently magical incantation, to destroy all the people of the serpent race. To prevent this annihilation, the supernatural being, Pundarika Nag, took a human form, and became the husband of the beautiful Parvati, daughter of a Brahman. But Pundarika Nag, being a serpent by nature, could not divest himself, even in human shape, of his forked tongue and venomed breath. And, just as Urvasi

---

[76] *Kitchi Gami*, p. 105.
[77] The sun-frog occurs seven times in Sir G. W. Cox's *Mythology of the Aryan Peoples*, and is used as an example to prove that animals in myth are usually the sun, like Bheki, 'the sun-frog.'

69

could not abide with her mortal lover, after he transgressed the prohibition to appear before her naked, so Pundarika Nag was compelled by fate to leave his bride, if she asked him any questions about his disagreeable peculiarities. She did, at last, ask questions, in circumstances which made Pundarika believe that he was bound to answer her. Now the curse came upon him, he plunged into a pool, like the beaver, and vanished. His wife became the mother of the serpent Rajas of Chutia Nagpur. Pundarika Nag, in his proper form as a great hooded snake, guarded his first-born child. The crest of the house is a hooded snake with human face. [78]

Here, then, we have many examples of the disappearance of the bride or bridegroom in consequence of infringement of various mystic rules. Sometimes the beloved one is seen when he or she should not be seen. Sometimes, as in a Maori story, the bride vanishes, merely because she is in a bad temper.[79] Among the Red Men, as in Sanskrit, the taboo on water is broken, with the usual results. Now for an example in which the rule against using *names* is infringed. [80]

This formula constantly occurs in the Welsh fairy tales published by Professor Rhys.[81] Thus the heir of Corwrion fell in love with a fairy: 'They were married on the distinct understanding that the husband was not to know her name, . . . and was not to strike her with iron, on pain of her leaving him at once.' Unluckily the man once tossed her a bridle, the iron bit touched the wife, and 'she at once flew through the air, and plunged headlong into Corwrion Lake.'

A number of tales turning on the same incident are published in 'Cymmrodor,' v. I. In these we have either the taboo on the name, or the taboo on the touch of iron. In a widely diffused superstition iron 'drives away devils and ghosts,' according to the Scholiast on the eleventh book of the 'Odyssey,' and the Oriental

---

[78] Dalton's *Ethnol. of Bengal,* pp. 165, 166.
[79] Taylor, *New Zealand,* p. 143.
[80] Liebrecht gives a Hindoo example, *Zur Volkskunde,* p. 239.
[81] *Cymmrodor,* iv. pt. 2.

70

Djinn also flee from iron.[82] Just as water is fatal to the Aryan frog-bride and to the Red Indian beaver-wife, restoring them to their old animal forms, so the magic touch of iron breaks love between the Welshman and his fairy mistress, the representative of the stone age.

In many tales of fairy-brides, they are won by a kind of force. The lover in the familiar Welsh and German *Märchen* sees the swan-maidens throw off their swan plumage and dance naked.. He steals the feather-garb of one of them, and so compels her to his love. Finally, she leaves him, in anger, or because he has broken some taboo. Far from being peculiar to Aryan mythology, this legend occurs, as Mr. Farrer has shown, [83]in Algonquin and Bornoese tradition. The Red Indian story told by Schoolcraft in his 'Algic Researches' is most like the Aryan version, but has some native peculiarities. Wampee was a great hunter, who, on the lonely prairie, once heard strains of music. Looking up he saw a speck in the sky: the speck drew nearer and nearer, and proved to be a basket containing twelve heavenly maidens. They reached the earth and began to dance, inflaming the heart of Wampee with love. But Wampee could not draw near the fairy girls in his proper form without alarming them. Like Zeus in his love adventures, Wampee exercised the medicine-man's power of metamorphosing himself. He assumed the form of a mouse, approached unobserved, and caught one of the dancing maidens. After living with Wampee for some time she wearied of earth, and, by virtue of a 'mystic chain of verse,' she ascended again to her heavenly home.

Now is there any reason to believe that this incident was once part of the myth of Pururavas and Urvasi? Was the fairy-love, Urvasi, originally caught and held by Pururavas among her naked and struggling companions? Though this does not appear to have been much noticed, it seems to follow from a speech of Pururavas in the Vedic dialogue [84] (x. 95, 8, 9). Mr. Max Müller translates

---

[82] *Prim. Cult.*, i. 140.
[83] Primitive Manners, p. 256.
[84] See Meyer, *Gandharven-Kentauren*, Benfey, *Pantsch.*, i. 263.

thus: 'When I, the mortal, threw my arms round those flighty immortals, they trembled away from me like a trembling doe, like horses that kick against the cart.'[85] Ludwig's rendering suits our view—that Pururavas is telling how he first caught Urvasi—still better: 'When I, the mortal, held converse with the immortals who had laid aside their raiment, like slippery serpents they glided from me, like horses yoked to the car.' These words would well express the adventure of a lover among the naked flying swan-maidens, an adventure familiar to the Red Men as to Persian legends of the Peris.

To end our comparison of myths like the tale of 'Cupid and Psyche,' we find an example among the Zulus. Here [86] the mystic lover came in when all was dark, and felt the damsel's face. After certain rites, 'in the morning he went away, he speaking continually, the girl not seeing him. During all those days he would not allow the girl (*sic*), when she said she would light a fire. Finally, after a magical ceremony, he said, "Light the fire!" and stood before her revealed, a shining shape.' This has a curious resemblance to the myth of Cupid and Psyche; but a more curious detail remains. In the Zulu story of Ukcombekcansini, the friends of a bride break a taboo and kill a tabooed animal. Instantly, like Urvasi and her companions in the Yajur Veda, the bride and her maidens disappear *and are turned into birds!* [87] They are afterwards surprised in human shape, and the bride is restored to her lover.

Here we conclude, having traced parallels to Cupid and Psyche in many non-Aryan lands. Our theory of the myth does not rest on etymology. We have seen that the most renowned scholars, Max Müller, Kuhn, Roth, all analyse the names Urvasi and Pururavas in different ways, and extract different interpretations. We have found the story where these names were probably never heard of. We interpret it as a tale of the intercourse between mortal men and immortal maids, or between

---

[85] *Selected Essays*, i. 411.
[86] *Callaway*, p. 63.
[87] *Ibid.*, p. 119.

men and metamorphosed animals, as in India and North America. We explain the separation of the lovers as the result of breaking a taboo, or law of etiquette, binding among men and women, as well as between men and fairies.

* * * * *

The taboos are, to see the beloved unveiled, to utter his or her name, to touch her with a metal 'terrible to ghosts and spirits,' or to do some action which will revive the associations of a former life. We have shown that rules of nuptial etiquette resembling these in character do exist, and have existed, even among Greeks—as where the Milesian, like the Zulu, women made a law not to utter their husbands' names. Finally, we think it a reasonable hypothesis that tales on the pattern of 'Cupid and Psyche' might have been evolved wherever a curious nuptial taboo required to be sanctioned, or explained, by a myth. On this hypothesis, the stories may have been separately invented in different lands; but there is also a chance that they have been transmitted from people to people in the unknown past of our scattered and wandering race. This theory seems at least as probable as the hypothesis that the meaning of an Aryan proverbial statement about sun and dawn was forgotten, and was altered unconsciously into a tale which is found among various non-Aryan tribes. That hypothesis again, learned and ingenious as it is, has the misfortune to be opposed by other scholarly hypotheses not less ingenious and learned.

* * * * *

As for the sun-frog, we may hope that he has sunk for ever beneath the western wave.

73

A FAR-TRAVELLED TALE.

A modern novelist has boasted that her books are read 'from Tobolsk to Tangiers.' This is a wide circulation, but the widest circulation in the world has probably been achieved by a story whose author, unlike Ouida, will never be known to fame. The tale which we are about to examine is, perhaps, of all myths the most widely diffused, yet there is no ready way of accounting for its extraordinary popularity. Any true 'nature-myth,' any myth which accounts for the processes of nature or the aspects of natural phenomena, may conceivably have been invented separately, wherever men in an early state of thought observed the same facts, and attempted to explain them by telling a story. Thus we have seen that the earlier part of the Myth of Cronus is a nature-myth, setting forth the cause of the separation of Heaven and Earth. Star-myths again, are everywhere similar, because men who believed all nature to be animated and personal, accounted for the grouping of constellations in accordance with these crude beliefs.[88] Once more, if a story like that of 'Cupid and Psyche' be found among the most diverse races, the distribution becomes intelligible if the myth was invented to illustrate or enforce a widely prevalent custom. But in the following story no such explanation is even provisionally acceptable.

The gist of the tale (which has many different 'openings,' and conclusions in different places) may be stated thus: A young man is brought to the home of a hostile animal, a giant, cannibal, wizard, or a malevolent king. He is put by his unfriendly host to various severe trials, in which it is hoped that he will perish. In each trial he is assisted by the daughter of his host. After achieving the adventures, he elopes with the girl, and is pursued

---

[88] *Primitive Culture*, i. 357: 'The savage sees individual stars as animate beings, or combines star-groups into living celestial creatures, or limbs of them, or objects connected with them.'

by her father. The runaway pair throw various common objects behind them, which are changed into magical obstacles and check the pursuit of the father. The myth has various endings, usually happy, in various places. Another form of the narrative is known, in which the visitors to the home of the hostile being are, not wooers of his daughter, but brothers of his wife.[89] The incidents of the flight, in this variant, are still of the same character. Finally, when the flight is that of a brother from his sister's malevolent ghost, in Hades (Japan), or of two sisters from a cannibal mother or step-mother (Zulu and Samoyed), the events of the flight and the magical aids to escape remain little altered. We shall afterwards see that attempts have been made to interpret one of these narratives as a nature-myth; but the attempts seem unsuccessful. We are therefore at a loss to account for the wide diffusion of this tale, unless it has been transmitted slowly from people to people, in the immense unknown prehistoric past of the human race.

* * * * *

Before comparing the various forms of the myth in its first shape—that which tells of the mortal lover and the giant's or wizard's daughter—let us give the Scottish version of the story. This version was written down for me, many years ago, by an aged lady in Morayshire. I published it in the 'Revue Celtique'; but it is probably new to story-comparers, in its broad Scotch variant.

NICHT NOUGHT NOTHING.

There once lived a king and a queen. They were long married and had no bairns; but at last the queen had a bairn, when the king was away in far countries. The queen would not christen the bairn till the king came back, and she said, 'We will just call him Nicht Nought Nothing until his father comes home.' But it was

---

[89] This formula occurs among Bushmen and Eskimo (Bleek and Rink).

long before he came home, and the boy had grown a nice little laddie. At length the king was on his way back; but he had a big river to cross, and there was a spate, and he could not get over the water. But a giant came up to him, and said, 'If you will give me Nicht Nought Nothing, I will carry you over the water on my back.' The king had never heard that his son was called Nicht Nought Nothing, and so he promised him. When the king got home again, he was very happy to see his wife again, and his young son. She told him that she had not given the child any name but Nicht Nought Nothing, until he should come home again himself. The poor king was in a terrible case. He said, 'What have I done? I promised to give the giant who carried me over the river on his back, Nicht Nought Nothing.' The king and the queen were sad and sorry, but they said, 'When the giant comes we will give him the hen-wife's bairn; he will never know the difference.' The next day the giant came to claim the king's promise, and he sent for the hen-wife's bairn; and the giant went away with the bairn on his back. He travelled till he came to a big stone, and there he sat down to rest. He said,

'Hidge, Hodge, on my back, what time of day is it?' The poor little bairn said, 'It is the time that my mother, the hen-wife, takes up the eggs for the queen's breakfast.'

The giant was very angry, and dashed the bairn on the stone and killed it.

*****

The same adventure is repeated with the gardener's son.

*****

Then the giant went back to the king's house, and said he would destroy them all if they did not give him Nicht Nought Nothing this time. They had to do it; and when he came to the big stone, the giant said, 'What time of day is it?' Nicht Nought Nothing said, 'It is the time that my father the king will be sitting down to supper.' The giant said, 'I've got the richt ane noo;' and took Nicht Nought Nothing to his own house and brought him up till he was a man.

The giant had a bonny dochter, and she and the lad grew very fond of each other. The giant said one day to Nicht Nought Nothing, 'I've work for you to-morrow. There is a stable seven miles long and seven miles broad, and it has not been cleaned for seven years, and you must clean it to-morrow, or I will have you for my supper.'

The giant's dochter went out next morning with the lad's breakfast, and found him in a terrible state, for aye as he cleaned out a bit, it aye fell in again. The giant's dochter said she would help him, and she cried a' the beasts of the field, and a' the fowls o' the air, and in a minute they a' came, and carried awa' everything that was in the stable and made a' clean before the giant came home. He said, 'Shame for the wit that helped you; but I have a worse job for you to-morrow.' Then he told Nicht Nought Nothing that there was a loch seven miles long, and seven miles deep, and seven miles broad, and he must drain it the next day, or else he would have him for his supper. Nicht Nought Nothing began early next morning and tried to lave the water with his pail, but the loch was never getting any less, and he did no ken what to do; but the giant's dochter called on all the fish in the sea to come and drink the water, and very soon they drank it dry. When the giant saw the work done he was in a rage, and said, 'I've a worse job for you to-morrow; there is a tree seven miles high, and no branch on it, till you get to the top, and there is a nest, and you must bring down the eggs without breaking one, or else I will have you for my supper.' At first the giant's dochter did not know how to help Nicht Nought Nothing; but she cut off first her fingers and then her toes, and made steps of them, and he clomb the tree, and got all the eggs safe till he came to the bottom, and then one was broken. The giant's dochter advised him to run away, and she would follow him. So he travelled till he came to a king's palace, and the king and queen took him in and were very kind to him. The giant's dochter left her father's house, and he pursued her and was drowned. Then she came to the king's palace where Nicht Nought Nothing was. And she went up into a tree to watch for him. The gardener's dochter, going to draw water in the well, saw the shadow of the lady in the water, and thought it was herself, and said, 'If I'm so bonny, if I'm so brave, do you send me to draw water?' The gardener's wife went out, and she said the same thing. Then the gardener went himself, and brought the lady from the tree, and led her in. And he told her that a stranger was to marry the king's dochter, and showed her the man: and it was Nicht Nought Nothing asleep in a chair. And she saw him, and cried to him, 'Waken, waken, and speak to me!' But he would not waken, and syne she cried,

> 'I cleaned the stable,
> I laved the loch,
> and I clamb the tree,
> And all for the love of thee,
> And thou wilt not waken and speak to me.'

The king and the queen heard this, and came to the bonny young lady, and she said,

'I canna get Nicht Nought Nothing to speak to me for all that I can do.'

Then were they greatly astonished when she spoke of Nicht Nought Nothing, and asked where he was, and she said, 'He that sits there in the chair.' Then they ran to him and kissed him and called him their own dear son, and he wakened, and told them all that the giant's dochter had done for him, and of all her kindness. Then they took her in their arms and kissed her, and said she should now be their dochter, for their son should marry her.

And they lived happy all their days.

In this variant of the story, which we may use as our text, it is to be noticed that a *lacuna* exists. The narrative of the flight omits to mention that the runaways threw things behind them which became obstacles in the giant's way. One of these objects probably turned into a lake, in which the giant was drowned. [90]A common incident is the throwing behind of a comb, which changes into a thicket. The formula of leaving obstacles behind occurs in the Indian collection, the 'Kathasarit sagara' (vii. xxxix.). The 'Battle of the Birds,' in Campbell's 'Tales of the West Highlands,' is a very copious Gaelic variant. Russian parallels are 'Vasilissa the Wise and the Water King,' and 'The King Bear.'[91] The incident of the flight and the magical obstacles is found in Japanese mythology.[92] The 'ugly woman of Hades' is sent to pursue the hero. He casts down his black head-dress, and it is instantly turned into grapes; he fled while she was eating them. Again, 'he cast down his multitudinous and close-toothed comb, and it instantly turned into bamboo sprouts.' In the Gaelic version, the pursuer is detained by talkative objects which the pursued leave at home, and this marvel recurs in Zululand, and is found among the Bushmen. The Zulu versions are numerous.[93] Oddly enough, in the last variant, the girl performs no magic feat, but merely throws sesamum on the ground to delay the cannibals, for cannibals are very fond of sesamum. [94]

✳ ✳ ✳ ✳ ✳

Here, then, we have the remarkable details of the flight, in Zulu, Gaelic, Norse, Malagasy, [95]Russian, Italian, Japanese. Of all incidents in the myth, the incidents of the flight are most widely known. But the whole connected series of events—the coming of the wooer; the love of the hostile being's daughter; the tasks imposed on the wooer; the aid rendered by the daughter; the

---

[90] The events of the flight are recorded correctly in the Gaelic variant 'The Battle of the Birds.' (Campbell, *Tales of the West Highlands*, vol. i. p. 25.)
[91] Ralston, *Russian Folk Tales*, 132; Köhler, *Orient und Occident*, ii. 107, 114.
[92] *Ko ti ki*, p. 36.
[93] Callaway, pp. 51, 53, 64, 145, 228.
[94] See also 'Petrosinella' in the *Pentamerone*, and 'The Mastermaid' in Dasent's *Tales from the Norse*.
[95] *Folk-Lore Journal*, August 1883.

flight of the pair; the defeat or destruction of the hostile being—all these, or most of these, are extant, in due sequence, among the following races. The Greeks have the tale, the people of Madagascar have it, the Lowland Scotch, the Celts, the Russians, the Italians, the Algonquins, the Finns, and the Samoans have it. Now if the story were confined to the Aryan race, we might account for its diffusion, by supposing it to be the common heritage of the Indo-European peoples, carried everywhere with them in their wanderings. But when the tale is found in Madagascar, North America, Samoa, and among the Finns, while many scattered incidents occur in even more widely severed races, such as Zulus, Bushmen, Japanese, Eskimo, Samoyeds, the Aryan hypothesis becomes inadequate.

To show how closely, all things considered, the Aryan and non-Aryan possessors of the tale agree, let us first examine the myth of Jason.

* * * * *

The earliest literary reference to the myth of Jason is in the 'Iliad' (vii. 467, xxiii. 747). Here we read of Euneos, a son whom Hypsipyle bore to Jason in Lemnos. Already, even in the 'Iliad,' the legend of Argo's voyage has been fitted into certain well-known geographical localities. A reference in the 'Odyssey' (xii. 72) has a more antique ring: we are told that of all barques Argo alone escaped the jaws of the Rocks Wandering, which clashed together and destroyed ships. Argo escaped, it is said, 'because Jason was dear to Hera.' It is plain, from various fragmentary notices, that Hesiod was familiar with several of the adventures in the legend of Jason. In the 'Theogony' (993-998) Hesiod mentions the essential facts of the legend: how Jason carried off from Æetes his daughter, 'after achieving the adventures, many and grievous,' which were laid upon him. At what period the home of Æetes was placed in Colchis, it is not easy to determine. Mimnermus, a contemporary of Solon, makes the home of Æetes

80

lie 'on the brink of ocean,' a very vague description.[96] Pindar, on the other hand, in the splendid Fourth Pythian Ode, already knows Colchis as the scene of the loves and flight of Jason and Medea.

* * * *

'Long were it for me to go by the beaten track,' says Pindar, 'and I know a certain short path.' Like Pindar, we may abridge the tale of Jason. He seeks the golden fleece in Colchis: Æetes offers it to him as a prize for success in certain labours. By the aid of Medea, the daughter of Æetes, the wizard-king, Jason tames the fire-breathing oxen, yokes them to the plough, and drives a furrow. By Medea's help he conquers the children of the teeth of the dragon, subdues the snake that guards the fleece of gold, and escapes, but is pursued by Æetes. To detain Æetes, Medea throws behind the mangled remains of her own brother, Apsyrtos, and the Colchians pursue no further than the scene of this bloody deed. The savagery of this act survives even in the work of a poet so late as Apollonius Rhodius (iv. 477), where we read how Jason performed a rite of savage magic, mutilating the body of Apsyrtos in a manner which was believed to appease the avenging ghost of the slain. 'Thrice he tasted the blood, thrice spat it out between his teeth,' a passage which the Scholiast says contains the description of an archaic custom popular among murderers.

Beyond Tomi, where a popular etymology fixed the 'cutting up' of Apsyrtos, we need not follow the fortunes of Jason and Medea. We have already seen the wooer come to the hostile being, win his daughter's love, achieve the adventures by her aid, and flee in her company, delaying, by a horrible device, the advance of the pursuers. To these incidents in the tale we confine our attention.

---

[96] *Poetæ Minores Gr.* ii.

Many explanations of the Jason myth have been given by Scholars who thought they recognised elemental phenomena in the characters. As usual these explanations differ widely. Whenever a myth has to be interpreted, it is certain that one set of Scholars will discover the sun and the dawn, where another set will see the thunder-cloud and lightning. The moon is thrown in at pleasure. Sir G. W. Cox determines [97] 'that the name Jason (Iasôn) must be classed with the many others, Iasion, Iamus, Iolaus, Iaso, belonging to the same root.' Well, what is the root? Apparently the root is 'the root *i*, as denoting a crying colour, that is, a loud colour' (ii. 81). Seemingly (i. 229) violet is a loud colour, and, wherever you have the root *i*, you have 'the violet-tinted morning from which the sun is born.' Medea is 'the daughter of the sun,' and most likely, in her 'beneficent aspect,' is the dawn. But (ii. 81, note) *ios* has another meaning, 'which, as a spear, represents the far-darting ray of the sun'; so that, in one way or another, Jason is connected with the violet-tinted morning or with the sun's rays. This is the gist of the theory of Sir George Cox.

Preller [98] is another Scholar, with another set of etymologies. Jason is derived, he thinks, from ιαομαι, to heal, because Jason studied medicine under the Centaur Chiron. This is the view of the Scholiast on Apollonius Rhodius (i. 554). Jason, to Preller's mind, is a form of Asclepius, 'a spirit of the spring with its soft suns and fertile rains.' Medea is the moon. Medea, on the other hand, is a lightning goddess, in the opinion of Schwartz. [99]No philological reason is offered. Meanwhile, in Sir George Cox's system, the equivalent of Medea, 'in her beneficent aspect,' is the dawn.

We must suppose, it seems, that either the soft spring rains and the moon, or the dawn and the sun, or the lightning and the thunder-cloud, in one arrangement or another, irresistibly suggested, to early Aryan minds, the picture of a wooer, arriving

---

[97] *Mythol. Ar.*, ii. 150.
[98] *Gr. My.*, ii. 318.
[99] *Sonne, Mond und Sterne*, pp. 213, 229.

in a hostile home, winning a maiden's love, achieving adventures by her aid, fleeing with her from her angry father and delaying his pursuit by various devices. Why the spring, the moon, the lightning, the dawn—any of them or all of them—should have suggested such a tale, let Scholars determine when they have reconciled their own differences. It is more to our purpose to follow the myth among Samoans, Algonquins, and Finns. None of these races speak an Aryan language, and none can have been beguiled into telling the same sort of tale by a disease of Aryan speech.

Samoa, where we find our story, is the name of a group of volcanic islands in Central Polynesia. They are about 3,000 miles from Sidney, were first observed by Europeans in 1722, and are as far removed as most spots from direct Aryan influences. Our position is, however, that in the shiftings and migrations of peoples, the Jason tale has somehow been swept, like a piece of drift-wood, on to the coasts of Samoa. In the islands, the tale has an epical form, and is chanted in a poem of twenty-six stanzas. There is something Greek in the free and happy life of the Samoans—something Greek, too, in this myth of theirs. There was once a youth, Siati, famous for his singing, a young Thamyris of Samoa. But as, according to Homer, 'the Muses met Thamyris the Thracian, and made an end of his singing, for he boasted and said that he would vanquish even the Muses if he sang against them,' so did the Samoan god of song envy Siati. The god and the mortal sang a match: the daughter of the god was to be the mortal's prize if he proved victorious. Siati won, and he set off, riding on a shark, as Arion rode the dolphin, to seek the home of the defeated deity. At length he reached the shores divine, and thither strayed Puapae, daughter of the god, looking for her comb which she had lost. 'Siati,' said she, 'how camest thou hither?' 'I am come to seek the song-god, and to wed his daughter.' 'My father,' said the maiden, 'is more a god than a man; eat nothing he hands you, never sit on a high seat, lest death follow.' So they were united in marriage. But the god, like Æetes, was wroth, and began to set Siati upon perilous tasks: 'Build me a house, and let it be finished this very day, else death and the oven await thee.'[100]

Siati wept, but the god's daughter had the house built by the evening. The other adventures were to fight a fierce dog, and to find a ring lost at sea. Just as the Scotch giant's daughter cut off her fingers to help her lover, so the Samoan god's daughter bade Siati cut her body into pieces and cast her into the sea. There she became a fish, and recovered the ring. They set off to the god's house, but met him pursuing them, with the help of his other daughter. 'Puapae and Siati threw down the comb, and it became a bush of thorns in the way to intercept the god and Puanli,' the other daughter. Next they threw down a bottle of earth which became a mountain; 'and then followed their bottle of water, and that became a sea, and drowned the god and Puanli.'[101]

This old Samoan song contains nearly the closest savage parallel to the various household tales which find their heroic and artistic shape in the Jason saga. Still more surprising in its resemblances is the Malagasy version of the narrative. In the Malagasy story, the conclusion is almost identical with the winding up of the Scotch fairy tale. The girl hides in a tree; her face, seen reflected in a well, is mistaken by women for their own faces, and the recognition follows in due course.[102]

Like most Red Indian versions of popular tales, the Algonquin form of the Jason saga is strongly marked with the peculiarities of the race. The story is recognisable, and that is all.

The opening, as usual, differs from other openings. Two children are deserted in the wilderness, and grow up to manhood. One of them loses an arrow in the water; the elder brother, Panigwun, wades after it. A magical canoe flies past: an old magician, who is alone in the canoe, seizes Panigwun and carries him off. The canoe fleets along, like the barques of the Phæacians, at the will of the magician, and reaches the isle where,

---

[100] This proves that the tale belongs to the pre-Christian cannibal age.
[101] Turner's *Samoa*, p. 102. In this tale only the names of the daughters are translated; they mean 'white fish' and 'dark fish.'
[102] *Folk-Lore Journal*, August 1883.

like the Samoan god of song, he dwells with his two daughters. 'Here, my daughter,' said he, 'is a young man for your husband.' But the daughter knew that the proposed husband was but another victim of the old man's magic arts. By the daughter's advice, Panigwun escaped in the magic barque, consoled his brother, and returned to the island. Next day the magician, Mishosha, set the young man to hard tasks and perilous adventures. He was to gather gulls' eggs; but the gulls attacked him in dense crowds. By an incantation he subdued the birds, and made them carry him home to the island. Next day he was sent to gather pebbles, that he might be attacked and eaten by the king of the fishes. Once more the young man, like the Finnish Ilmarinen in Pohjola, subdued the mighty fish, and went back triumphant. The third adventure, as in 'Nicht Nought Nothing,' was to climb a tree of extraordinary height in search of a bird's nest. Here, again, the youth succeeded, and finally conspired with the daughters to slay the old magician. Lastly the boy turned the magician into a sycamore tree, and won his daughter. The other daughter was given to the brother who had no share in the perils.[103] Here we miss the incident of the flight; and the magician's daughter, though in love with the hero, does not aid him to perform the feats. Perhaps an Algonquin brave would scorn the assistance of a girl. In the 'Kalevala,' the old hero, Wäinämöinen, and his friend Ilmarinen, set off to the mysterious and hostile land of Pohjola to win a bride. The maiden of Pohjola loses her heart to Ilmarinen, and, by her aid, he bridles the wolf and bear, ploughs a field of adders with a plough of gold, and conquers the gigantic pike that swims in the Styx of Finnish mythology. After this point the story is interrupted by a long sequel of popular bridal songs, and, in the wandering course of the rather aimless epic, the flight and its incidents have been forgotten, or are neglected. These incidents recur, however, in the thread of somewhat different plots. We have seen that they are found in Japan, among the Eskimo, among the Bushmen, the

---

[103] Schoolcraft, *Algic Researches*, ii. 94-104.

Samoyeds, and the Zulus, as well as in Hungarian, Magyar, Celtic, and other European household tales.

The conclusion appears to be that the central part of the Jason myth is incapable of being explained, either as a nature-myth, or as a myth founded on a disease of language. So many languages could not take the same malady in the same way; nor can we imagine any series of natural phenomena that would inevitably suggest this tale to so many diverse races.

We must suppose, therefore, either that all wits jumped and invented the same romantic series of situations by accident, or that all men spread from one centre, where the story was known, or that the story, once invented, has drifted all round the world. If the last theory be approved of, the tale will be like the Indian Ocean shell found lately in the Polish bone-cave, [104]or like the Egyptian beads discovered in the soil of Dahomey. The story will have been carried hither and thither, in the remotest times, to the remotest shores, by traders, by slaves, by captives in war, or by women torn from their own tribe and forcibly settled as wives among alien peoples.

Stories of this kind are everywhere the natural property of mothers and grandmothers. When we remember how widely diffused is the law of exogamy, which forbids marriage between a man and woman of the same stock, we are impressed by the number of alien elements which must have been introduced with alien wives. Where husband and wife, as often happened, spoke different languages, the woman would inevitably bring the hearthside tales of her childhood among a people of strange speech. By all these agencies, working through dateless time, we may account for the diffusion, if we cannot explain the origin, of tales like the central arrangement of incidents in the career of Jason. [105]

---

[104] *Nature*, March 14, 1884.
[105] The earlier part of the Jason cycle is analysed in the author's preface to Grimm's *Märchen* (Bell & Sons).

APOLLO AND THE MOUSE.

Why is Apollo, especially the Apollo of the Troad, he who showered the darts of pestilence among the Greeks, so constantly associated with a mouse? The very name, Smintheus, by which his favourite priest calls on him in the 'Iliad' (i. 39), might be rendered 'Mouse Apollo,' or 'Apollo, Lord of Mice.' As we shall see later, mice lived beneath the altar, and were fed in the holy of holies of the god, and an image of a mouse was placed beside or upon his sacred tripod. The ancients were puzzled by these things, and, as will be shown, accounted for them by 'mouse-stories,' Σμινθιακοι λογοι, so styled by Eustathius, the mediæval interpreter of Homer. Following our usual method, let us ask whether similar phenomena occur elsewhere, in countries where they are intelligible. Did insignificant animals elsewhere receive worship: were their effigies elsewhere placed in the temples of a purer creed? We find answers in the history of Peruvian religion.

After the Spanish conquest of Peru, one of the European adventurers, Don Garcilasso de la Vega, married an Inca princess. Their son, also named Garcilasso, was born about 1540. His famous book, 'Commentarias Reales,' contains the most authentic account of the old Peruvian beliefs. Garcilasso was learned in all the learning of the Europeans, and, as an Inca on the mother's side, had claims on the loyalty of the defeated race. He set himself diligently to collect both their priestly and popular traditions, and his account of them is the more trustworthy as it coincides with what we know to have been true in lands with which Garcilasso had little acquaintance.

✳ ✳ ✳ ✳ ✳

To Garcilasso's mind, Peruvian religion seems to be divided into two periods—the age before, and the age which followed the accession of the Incas, and their establishment of sun-worship as the creed of the State. In the earlier period, the pre-Inca period, he tells us 'an Indian was not accounted honourable unless he was

87

descended from a fountain, river, or lake, or even from the sea, or from a wild animal, such as a bear, lion, tiger, eagle, or the bird they call *cuntur* (condor), or some other bird of prey.' [106]To these worshipful creatures 'men offered what they usually saw them eat' (i. 53). But men were not content to adore large and dangerous animals. 'There was not an animal, how vile and filthy soever, that they did not worship as a god,' including 'lizards, toads, and frogs.' In the midst of these superstitions the Incas appeared. Just as the tribes claimed descent from animals, great or small, so the Incas drew *their* pedigree from the sun, which they adored like the *gens* of the Aurelii in Rome.[107] Thus every Indian had his *pacarissa*, or, as the North American Indians say, *totem*, [108]a natural object from which he claimed descent, and which, in a certain degree, he worshipped. Though sun-worship became the established religion, worship of the animal *pacarissas* was still tolerated. The sun-temples also contained *huacas*, or images, of the beasts which the Indians had venerated.[109] In the great temple of Pachacamac, the most spiritual and abstract god of Peruvian faith, 'they worshipped a she-fox and an emerald. The devil also appeared to them, and spoke in the form of a tiger, very fierce.'[110] This toleration of an older and cruder, in subordination to a purer, faith is a very common feature in religious evolution. In Catholic countries, to this day, we may watch, in Holy Week, the Adonis feast described by Theocritus, [111]and the procession and entombment of the old god of spring.

'The Incas had the good policy to collect all the tribal animal gods into their temples in and round Cuzco, in which the two leading gods were the Master of Life, and the Sun.' Did a process

---

[106] *Comm. Real.* i. 75.

[107] See Early History of the Family, infra.

[108] The names *Totem* and *Totemism* have been in use at least since 1792, among writers on the North American tribes. Prof. Max Müller (*Academy*, Jan. 1884) says the word should be, not *Totem*, but *Ote* or *Otem*. Long, an interpreter among the Indians, introduced the word *Totamism* in 1792.

[109] Christoval de Moluna (1570), p. 5.

[110] Cieza de Leon, p. 183.

[111] *Idyll* xv.

of this sort ever occur in Greek religion, and were older animal gods ever collected into the temples of such deities as Apollo?

* * * * *

While a great deal of scattered evidence about many animals consecrated to Greek gods points in this direction, it will be enough, for the present, to examine the case of the Sacred Mice. Among races which are still in the totemistic stage, which still claim descent from animals and from other objects, a peculiar marriage law generally exists, or can be shown to have existed. No man may marry a woman who is descended from the same ancestral animal, and who bears the same totem-name, and carries the same badge or family crest, as himself. A man descended from the Crane, and whose family name is Crane, cannot marry a woman whose family name is Crane. He must marry a woman of the Wolf, or Turtle, or Swan, or other name, and her children keep her family title, not his. Thus, if a Crane man marries a Swan woman, the children are Swans, and none of them may marry a Swan; they must marry Turtles, Wolves, or what not, and *their* children, again, are Turtles, or Wolves. Thus there is necessarily an eternal come and go of all the animal names known in a district. As civilisation advances these rules grow obsolete. People take their names from the father, as among ourselves. Finally the dwellers in a given district, having become united into a local tribe, are apt to drop the various animal titles and to adopt, as the name of the whole tribe, the name of the chief, or of the predominating family. Let us imagine a district of some twenty miles in which there are Crane, Wolf, Turtle, and Swan families. Long residence together, and common interests, have welded them into a local tribe. The chief is of the Wolf family, and the tribe, sinking family differences and family names, calls itself 'the Wolves.' Such tribes were probably, in the beginning, the inhabitants of the various Egyptian towns which severally worshipped the wolf, or the sheep, or the crocodile, and abstained religiously (except on certain sacrificial occasions) from the flesh of the animal that gave them its name. [112]

* * * * *

It has taken us long to reach the Sacred Mice of Greek religion, but we are now in a position to approach their august divinity. We have seen that the sun-worship superseded, without abolishing, the tribal *pacarissas* in Peru, and that the *huacas*, or images, of the sacred animals were admitted under the roof of the temple of the Sun. Now it is recognised that the temples of the Sminthian Apollo contained images of sacred mice among other animals, and our argument is that here, perhaps, we have another example of the Peruvian religious evolution. Just as, in Peru, the tribes adored 'vile and filthy' animals, just as the solar worship of the Incas subordinated these, just as the *huacas* of the beasts remained in the temples of the Peruvian Sun; so, we believe, the tribes along the Mediterranean coasts had, at some very remote prehistoric period, their animal *pacarissas*; these were subordinated to the religion (to some extent solar) of Apollo; and the *huacas*, or animal idols, survived in Apollo's temples.

* * * * *

If this theory be correct, we shall probably find the mouse, for example, revered as a sacred animal in many places. This would necessarily follow, if the marriage customs which we have described ever prevailed on Greek soil, and scattered the mouse-name far and wide. [113] Traces of the Mouse families, and of

---

[112] Sayce, *Herodotos*, p. 344; Herodotus, ii. 42; Wilkinson's *Ancient Egyptians* (1878, ii. 475, note 2); Plutarch, *De Is. et Os.*, 71, 72; Athenæus, vii. 299; Strabo, xvii. 813.

[113] The Mouse, according to Dalton, is still a totem among the Oraons of Bengal. A man of the Mouse 'motherhood,' as the totem kindred is locally styled, may not eat mice (esteemed a delicacy), nor marry a girl who is a Mouse.

adoration, if adoration there was of the mouse, would linger on in the following shapes:—(1) Places would be named from mice, and mice would be actually held sacred in themselves. (2) The mouse-name would be given locally to the god who superseded the mouse. (3) The figure of the mouse would be associated with the god, and used as a badge, or a kind of crest, or local mark, in places where the mouse has been a venerated animal. (4) Finally, myths would be told to account for the sacredness of a creature so undignified.

Let us take these considerations in their order:—

(1) If there were local mice tribes, deriving their name from the worshipful mouse, certain towns settled by these tribes would retain a reverence for mice.

In Chrysa, a town of the Troad, according to Heraclides Ponticus, mice were held sacred, the local name for mouse being σμινθος. Many places bore this mouse-name, according to Strabo.[114] This is precisely what would have occurred had the Mouse totem, and the Mouse stock, been widely distributed.[115] The Scholiast [116] mentions Sminthus as a place in the Troad. Strabo speaks of two places deriving their name from Sminthus, or mouse, near the Sminthian temple, and others near Larissa. In Rhodes and Lindus, the mouse place-name recurs, 'and in many other districts' (Και αλλοθι δε πολλαχοθι). Strabo (x. 486) names Caressus, and Poeessa, in Ceos, among the other places which had Sminthian temples, and, presumably, were once centres of tribes named after the mouse.

Here, then, are a number of localities in which the Mouse Apollo was adored, and where the old mouse-name lingered. That the mice were actually held sacred in their proper persons we learn from Ælian. 'The dwellers in Hamaxitus of the Troad worship mice,' says Ælian. 'In the temple of Apollo Smintheus, mice are nourished, and food is offered to them, at the public

---

[114] xiii. 604. Casaub. 1620.
[115] There were Sminthiac feasts at Rhodes, Gela, Lesbos, and Crete (De Witte, *Revue Numismatique*, N.S. iii. 3-11).
[116] *Iliad*, i. 39.

91

expense, and white mice dwell beneath the altar.'[117] In the same way we found that the Peruvians fed their sacred beasts on what they usually saw them eat.

(2) The second point in our argument has already been sufficiently demonstrated. The mouse-name 'Smintheus' was given to Apollo in all the places mentioned by Strabo, 'and many others.'

(3) The figure of the mouse will be associated with the god, and used as a badge, or crest, or local mark, in places where the mouse has been a venerated animal.

The passage already quoted from Ælian informs us that there stood 'an effigy of the mouse beside the tripod of Apollo.' In Chrysa, according to Strabo (xiii. 604), the statue of Apollo Smintheus had a mouse beneath his foot. The mouse on the tripod of Apollo is represented on a bas-relief illustrating the plague, and the offerings of the Greeks to Apollo Smintheus, as described in the first book of the 'Iliad.' [118]

* * * * *

The mouse is a not uncommon local badge or crest in Greece. The animals whose figures are stamped on coins, like the Athenian owl, are the most ancient marks of cities. It is a plausible conjecture that, just as the Iroquois when they signed treaties with the Europeans used their totems—bear, wolf, and turtle—as seals, [119]so the animals on archaic Greek city coins represented crests or badges which, at some far more remote period, had been totems.

---

[117] Ælian, *H. A.* xii. 5.
[118] The bas-relief is published in Paoli's *Della Religione de' Gentili*, Naples, 1771, p. 9; also by Fabretti, *Ad Cal. Oper. de Colum. Trajan.* p. 315. Paoli's book was written after the discovery in Neapolitan territory of a small bronze image, hieratic in character, representing a man with a mouse on his hand. Paoli's engraving of this work of art, unluckily, does not enable us to determine its date or *provenance*. The book is a mine of mouse-lore.
[119] Colden, *History of the Five Nations*, p. 15 (1727).

The Argives, according to Pollux, [120]stamped the mouse on their coins.[121] As there was a temple of Apollo Smintheus in Tenedos, we naturally hear of a mouse on the coins of the island.[122] Golzio has published one of these mouse coins. The people of Metapontum stamped their money with a mouse gnawing an ear of corn. The people of Cumæ employed a mouse dormant. Paoli fancied that certain mice on Roman medals might be connected with the family of *Mus*, but this is rather guesswork. [123]

We have now shown traces, at least, of various ways in which an early tribal religion of the mouse—the mouse *pacarissa*, as the Peruvians said—may have been perpetuated. When we consider that the superseding of the mouse by Apollo must have occurred, if it did occur, long before Homer, we may rather wonder that the mouse left his mark on Greek religion so long. We have seen mice revered, a god with a mouse-name, the mouse-name recurring in many places, the *huaca*, or idol, of the mouse preserved in the temples of the god, and the mouse-badge used in several widely severed localities. It remains (4) to examine the myths about mice. These, in our opinion, were probably told to account for the presence of the *huaca* of the mouse in temples, and for the occurrence of the animal in religion, and his connection with Apollo.

A singular mouse-myth, narrated by Herodotus, is worth examining for reasons which will appear later, though the events are said to have happened on Egyptian soil.[124] According to Herodotus, one Sethos, a priest of Hephæstus (Ptah), was king of

---

[120] *Onomast.*, ix. 6, segm. 84, p. 1066.
[121] De Witte says Pollux was mistaken here. In the *Revue Numismatique*, N.S. iii., De Witte publishes coins of Alexandria, the more ancient Hamaxitus, in the Troad. The Sminthian Apollo is represented with his bow, and the mouse on his hand. Other coins show the god with the mouse at his foot, or show us the lyre of Apollo supported by mice. A bronze coin in the British Museum gives Apollo with the mouse beside his foot.
[122] *Spanheim*, ad Fl. Joseph., vi. I, p. 312.
[123] *Della Rel.*, p. 174.
[124] Herodotus, ii. 141.

Egypt. He had disgraced the military class, and he found himself without an army when Sennacherib invaded his country. Sethos fell asleep in the temple, and the god, appearing to him in a vision, told him that divine succour would come to the Egyptians.[125] In the night before the battle, field-mice gnawed the quivers and shield-handles of the foe, who fled on finding themselves thus disarmed. 'And now,' says Herodotus, 'there standeth a stone image of this king in the temple of Hephæstus, and in the hand of the image a mouse, and there is this inscription, "Let whoso looketh on me be pious."'

Prof. Sayce [126] holds that there was no such person as Sethos, but that the legend 'is evidently Egyptian, not Greek, and the name of Sennacherib, as well as the fact of the Assyrian attack, is correct.' The legend also, though Egyptian, is 'an echo of the biblical account of the destruction of the Assyrian army,' an account which omits the mice. 'As to the mice, here,' says Prof. Sayce, 'we have to do again with the Greek dragomen (sic). The story of Sethos was attached to the statue of some deity which was supposed to hold a mouse in its hand.' It must have been easy to verify this supposition; but Mr. Sayce adds, 'mice were not sacred in Egypt, nor were they used as symbols, or found on the monuments.' To this remark we may suggest some exceptions. Apparently this one mouse *was* found on the monuments. Wilkinson (iii. 264) says mice do occur in the sculptures, but they were not sacred. Rats, however, were certainly sacred, and as little distinction is taken, in myth, between rats and mice as between rabbits and hares. The rat was sacred to Ra, the Sungod, and (like all totems) was not to be eaten.[127] This association

---

[125] Liebrecht (*Zur Volkskunde,* p. 13, quoting *Journal Asiatique,* 1st series, 3, 307) finds the same myth in Chinese annals. It is not a god, however, but the king of the rats, who appears to the distressed monarch in his dream. Rats then gnaw the bowstrings of his enemies. The invaders were Turks, the rescued prince a king of Khotan. The king raised a temple, and offered sacrifice—to the rats?

[126] *Herodotos,* p. 204.

[127] Wilkinson, iii. 294, quoting the *Ritual* xxxiii.: 'Thou devourest the abominable rat of Ra, or the sun.'

of the rat and the Sun cannot but remind us of Apollo and his mouse. According to Strabo, a certain city of Egypt did worship the shrew-mouse. The Athribitæ, or dwellers in Crocodilopolis, are the people to whom he attributes this cult, which he mentions (xvii. 813) among the other local animal-worships of Egypt.[128] Several porcelain examples of the field-mouse sacred to Horus (commonly called Apollo by the Greeks) may be seen in the British Museum.

That rats and field-mice were sacred in Egypt, then, we may believe on the evidence of the Ritual, of Strabo, and of many relics of Egyptian art. Herodotus, moreover, is credited when he says that the statue 'had a mouse on its hand.' Elsewhere, it is certain that the story of mice gnawing the bowstrings occurs frequently as an explanation of mouse-worship. One of the Trojan 'mouse-stories' ran—That emigrants had set out in prehistoric times from Crete. The oracle advised them to settle 'wherever they were attacked by the children of the soil.' At Hamaxitus in the Troad, they were assailed in the night by mice, which ate all that was edible of their armour and bowstrings. The colonists made up their mind that these mice were 'the children of the soil,' settled there, and adored the mouse Apollo.[129] A myth of this sort may either be a story invented to explain the mouse-name; or a Mouse tribe, like the Red Indian Wolves, or Crows, may actually have been settled on the spot, and may even have resisted invasion.[130] Another myth of the Troad accounted for

---

[128] Mr. Loftie has kindly shown me a green mouse containing the throne-name of Thothmes III. The animals thus used as substitutes for scarabs were also sacred, as the fish, rhinoceros, fly, all represented in Mr. Loftie's collection. See his *Essay of Scarabs*, p. 27. It may be admitted that, in a country where Cats were gods, the religion of the Mouse must have been struggling and oppressed.

[129] Strabo, xiii. 604.
[130] Eustathius on *Iliad*, i. 39.

the worship of the mouse Apollo on the hypothesis that he had once freed the land from mice, like the Pied Piper of Hamelin, whose pipe (still serviceable) is said to have been found in his grave by men who were digging a mine. [131]

Stories like these, stories attributing some great deliverance to the mouse, or some deliverance from mice to the god, would naturally spring up among people puzzled by their own worship of the mouse-god or of the mouse. We have explained the religious character of mice as the relics of a past age in which the mouse had been a totem and mouse family names had been widely diffused. That there are, and have been, mice totems and mouse family names among Semitic stocks round the Mediterranean is proved by Prof. Robertson Smith: [132]'Achbor, the mouse, is an Edomite name, apparently a stock name, as the jerboa and another mouse-name are among the Arabs. The same name occurs in Judah.' Where totemism exists, the members of each stock either do not eat the ancestral animal at all, or only eat him on rare sacrificial occasions. The totem of a hostile stock may be eaten by way of insult. In the case of the mouse, Isaiah seems to refer to one or other of these practices (lxvi.): 'They that sanctify themselves, and purify themselves in the gardens behind one tree in the midst, eating swine's flesh, and the abomination, and the *mouse*, shall be consumed together, saith the Lord.' This is like the Egyptian prohibition to eat 'the abominable' (that is, tabooed or forbidden) 'Rat of Ra.' If the unclean animals of Israel were originally the totems of each clan, then the mouse was a totem, [133]for the chosen people were forbidden to eat 'the weasel, and the mouse, and the tortoise after his kind.' That unclean beasts, beasts not to be eaten, were originally totems, Prof. Robertson Smith infers from Ezekiel (viii. 10, 11), where 'we find seventy of the elders of Israel—that is, the heads of houses—worshipping in a chamber which had on its walls the figures of all manner of unclean' (tabooed) 'creeping things, and

---

[131] A Strange and True Relation of the Prodigious Multitude of Mice, 1670.
[132] *Journal of Philol.*, xvii. p. 96.
[133] Leviticus xi. 29.

quadrupeds, *even all the idols of the House of Israel.*' Some have too hastily concluded that the mouse was a sacred animal among the neighbouring Philistines. After the Philistines had captured the Ark and set it in the house of Dagon, the people were smitten with disease. They therefore, in accordance with a well-known savage magical practice, made five golden representations of the diseased part, and five golden mice, as 'a trespass offering to the Lord of Israel,' and so restored the Ark.[134] Such votive offerings are common still in Catholic countries, and the mice of gold by no means prove that the Philistines had ever worshipped mice.

* * * * *

Turning to India from the Mediterranean basin, and the Aryan, Semitic, and Egyptian tribes on its coasts, we find that the mouse was the sacred animal of Rudra. 'The mouse, Rudra, is thy beast,' says the Yajur Veda, as rendered by Grohmann in his 'Apollo Smintheus.' Grohmann recognises in Rudra a deity with most of the characteristics of Apollo. In later Indian mythology, the mouse is an attribute of Ganeça, who, like Apollo Smintheus, is represented in art with his foot upon a mouse.

Such are the chief appearances of the mouse in ancient religion. If he really was a Semitic totem, it may, perhaps, be argued that his prevalence in connection with Apollo is the result of a Semitic leaven in Hellenism. Hellenic invaders may have found Semitic mouse-tribes at home, and incorporated the alien stock deity with their own Apollo-worship. In that case the mouse, while still originally a totem, would not be an Aryan totem. But probably the myths and rites of the mouse, and their diffusion, are more plausibly explained on our theory than on that of De Gubernatis: 'The Pagan sun-god crushes under his foot the Mouse of Night. When the cat's away, the mice may play; the shadows of night dance when the moon is absent.'[135] This is one of the quaintest pieces of mythological logic. Obviously, when

---

[134] Samuel i. 5, 6.
[135] *Zool. Myth,* ii. 68.

the cat (the moon) is away, the mice (the shadows) *cannot* play: there is no light to produce a shadow. As usually chances, the scholars who try to resolve all the features of myth into physical phenomena do not agree among themselves about the mouse. While the mouse is the night, according to M. de Gubernatis, in Grohmann's opinion the mouse is the lightning. He argues that the lightning was originally regarded by the Aryan race as the 'flashing tooth of a beast,' especially of a mouse. Afterwards men came to identify the beast with his teeth, and, behold, the lightning and the mouse are convertible mythical terms! Now it is perfectly true that savages regard many elemental phenomena, from eclipses to the rainbow, as the result of the action of animals. The rainbow is a serpent; [136]thunder is caused by the thunder-bird, who has actually been shot in Dacotah, and who is familiar to the Zulus; while rain is the milk of a heavenly cow— an idea recurring in the 'Zend Avesta.' But it does not follow because savages believe in these meteorological beasts that all the beasts in myth were originally meteorological. Man raised a serpent to the skies, perhaps, but his interest in the animal began on earth, not in the clouds. It is excessively improbable, and quite unproved, that any race ever regarded lightning as the flashes of a mouse's teeth. The hypothesis is a *jeu d'esprit*, like the opposite hypothesis about the mouse of Night. In these, and all the other current theories of the Sminthian Apollo, the widely diffused worship of ordinary mice, and such small deer, has been either wholly neglected, or explained by the first theory of symbolism that occurred to the conjecture of a civilised observer. The facts of savage animal-worship, and their relations to totemism, seem still unknown to or unappreciated by scholars, with the exception of Mr. Sayce, who recognises totemism as the origin of the zoomorphic element in Egyptian religion.

Our explanation, whether adequate or not, is not founded on an isolated case. If Apollo superseded and absorbed the worship of the mouse, he did no less for the wolf, the ram, the dolphin,

---

[136] *Mélusine*, N.S. i.

and several other animals whose images were associated with his own. The Greek religion was more refined and anthropomorphic than that of Egypt. In Egypt the animals were still adored, and the images of the gods had bestial heads. In Greece only a few gods, and chiefly in very archaic statues, had bestial heads; but beside the other deities the sculptor set the owl, eagle, wolf, serpent, tortoise, mouse, or whatever creature was the local favourite of the deity.[137] Probably the deity had, in the majority of cases, superseded the animal and succeeded to his honours. But the conservative religious sentiment retained the beast within the courts and in the suit and service of the anthropomorphic god.[138]

The process by which the god ousted the beasts may perhaps be observed in Samoa. There (as Dr. Turner tells us in his 'Samoa') each family has its own sacred animal, which it may not eat. If this law be transgressed, the malefactor is supernaturally punished in a variety of ways. But, while each family has thus its totem, four or five different families recognise, in owl, crab, lizard, and so on, incarnations of the same god, say of Tongo. If Tongo had a temple among these families, we can readily believe that images of the various beasts in which he was incarnate would be kept within the consecrated walls. Savage ideas like these, if they were ever entertained in Greece, would account for the holy animals of the different deities. But it is obvious that the phenomena which we have been studying may be otherwise explained. It may be said that the Sminthian Apollo was only revered as the enemy and opponent of mice. St. Gertrude (whose heart was eaten by mice) has the same *rôle* in France.[139] The

---

[137] *De Iside et Osiride*, lxxvi.

[138] This hypothesis does not maintain that totemism prevailed in Greece during historic times. Though Plutarch mentions an Athenian γενος, the Ioxidæ, which claimed descent from and revered asparagus, it is probable that genuine totemism had died out of Greece many hundreds of years before even Homer's time. But this view is not inconsistent with the existence of survivals in religion and ritual.

[139] Rolland, *Faune populaire.*

worship of Apollo, and the badge of the mouse, would, on this principle, be diffused by colonies from some centre of the faith. The images of mice in Apollo's temples would be nothing more than votive offerings. Thus, in the church of a Saxon town, the verger shows a silver mouse dedicated to Our Lady. 'This is the greatest of our treasures,' says the verger. 'Our town was overrun with mice till the ladies of the city offered this mouse of silver. Instantly all the mice disappeared.' 'And are you such fools as to believe that the creatures went away because a silver mouse was dedicated?' asked a Prussian officer. 'No,' replied the verger, rather neatly; 'or long ago we should have offered a silver Prussian.'

STAR MYTHS.

Artemus Ward used to say that, while there were many things in the science of astronomy hard to be understood, there was one fact which entirely puzzled him. He could partly perceive how we 'weigh the sun,' and ascertain the component elements of the heavenly bodies, by the aid of *spectrum* analysis. 'But what beats me about the stars,' he observed plaintively, 'is how we come to know their names.' This question, or rather the somewhat similar question, 'How did the constellations come by their very peculiar names?' has puzzled Professor Pritchard and other astronomers more serious than Artemus Ward. Why is a group of stars called the *Bear*, or the *Swan*, or the *Twins*, or named after the *Pleiades*, the fair daughters of the Giant Atlas? [140]These are difficulties that meet even children when they examine a 'celestial globe.' There they find the figure of a bear, traced out with lines in the intervals between the stars of the constellations, while a very imposing giant is so drawn that Orion's belt just fits his waist. But when he comes to look at the heavens, the infant speculator sees no sort of likeness to a bear in the stars, nor anything at all resembling a giant in the neighbourhood of Orion. The most eccentric modern fancy which can detect what shapes it will in clouds, is unable to find any likeness to human or animal forms in the stars, and yet we call a great many of the stars by the names of men and beasts and gods. Some resemblance to terrestrial things, it is true, everyone can behold in the heavens. *Corona*, for example, is like a crown, or, as the Australian black fellows know, it is like a boomerang, and we can understand why they give it the name of that curious curved missile. The *Milky Way*, again, does resemble a path in the sky; our English ancestors called it *Watling Street*—the path of the Watlings, mythical giants—and Bushmen in Africa and Red Men in North America name it the 'ashen path,' or 'the path of souls.' The ashes of the path, of course, are supposed to be hot and glowing, not dead and black like the ash-

---

[140] The attempt is not to explain the origin of each separate name but only of the general habit of giving animal or human names stars.

paths of modern running-grounds. Other and more recent names for certain constellations are also intelligible. In Homer's time the Greeks had two names for the *Great Bear*; they called it the *Bear*, or the *Wain*: and a certain fanciful likeness to a wain may be made out, though no resemblance to a bear is manifest. In the United States the same constellation is popularly styled the *Dipper*, and every one may observe the likeness to a dipper or toddy-ladle.

But these resemblances take us only a little way towards appellations. We know that we derive many of the names straight from the Greek; but whence did the Greeks get them? Some, it is said, from the Chaldæans; but whence did they reach the Chaldæans? To this we shall return later, but, as to early Greek star-lore, Goguet, the author of 'L'Origine des Lois,' a rather learned but too speculative work of the last century, makes the following characteristic remarks: 'The Greeks received their astronomy from Prometheus. This prince, as far as history teaches us, made his observations on Mount Caucasus.' That was the eighteenth century's method of interpreting mythology. The myth preserved in the 'Prometheus Bound' of Æschylus tells us that Zeus crucified the Titan on Mount Caucasus. The French philosopher, rejecting the supernatural elements of the tale, makes up his mind that Prometheus was a prince of a scientific bent, and that he established his observatory on the frosty Caucasus. But, even admitting this, why did Prometheus give the stars animal names? Goguet easily explains this by a hypothetical account of the manners of primitive men. 'The earliest peoples,' he says, 'must have used writing for purposes of astronomical science. They would be content to design the constellations of which they wished to speak by the hieroglyphical symbols of their names; hence the constellations have insensibly taken the names of the chief symbols.' Thus, a drawing of a bear or a swan was the hieroglyphic of the name of a star, or group of stars. But whence came the name which was represented by the hieroglyphic? That is precisely what our author forgets to tell us. But he remarks that the meaning of the hieroglyphic came to be forgotten, and 'the symbols gave rise to all the ridiculous tales about the heavenly signs.' This explanation is attained by the process of reasoning in a vicious circle from hypothetical premises ascertained to be false. All the known savages of the world, even those which have scarcely the elements of picture-writing, call the constellations by the names of men and animals, and all tell 'ridiculous tales' to account for the names.

As the star-stories told by the Greeks, the ancient Egyptians, and other civilised people of the old world, exactly correspond in character, and sometimes even in incident, with the star-stories of modern savages, we have the choice of three hypotheses to explain this curious coincidence. Perhaps the star-stories, about nymphs changed into bears, and bears changed into stars, were invented by the civilised races of old, and gradually found their way amongst people like the Eskimo, and the Australians, and Bushmen. Or it may be insisted that the ancestors of Australians, Eskimo, and Bushmen were once civilised, like the Greeks and Egyptians, and invented star-stories, still remembered by their degenerate descendants. These are the two forms of the explanation which will be advanced by persons who believe that the star-stories were originally the fruit of the civilised imagination. The third theory would be, that the 'ridiculous tales' about the stars were originally the work of the savage imagination, and that the Greeks, Chaldæans, and Egyptians, when they became civilised, retained the old myths that their ancestors had invented when they were savages. In favour of this theory it may be said, briefly, that there is no proof that the fathers of Australians, Eskimo, and Bushmen had ever been civilised, while there is a great deal of evidence to suggest that the fathers of the Greeks had once been savages.[141] And, if we incline to the theory that the star-myths are the creation of savage fancy, we at once learn why they are, in all parts of the world, so much alike. Just as the flint and bone weapons of rude races resemble each other much more than they resemble

---

[141] Mr. Herbert Spencer believes that the Australians were once more civilised than at present. But there has never been found a trace of pottery on the Australian continent, which says little for their civilisation in the past.

the metal weapons and the artillery of advanced peoples, so the mental products, the fairy tales, and myths of rude races have everywhere a strong family resemblance. They are produced by men in similar mental conditions of ignorance, curiosity, and credulous fancy, and they are intended to supply the same needs, partly of amusing narrative, partly of crude explanation of familiar phenomena.

Now it is time to prove the truth of our assertion that the star-stories of savage and of civilised races closely resemble each other. Let us begin with that well-known group the *Pleiades*. The peculiarity of the *Pleiades* is that the group consists of seven stars, of which one is so dim that it seems entirely to disappear, and many persons can only detect its presence through a telescope. The Greeks had a myth to account for the vanishing of the lost Pleiad. The tale is given in the 'Catasterismoi' (stories of metamorphoses into stars) attributed to Eratosthenes. This work was probably written after our era; but the author derived his information from older treatises now lost. According to the Greek myth, then, the seven stars of the Pleiad were seven maidens, daughters of the Giant Atlas. Six of them had gods for lovers; Poseidon admired two of them, Zeus three, and Ares one; but the seventh had only an earthly wooer, and when all of them were changed into stars, the maiden with the mortal lover hid her light for shame.

Now let us compare the Australian story. According to Mr. Dawson ('Australian Aborigines'), a writer who understands the natives well, 'their knowledge of the heavenly bodies greatly exceeds that of most white people,' and 'is taught by men selected for their intelligence and information. The knowledge is important to the aborigines on their night journeys;' so we may be sure that the natives are careful observers of the heavens, and are likely to be conservative of their astronomical myths. The 'Lost Pleiad' has not escaped them, and this is how they account for her disappearance. The *Pirt Kopan noot* tribe have a tradition that the *Pleiades* were a queen and her six attendants. Long ago the *Crow* (our *Canopus*) fell in love with the queen, who refused to

104

be his wife. The *Crow* found that the queen and her six maidens, like other Australian *gins*, were in the habit of hunting for white edible grubs in the bark of trees. The Crow at once changed himself into a grub (just as Jupiter and Indra used to change into swans, horses, ants, or what not) and hid in the bark of a tree. The six maidens sought to pick him out with their wooden hooks, but he broke the points of all the hooks. Then came the queen, with her pretty bone hook; he let himself be drawn out, took the shape of a giant, and ran away with her. Ever since there have only been six stars, the six maidens, in the *Pleiad.* This story is well known, by the strictest inquiry, to be current among the blacks of the West District and in South Australia.

Mr. Tylor, whose opinion is entitled to the highest respect, thinks that this may be a European myth, told by some settler to a black in the Greek form, and then spread about among the natives. He complains that the story of the loss of the *brightest* star does not fit the facts of the case.

We do not know, and how can the Australians know, that the lost star was once the brightest? It appears to me that the Australians, remarking the disappearances of a star, might very naturally suppose that the *Crow* had selected for his wife that one which had been the most brilliant of the cluster. Besides, the wide distribution of the tale among the natives, and the very great change in the nature of the incidents, seem to point to a native origin. Though the main conception—the loss of one out of seven maidens—is identical in Greek and in *Murri*, the manner of the disappearance is eminently Hellenic in the one case, eminently savage in the other. However this may be, nothing of course is proved by a single example. Let us next examine the stars *Castor* and *Pollux.* Both in Greece and in Australia these are said once to have been two young men. In the 'Catasterismoi,' already spoken of, we read: 'The *Twins*, or *Dioscouroi.*—They were nurtured in Lacedæmon, and were famous for their brotherly love, wherefore, Zeus, desiring to make their memory immortal, placed them both among the stars.' In Australia, according to Mr. Brough Smyth ('Aborigines of Victoria'), *Turree* (*Castor*) and *Wanjel* (*Pollux*) are two young men who pursue *Purra* and kill him at the commencement of the great heat. *Coonar toorung* (the mirage) is the smoke of the fire by which they roast him. In Greece it was not Castor and Pollux, but *Orion* who was the great hunter placed among the stars. Among the Bushmen of South Africa, *Castor* and *Pollux* are not young men, but young women, the wives of the Eland, the great native antelope. In Greek star-stories the *Great Bear* keeps watch, Homer says, on the hunter Orion for fear of a sudden attack. But how did the Bear get its name in Greece? According to Hesiod, the oldest Greek poet after Homer, the Bear was once a lady, daughter of Lycaon, King of Arcadia. She was a nymph of the train of chaste Artemis, but yielded to the love of Zeus, and became the ancestress of all the Arcadians (that is, *Bear-folk*). In her bestial form she was just about to be slain by her own son when Zeus rescued her by raising her to the stars. Here we must notice first, that the Arcadians, like Australians, Red Indians, Bushmen, and many other wild races, and like the Bedouins, believed themselves to be descended from an animal. That the early Egyptians did the same is not improbable; for names of animals are found among the ancestors in the very oldest genealogical papyrus, [142]as in the genealogies of the old English kings. Next the Arcadians transferred the ancestral bear to the heavens, and, in doing this, they resembled the Peruvians, of whom Acosta says: 'They adored the star *Urchuchilly*, feigning it to be a *Ram*, and worshipped two others, and say that one of them is a *sheep*, and the other a lamb . . . others worshipped the star called the *Tiger. They were of opinion that there was not any beast or bird upon the earth, whose shape or image did not shine in the heavens.*'

But to return to our bears. The Australians have, properly speaking, no bears, though the animal called the native bear is looked up to by the aborigines with superstitious regard. But among the North American Indians, as the old missionaries Lafitau and Charlevoix observed, 'the four stars in front of our

---

[142] Brugsch, *History of Egypt*, i. 32.

constellation are a bear; those in the tail are hunters who pursue him; the small star apart is the pot in which they mean to cook him.'

It may be held that the Red Men derived their bear from the European settlers. But, as we have seen, an exact knowledge of the stars has always been useful if not essential to savages; and we venture to doubt whether they would confuse their nomenclature and sacred traditions by borrowing terms from trappers and squatters. But, if this is improbable, it seems almost impossible that all savage races should have borrowed their whole conception of the heavenly bodies from the myths of Greece. It is thus that Egede, a missionary of the last century, describes the Eskimo philosophy of the stars: 'The notions that the Greenlanders have as to the origin of the heavenly lights—as sun, moon, and stars— are very nonsensical; in that they pretend they have formerly been as many of their own ancestors, who, on different accounts, were lifted up to heaven, and became such glorious celestial bodies.' Again, he writes: 'Their notions about the stars are that some of them have been men, and others different sorts, of animals and fishes.' But every reader of Ovid knows that this was the very mythical theory of the Greeks and Romans. The Egyptians, again, worshipped Osiris, Isis, and the rest as *ancestors*, and there are even modern scholars, like Mr. Loftie in his 'Essay of Scarabs,' who hold Osiris to have been originally a real historical person. But the Egyptian priests who showed Plutarch the grave of Osiris, showed him, too, the stars into which Osiris, Isis, and Horus had been metamorphosed. Here, then, we have Greeks, Egyptians, and Eskimo, all agreed about the origin of the heavenly lights, all of opinion that 'they have formerly been as many of their own ancestors.'

The Australian general theory is: 'Of the good men and women, after the deluge, Pundjel (a kind of Zeus, or rather a sort of Prometheus of Australian mythology) made stars. Sorcerers (*Biraark*) can tell which stars were once good men and women.' Here the sorcerers have the same knowledge as the Egyptian priests. Again, just as among the Arcadians, 'the progenitors of

107

the existing tribes, whether birds, or beasts, or men, were set in the sky, and made to shine as stars.' [143]

We have already given some Australian examples in the stories of the *Pleiades*, and of *Castor* and *Pollux*. We may add the case of the *Eagle*. In Greece the *Eagle* was the bird of Zeus, who carried off Ganymede to be the cup-bearer of Olympus. Among the Australians this same constellation is called *Totyarguil*; he was a man who, when bathing, was killed by a fabulous animal, a kind of kelpie; as Orion, in Greece, was killed by the *Scorpion*. Like Orion, he was placed among the stars. The Australians have a constellation named *Eagle*, but he is our *Sinus*, or *Dog-star*.

The Indians of the Amazon are in one tale with the Australians and Eskimo. 'Dr. Silva de Coutinho informs me,' says Professor Hartt, [144]'that the Indians of the Amazonas not only give names to many of the heavenly bodies, but also tell stories about them. The two stars that form the shoulders of Orion are said to be an old man and a boy in a canoe, chasing *a peixe boi*, by which name is designated a dark spot in the sky near the above constellation.' The Indians also know monkey-stars, crane-stars, and palm-tree stars.

The Bushmen, almost the lowest tribe of South Africa, have the same star-lore and much the same myths as the Greeks, Australians, Egyptians, and Eskimo. According to Dr. Bleek, 'stars, and even the sun and moon, were once mortals on earth, or even animals or inorganic substances, which happened to get translated to the skies. The sun was once a man, whose arm-pit radiated a limited amount of light round his house. Some children threw him into the sky, and there he shines.' The Homeric hymn to Helios, in the same way, as Mr. Max Müller observes, 'looks on the sun as a half-god, almost a hero, who had once lived on earth.' The pointers of the Southern Cross were 'two men who were lions,' just as Callisto, in Arcadia, was a woman who was a bear. It is not at all rare in those queer

---

[143] Brough Smith.
[144] Amazonian Tortoise Myths, p. 39.

philosophies, as in that of the Scandinavians, to find that the sun or moon has been a man or woman. In Australian fable the moon was a man, the sun a woman of indifferent character, who appears at dawn in a coat of red kangaroo skins, the present of an admirer. In an old Mexican text the moon was a man, across whose face a god threw a rabbit, thus making the marks in the moon. [145]

Many separate races seem to recognise the figure of a hare, where we see 'the Man in the Moon.' In a Buddhist legend, an exemplary and altruistic hare was translated to the moon. 'To the common people in India the spots on the moon look like a hare, and Chandras, the god of the moon, carries a hare: hence the moon is called *sasin* or *sasanka*, hare-mark. The Mongolians also see in these shadows the figure of a hare.'[146] Among the Eskimo, the moon is a girl, who always flees from her cruel brother, the sun, because he disfigured her face. Elsewhere the sun is the girl, beloved by her own brother, the moon; she blackens her face to avert his affection. On the Rio Branco, and among the Tomunda, the moon is a girl who loved her brother and visited him in the dark. He detected her wicked passion by drawing his blackened hand over her face. The marks betrayed her, and, as the spots on the moon, remain to this day. [147]

Among the New Zealanders and North American Indians the sun is a great beast, whom the hunters trapped and thrashed with cudgels. His blood is used in some New Zealand incantations; and, according to an Egyptian myth, was kneaded into clay at the making of man. But there is no end to similar sun-myths, in all of which the sun is regarded as a man, or even as a beast.

To return to the stars—

The Red Indians, as Schoolcraft says, 'hold many of the planets to be transformed adventurers.' The Iowas 'believed stars to be a sort of living creatures.' One of them came down and talked to a hunter, and showed him where to find game. The

---

[145] Sahagun, vii. 3.
[146] Grimm, *D. M.*, Engl. transl., p. 716.
[147] Hartt, *op. cit.*, p. 40.

Gallinomeros of Central California, according to Mr. Bancroft, believe that the sun and moon were made and lighted up by the Hawk and the Coyote, who one day flew into each other's faces in the dark, and were determined to prevent such accidents in the future. But the very oddest example of the survival of the notion that the stars are men or women is found in the 'Pax' of Aristophanes. Trygæus in that comedy has just made an expedition to heaven. A slave meets him, and asks him, 'Is not the story true, then, that we become stars when we die?' The answer is 'Certainly;' and Trygæus points out the star into which Ios of Chios has just been metamorphosed. Aristophanes is making fun of some popular Greek superstition. But that very superstition meets us in New Zealand. 'Heroes,' says Mr. Taylor, 'were thought to become stars of greater or less brightness, according to the number of their victims slain in fight.' The Aryan race is seldom far behind, when there are ludicrous notions to be credited or savage tales to be told. We have seen that Aristophanes, in Greece, knew the Eskimo doctrine that stars are souls of the dead. The Persians had the same belief, [148]'all the unnumbered stars were reckoned ghosts of men.'[149] The German folklore clings to the same belief, 'Stars are souls; when a child dies God makes a new star.' Kaegi quotes [150] the same idea from the Veda, and from the Satapatha Brahmana the thoroughly Australian notion that 'good men become stars.' For a truly savage conception, it would be difficult, in South Africa or on the Amazons, to beat the following story from the 'Aitareya Brahmana' (iii. 33.) Pragapati, the Master of Life, conceived an incestuous passion for his own daughter. Like Zeus, and Indra, and the Australian wooer in the Pleiad tale, he concealed himself under the shape of a beast, a roebuck, and approached his own daughter, who had assumed the form of a doe. The gods, in anger at the awful crime, made a monster to punish Pragapati. The monster sent an arrow through the god's body; he sprang

---

[148] Kaegi, *Der Rig Veda*, p. 217.
[149] *Mainjo-i-Khard*, 49, 22, ed. West.
[150] *Op. cit.* p. 98.

110

into heaven, and, like the Arcadian bear, this Aryan roebuck became a constellation. He is among the stars of Orion, and his punisher, also now a star, is, like the Greek Orion, a hunter. The daughter of Pragapati, the doe, became another constellation, and the avenging arrow is also a set of stars in the sky. What follows, about the origin of the gods called Adityas, is really too savage to be quoted by a chaste mythologist.

It would be easy to multiply examples of this stage of thought among Aryans and savages. But we have probably brought forward enough for our purpose, and have expressly chosen instances from the most widely separated peoples. These instances, it will perhaps be admitted, suggest, if they do not prove, that the Greeks had received from tradition precisely the same sort of legends about the heavenly bodies as are current among Eskimo and Bushmen, New Zealanders and Iowas. As much, indeed, might be inferred from our own astronomical nomenclature. We now give to newly discovered stars names derived from distinguished people, as *Georgium Sidus*, or *Herschel*; or, again, merely technical appellatives, as *Alpha*, *Beta*, and the rest. We should never think when 'some new planet swims into our ken' of calling it *Kangaroo*, or *Rabbit*, or after the name of some hero of romance, as *Rob Roy*, or *Count Fosco*. But the names of stars which we inherit from Greek mythology— the *Bear*, the *Pleiads*, *Castor* and *Pollux*, and so forth—are such as no people in our mental condition would originally think of bestowing. When Callimachus and the courtly astronomers of Alexandria pretended that the golden locks of Berenice were raised to the heavens, that was a mere piece of flattery constructed on the inherited model of legends about the crown (*Corona*) of Ariadne. It seems evident enough that the older Greek names of stars are derived from a time when the ancestors of the Greeks were in the mental and imaginative condition of Iowas, Kanekas, Bushmen, Murri, and New Zealanders. All these, and all other savage peoples, believe in a kind of equality and intercommunion among all things animate and inanimate. Stones are supposed in the Pacific Islands to be male and female and to propagate their species. Animals are believed to have human or superhuman intelligence, and speech, if they choose to exercise the gift. Stars are just on the same footing, and their movements are explained by the same ready system of universal anthropomorphism. Stars, fishes, gods, heroes, men, trees, clouds, and animals, all play their equal part in the confused dramas of savage thought and savage mythology. Even in practical life the change of a sorcerer into an animal is accepted as a familiar phenomenon, and the power of soaring among the stars is one on which the Australian Biraark, or the Eskimo Shaman, most plumes himself. It is not wonderful that things which are held possible in daily practice should be frequent features of mythology. Hence the ready invention and belief of star-legends, which in their turn fix the names of the heavenly bodies. Nothing more, except the extreme tenacity of tradition and the inconvenience of changing a widely accepted name, is needed to account for the human and animal names of the stars. The Greeks received from the dateless past of savage intellect the myths, and the names of the constellations, and we have taken them, without inquiry, from the Greeks. Thus it happens that our celestial globes are just as queer menageries as any globes could be that were illustrated by Australians or American Indians, by Bushmen or Peruvian aborigines, or Eskimo. It was savages, we may be tolerably certain, who first handed to science the names of the constellations, and provided Greece with the raw material of her astronomical myths—as Bacon prettily says, that we listen to the harsh ideas of earlier peoples 'blown softly through the flutes of the Grecians.'

This position has been disputed by Mr. Brown, in a work rather komically called 'The Law of Kosmic Order.' Mr. Brown's theory is that the early Accadians named the zodiacal signs after certain myths and festivals connected with the months. Thus the crab is a figure of 'the darkness power' which seized the Akkadian solar hero, Dumuzi, and 'which is constantly represented in monstrous and drakontic form.' The bull, again, is connected with night and darkness, 'in relation to the horned moon,' and is, for other reasons, 'a nocturnal potency.' Few stars, to tell the truth, are diurnal potencies. Mr. Brown's explanations appear to me far-fetched and unconvincing. But, granting that the zodiacal signs reached Greece from Chaldæa, Mr. Brown will hardly maintain that Australians, Melanesians, Iowas, Amazon Indians, Eskimo, and the rest, borrowed their human and animal stars from 'Akkadia.' The belief in animal and human stars is practically universal among savages who have not attained the 'Akkadian' degree of culture. The belief, as Mr. Tylor has shown, [151]is a natural result of savage ideas. We therefore infer that the 'Akkadians,' too, probably fell back for star-names on what they inherited from the savage past. If the Greeks borrowed certain star-names from the Akkadians, they also, like the Aryans of India, retained plenty of savage star-myths of their own, fables derived from the earliest astronomical guesses of early thought.

The first moment in astronomical science arrives when the savage, looking at a star, says, like the child in the nursery poem, 'How I wonder what you are!' The next moment comes when the savage has made his first rough practical observations of the movements of the heavenly body. His third step is to explain these to himself. Now science cannot offer any but a fanciful explanation beyond the sphere of experience. The experience of the savage is limited to the narrow world of his tribe, and of the beasts, birds, and fishes of his district. His philosophy, therefore, accounts for all phenomena on the supposition that the laws of the animate nature he observes are working everywhere. But his observations, misguided by his crude magical superstitions, have led him to believe in a state of equality and kinship between men and animals, and even inorganic things. He often worships the very beasts he slays; he addresses them as if they understood him; he believes himself to be descended from the animals, and of their kindred. These confused ideas he applies to the stars, and recognises in them men like himself, or beasts like those with which he conceives himself to be in such close human relations. There is scarcely a bird or beast but the Red Indian or the

---

[151] *Prim. Cult.*, i. 357.

113

Australian will explain its peculiarities by a myth, like a page from Ovid's 'Metamorphoses.' It was once a man or a woman, and has been changed to bird or beast by a god or a magician. Men, again, have originally been beasts, in his philosophy, and are descended from wolves, frogs or serpents, or monkeys. The heavenly bodies are traced to precisely the same sort of origin; and hence, we conclude, come their strange animal names, and the strange myths about them which appear in all ancient poetry. These names, in turn, have curiously affected human beliefs. Astrology is based on the opinion that a man's character and fate are determined by the stars under which he is born. And the nature of these stars is deduced from their names, so that the bear should have been found in the horoscope of Dr. Johnson. When Giordano Bruno wrote his satire against religion, the famous 'Spaccio della bestia trionfante,' he proposed to banish not only the gods but the beasts from heaven. He would call the stars, not the *Bear*, or the *Swan*, or the *Pleiads*, but Truth, Mercy, Justice, and so forth, that men might be born, not under bestial, but moral influences. But the beasts have had too long possession of the stars to be easily dislodged, and the tenure of the *Bear* and the *Swan* will probably last as long as there is a science of Astronomy. Their names are not likely again to delude a philosopher into the opinion of Aristotle that the stars are animated.

This argument had been worked out to the writer's satisfaction when he chanced to light on Mr. Max Müller's explanation of the name of the *Great Bear*. We have explained that name as only one out of countless similar appellations which men of every race give to the stars. These names, again, we have accounted for as the result of savage philosophy, which takes no great distinction between man and the things in the world, and looks on stars, beasts, birds, fishes, flowers, and trees as men and women in disguise. Mr. Müller's theory is based on philological considerations. He thinks that the name of the *Great Bear* is the result of a mistake as to the meaning of words. There was in

Sanskrit, he says, [152]a root *ark*, or *arch*, meaning 'to be bright.' The stars are called *riksha*, that is, bright ones, in the Veda. 'The constellations here called the Rikshas, in the sense of the "bright ones," would be homonymous in Sanskrit with the Bears. Remember also that, apparently without rhyme or reason, the same constellation is called by Greeks and Romans the Bear. . . . There is not the shadow of a likeness with a bear. You will now perceive the influence of words on thought, or the spontaneous growth of mythology. The name *Riksha* was applied to the bear in the sense of the bright fuscous animal, and in that sense it became most popular in the later Sanskrit, and in Greek and Latin. The same name, "in the sense of the bright ones," had been applied by the Vedic poets to the stars in general, and more particularly to that constellation which in the northern parts of India was the most prominent. The etymological meaning, "the bright stars," was forgotten; the popular meaning of Riksha (bear) was known to everyone. And thus it happened that, when the Greeks had left their central home and settled in Europe, they retained the name of Arktos for the same unchanging stars; but, not knowing why those stars had originally received that name, they ceased to speak of them as *arktoí*, or many bears, and spoke of them as the Bear.'

This is a very good example of the philological way of explaining a myth. If once we admit that *ark*, or *arch*, in the sense of 'bright' and of 'bear,' existed, not only in Sanskrit, but in the undivided Aryan tongue, and that the name Riksha, bear, 'became in that sense most popular in Greek and Latin,' this theory seems more than plausible. But the explanation does not look so well if we examine, not only the Aryan, but all the known myths and names of the Bear and the other stars. Professor Sayce, a distinguished philologist, says we may not compare non-Aryan with Aryan myths. We have ventured to do so, however, in this paper, and have shown that the most widely severed races give the stars animal names, of which the *Bear* is one example. Now, if

---

[152] *Lectures on Language*, pp. 359, 362.

115

the philologists wish to persuade us that it was decaying and half-forgotten language which caused men to give the names of animals to the stars, they must prove their case on an immense collection of instances—on Iowa, Kaneka, Murri, Maori, Brazilian, Peruvian, Mexican, Egyptian, Eskimo, instances. It would be the most amazing coincidence in the world if forgetfulness of the meaning of their own speech compelled tribes of every tongue and race to recognise men and beasts, cranes, cockatoos, serpents, monkeys, bears, and so forth, in the heavens. How came the misunderstood words always to be misunderstood in the same way? Does the philological explanation account for the enormous majority of the phenomena? If it fails, we may at least doubt whether it solves the one isolated case of the Great Bear among the Greeks and Romans. It must be observed that the philological explanation of Mr. Müller does not clear up the Arcadian story of their own descent from a she-bear who is now a star. Yet similar stories of the descent of tribes from animals are so widespread that it would be difficult to name the race or the quarter of the globe where they are not found. Are they all derived from misunderstood words meaning 'bright'? These considerations appear to be a strong argument for comparing not only Aryan, but all attainable myths. We shall often find, if we take a wide view, that the philological explanation which seemed plausible in a single case is hopelessly narrow when applied to a large collection of parallel cases in languages of various families.

Finally, in dealing with star myths, we adhere to the hypothesis of Mr. Tylor: 'From savagery up to civilisation,' Akkadian, Greek, or English, 'there may be traced in the mythology of the stars a course of thought, changed, indeed, in application, yet never broken in its evident connection from first to last. The savage sees individual stars as animate beings, or combines star-groups into living celestial creatures, or limbs of them, or objects connected with them; while at the other extremity of the scale of civilisation the modern astronomer keeps up just such ancient fancies, turning them to account in useful survival, as a means of mapping out the celestial globe.'

MOLY AND MANDRAGORA.

'I have found out a new cure for rheumatism,' said the lady beside whom it was my privilege to sit at dinner. 'You carry a potato about in your pocket!'

Some one has written an amusing account of the behaviour of a man who is finishing a book. He takes his ideas everywhere with him and broods over them, even at dinner, in the pauses of conversation. But here was a lady who kindly contributed to my studies and offered me folklore and survivals in cultivated Kensington.

My mind had strayed from the potato cure to the New Zealand habit of carrying a baked yam at night to frighten away ghosts, and to the old English belief that a bit of bread kept in the pocket was sovereign against evil spirits. Why should ghosts dread the food of mortals when it is the custom of most races of mortals to feed ancestral ghosts? The human mind works pretty rapidly, and all this had passed through my brain while I replied, in tones of curiosity: 'A potato!'

'Yes; but it is not every potato that will do. I heard of the cure in the country, and when we came up to town, and my husband was complaining of rheumatism, I told one of the servants to get me a potato for Mr. Johnson's rheumatism. "Yes, ma'am," said the man; "but it must be a *stolen* potato." I had forgotten that. Well, one can't ask one's servants to steal potatoes. It is easy in the country, where you can pick one out of anybody's field.' 'And what did you do?' I asked. 'Oh, I drove to Covent Garden and ordered a lot of fruit and flowers. While the man was not looking, I stole a potato—a very little one. I don't think there was any harm in it.' 'And did Mr. Johnson try the potato cure?' 'Yes, he carried it in his pocket, and now he is quite well. I told the doctor, and he says he knows of the cure, but he dares not recommend it.'

How oddly superstitions survive! The central idea of this modern folly about the potato is that you must pilfer the root. Let us work the idea of the healing or magical herb backwards,

117

from Kensington to European folklore, and thence to classical times, to Homer, and to the Hottentots. Turning first to Germany, we note the beliefs, not about the potato, but about another vegetable, the mandrake. Of all roots, in German superstition, the Alraun, or mandrake, is the most famous. The herb was conceived of, in the savage fashion, as a living human person, a kind of old witch-wife. [153]

Again, the root has a human shape. 'If a hereditary thief who has preserved his chastity gets hung,' the broad-leafed, yellow-flowered mandrake grows up, in his likeness, beneath the gallows from which he is suspended. The mandrake, like the moly, the magical herb of the Odyssey, is 'hard for men to dig.' He who desires to possess a mandrake must stop his ears with wax, so that he may not hear the deathly yells which the plant utters as it is being dragged out of the earth. Then before sunrise, on a Friday, the amateur goes out with a dog, 'all black,' makes three crosses round the mandrake, loosens the soil about the root, ties the root to the dog's tail, and offers the beast a piece of bread. The dog runs at the bread, drags out the mandrake root, and falls dead, killed by the horrible yell of the plant. The root is now taken up, washed with wine, wrapped in silk, laid in a casket, bathed every Friday, 'and clothed in a little new white smock every new moon.' The mandrake acts, if thus considerately treated, as a kind of familiar spirit. 'Every piece of coin put to her over night is found doubled in the morning.' Gipsy folklore, and the folklore of American children, keep this belief in doubling deposits. The gipsies use the notion in what they call 'The Great Trick.' Some foolish rustic makes up his money in a parcel which he gives to the gipsy. The latter, after various ceremonies performed, returns the parcel, which is to be buried. The money will be found doubled by a certain date. Of course when the owner unburies the parcel he finds nothing in it but brass buttons. In the same way, and with pious confidence, the American boy buries a marble in a hollow log, uttering the

---

[153] Grimm, *D. M.*, Engl., Trans. p. 1202.

118

formula, 'What hasn't come here, *come!* what's here, *stay* here!' and expects to find all the marbles he has ever lost.[154] Let us follow the belief in magical roots into the old Pagan world.

The ancients knew mandragora and the superstitions connected with it very well. Dioscorides mentions *mandragorus*, or *antimelon*, or *dircæa*, or *Circæa*, and says the Egyptians call it *apemoum*, and Pythagoras 'anthropomorphon.' In digging the root, Pliny says, 'there are some ceremonies observed, first they that goe about this worke, look especially to this that the wind be not in their face, but blow upon their backs. Then with the point of a sword they draw three circles round about the plant, which don, they dig it up afterwards with their face unto the west.' Pliny says nothing of the fetich qualities of the plant, as credited in modern and mediæval Germany, but mentions 'sufficient it is with some bodies to cast them into sleep with the smel of mandrago.' This is like Shakespeare's 'poppy and mandragora, and all the drowsy syrups of the world.' Plato and Demosthenes [155] also speak of mandragora as a soporific. It is more to the purpose of magic that Columella mentions 'the *half-human* mandragora.' Here we touch the origin of the mandrake superstitions. The roots have a kind of fantastic resemblance to the human shape; Pliny describes them as being 'of a fleshy substance and tender.' Now it is one of the recognised principles in magic, that things like each other, however superficially, affect each other in a mystic way, and possess identical properties. Thus, in Melanesia, according to Mr. Codrington, [156]'a stone in the shape of a pig, of a bread-fruit, of a yam, was a most valuable find,' because it made pigs prolific, and fertilised bread-fruit trees and yam-plots. In Scotland, too, 'stones were called by the names of the limbs they resembled, as "eye-stane," "head-stane." A patient washed the affected part of his body, and rubbed it well with the stone corresponding.'[157] In precisely the same way, the

---

[154] *Tom Sawyer*, p. 87.
[155] *Rep.* vi. 488. Dem. 10, 6.
[156] *Journal Anthrop. Inst.*, Feb. 1881.
[157] Gregor, *Folklore of North-east Counties*, p, 40.

mandrake root, being thought to resemble the human body, was credited with human and superhuman powers. Josephus mentions [158] a plant 'not easily caught, which slips away from them that wish to gather it, and never stands still' till certain repulsive rites are performed. These rites cannot well be reported here, but they are quite familiar to Red Indian and to Bushman magic. Another way to dig the plant spoken of by Josephus is by aid of the dog, as in the German superstition quoted from Grimm. Ælian also recommends the use of the dog to pluck the herb aglaophotis, which shines at night.[159] When the dog has dragged up the root, and died of terror, his body is to be buried on the spot with religious honours and secret sacred rites.

So much for mandragora, which, like the healing potato, has to be acquired stealthily and with peril. Now let us examine the Homeric herb moly. The plant is thus introduced by Homer: In the tenth book of the 'Odyssey,' Circe has turned Odysseus's men into swine. He sets forth to rescue them, trusting only to his sword. The god Hermes meets him, and offers him 'a charmed herb,' 'this herb of grace' (φαρμακον εσθλον) whereby he may subdue the magic wiles of Circe.

The plant is described by Homer with some minuteness. 'It was black at the root, but the flower was like to milk. "Moly," the gods call it, but it is hard for mortal men to dig, howbeit with the gods all things are possible.' The etymologies given of 'moly' are almost as numerous as the etymologists. One derivation, from the old 'Turanian' tongue of Accadia, will be examined later. The Scholiast offers the derivation 'μωλυειν, to make charms of no avail'; but this is exactly like Professor Blackie's etymological discovery that Erinys is derived from ερινυειν: 'he might as well derive *critic* from *criticise*.'[160] The Scholiast adds that moly caused death to the person who dragged it out of the ground. This identification of moly with mandrake is probably based on Homer's remark that moly is 'hard to dig.' The black root and

---

[158] *Wars of Jews*, vii. 6, 3.
[159] *Var. Hist.*, 14, 27.
[160] Max Müller, *Selected Essays*, ii. 622.

white flower of moly are quite unlike the yellow flower and white fleshy root ascribed by Pliny to mandrake. Only confusion is caused by regarding the two magical herbs as identical.

But why are any herbs or roots magical? While some scholars, like De Gubernatis, seek an explanation in supposed myths about clouds and stars, it is enough for our purpose to observe that herbs really have medicinal properties, and that untutored people invariably confound medicine with magic. A plant or root is thought to possess virtue, not only when swallowed in powder or decoction, but when carried in the hand. St. John's wort and rowan berries, like the Homeric moly, still 'make evil charms of none avail;'

> Rowan, ash, and red threed
> Keep the devils from their speed,

says the Scotch rhyme. Any fanciful resemblance of leaf or flower or root to a portion of the human body, any analogy based on colour, will give a plant reputation for magical virtues. This habit of mind survives from the savage condition. The Hottentots are great herbalists. Like the Greeks, like the Germans, they expect supernatural aid from plants and roots. Mr. Hahn, in his 'Tsui Goam, the Supreme Being of the Khoi Khoi' (p. 82), gives the following examples:—

Dapper, in his description of Africa, p. 621, tells us:—'Some of them wear round the neck roots, which they find far inland, in rivers, and being on a journey they light them in a fire or chew them, if they must sleep the night out in the field. They believe that these roots keep off the wild animals. The roots they chew are spit out around the spot where they encamp for the night; and in a similar way if they set the roots alight, they blow the smoke and ashes about, believing that the smell will keep the wild animals off.

I had often occasion to observe the practice of these superstitious ceremonies, especially when we were in a part of the country where we heard the roaring of the lions, or had the day previously met with the footprints of the king of the beasts.

The Korannas also have these roots as safeguards with them. If a Commando (a warlike expedition) goes out, every man will put such roots in his pockets and in the pouch where he keeps his bullets, believing that the arrows or bullets of the enemy have no effect, but that his own bullets will surely kill the enemy. And also before they lie down to sleep, they set these roots alight, and murmur, 'My grandfather's root, bring sleep on the eyes of the lion and leopard and the hyena. Make them blind, that they cannot find us, and cover their noses, that they cannot smell us out.' Also, if they have carried off large booty, or stolen cattle of the enemy, they light these roots and say: 'We thank thee, our grandfather's root, that thou hast given us cattle to eat. Let the enemy sleep, and lead him on the wrong track, that he may not follow us until we have safely escaped.'

Another sort of shrub is called ābib. Herdsmen, especially, carry pieces of its wood as charms, and if cattle or sheep have gone astray, they burn a piece of it in the fire, that the wild animals may not destroy them. And they believe that the cattle remain safe until they can be found the next morning.

Schweinfurth found the same belief in magic herbs and roots among the Bongoes and Niam Niams in 'The Heart of Africa.' The Bongoes believe, like the Homeric Greeks, that 'certain roots ward off the evil influences of spirits.' Like the German amateurs of the mandrake, they assert that 'there is no other resource for obtaining communication with spirits, except by means of certain roots' (i. 306).

Our position is that the English magical potato, the German mandrake, the Greek moly, are all survivals from a condition of mind like that in which the Hottentots still pray to roots.

Now that we have brought mandragora and moly into connection with the ordinary magical superstitions of savage peoples, let us see what is made of the subject by another method. Mr. R. Brown, the learned and industrious author of 'The Great Dionysiak Myth,' has investigated the traditions about the Homeric moly. He first [161] 'turns to Aryan philology.' Many guesses at the etymology of 'moly' have been made. Curtius suggests *mollis, molvis*, μωλυ-ς, akin to μαλακος, 'soft.' This does not suit Mr. Brown, who, to begin with, is persuaded that the herb is not a magical herb, *sans phrase*, like those which the Hottentots use, but that the basis of the myth 'is simply the effect of night upon the world of day.' Now, as moly is a name in use among the gods, Mr. Brown thinks 'we may fairly examine the hypothesis of a foreign origin of the term.' Anyone who holds that certain Greek gods were borrowed from abroad, may be allowed to believe that the gods used foreign words, and, as Mr. Brown points out, there are foreign elements in various Homeric names of imported articles, peoples, persons, and so forth. Where, then, is a foreign word like moly, which might have reached Homer? By a long process of research, Mr. Brown finds his word in ancient 'Akkadian.' From Professor Sayce he borrows a reference to Apuleius Barbarus, about whose life nothing is known, and whose date is vague. Apuleius Barbarus may have lived about four centuries after our era, and *he* says that 'wild rue was called moly by the Cappadocians.' Rue, like rosemary, and indeed like most herbs, has its magical repute, and if we supposed that Homer's moly was rue, there would be some interest in the knowledge. Rue was called 'herb of grace' in English, holy water was sprinkled with it, and the name is a translation of Homer's φαρμακον εσθλον. Perhaps rue was used in sprinkling, because in pre-Christian times rue had, by itself, power against sprites and powers of evil. Our ancestors may have thought it as well to combine the old charm of rue and the new Christian potency of holy water. Thus there would be a distinct analogy between Homeric moly and English 'herb of grace.'

'Euphrasy and rue' were employed to purge and purify mortal eyes. Pliny is very learned about the magical virtues of rue. Just as the stolen potato is sovran for rheumatism, so 'rue stolen thriveth the best.' The Samoans think that their most valued

---

[161] *Myth of Kirkê*, p. 80.

vegetables were stolen from heaven by a Samoan visitor. [162]It is remarkable that rue, according to Pliny, is killed by the touch of a woman in the same way as, according to Josephus, the mandrake is tamed.[163] These passages prove that the classical peoples had the same extraordinary superstitions about women as the Bushmen and Red Indians. Indeed Pliny [164] describes a magical manner of defending the crops from blight, by aid of women, which is actually practised in America by the Red Men. [165]

Here, then, are proofs enough that rue was magical outside of Cappadocia. But this is not an argument on Mr. Brown's lines. The Cappadocians called rue 'moly'; what language, he asks, was spoken by the Cappadocians? Prof. Sayce (who knows so many tongues) says that 'we know next to nothing of the language of the Cappadocians, or of the Moschi who lived in the same locality.' But where Prof. Sayce is, the Hittites, if we may say so respectfully, are not very far off. In this case he thinks the Moschi (though he admits we know next to nothing about it) 'seem to have spoken a language allied to that of the Cappadocians and Hittites.' That is to say, it is not impossible that the language of the Moschi, about which next to nothing is known, may have been allied to that of the Cappadocians, about which we know next to nothing. All that we do know in this case is, that four hundred years after Christ the dwellers in Cappadocia employed a word 'moly,' which had been Greek for at least twelve hundred years. But Mr. Brown goes on to quote that one of the languages of which we know next to nothing, Hittite, was 'probably allied to Proto-Armenian, and perhaps Lykian, and was above all not Semitic.' In any case 'the cuneiform mode of writing was used in Cappadocia at an early period.' As even

---

[162] Turner's *Samoa.*
[163] Josephus, *loc. cit.* For this, and many other references, I am indebted to Schwartz's *Prähistorisch-änthropologische Studien.* In most magic herbs the learned author recognises thunder and lightning—a theory no less plausible than Mr. Brown's.
[164] Lib. xxviii.
[165] Schoolcraft.

Professor Sayce declines to give more than a tentative reading of a Cappadocian cuneiform inscription, it seems highly rash to seek in this direction for an interpretation of a Homeric word 'moly,' used in Cappadocia very many centuries after the tablets were scratched. But, on the evidence of the Babylonian character of the cuneiform writing on Cappadocian tablets, Mr. Brown establishes a connection between the people of Accadia (who probably introduced the cuneiform style) and the people of Cappadocia. The connection amounts to this. Twelve hundred years after Homer, the inhabitants of Cappadocia are said to have called rue 'moly.' At some unknown period, the Accadians appear to have influenced the art of writing in Cappadocia. Apparently Mr. Brown thinks it not too rash to infer that the Cappadocian use of the word 'moly' is not derived from the Greeks, but from the Accadians. Now in Accadian, according to Mr. Brown, *mul* means 'star.' 'Hence *ulu* or *mulu* = μῶλυ, the mysterious Homerik counter-charm to the charms of Kirkê' (p. 60). Mr. Brown's theory, therefore, is that moly originally meant 'star.' Circe is the moon, Odysseus is the sun, and 'what *watches over* the solar hero at night when exposed to the hostile lunar power, but the stars?' especially the dog-star.

The truth is, that Homer's moly, whatever plant he meant by the name, is only one of the magical herbs in which most peoples believe or have believed. Like the Scottish rowan, or like St. John's wort, it is potent against evil influences. People have their own simple reasons for believing in these plants, and have not needed to bring down their humble, early botany from the clouds and stars. We have to imagine, on the other hand (if we follow Mr. Brown), that in some unknown past the Cappadocians turned the Accadian word for a star into a local name of a plant, that this word reached Homer, that the supposed old Accadian myth of the star which watches over the solar hero retained its vitality in Greek, and leaving the star clung to the herb, that Homer used an 'Akkado-Kappadokian' myth, and that, many ages after, the Accadian star-name in its perverted sense of 'rue' survived in Cappadocia. This structure of argument is based on tablets

125

which even Prof. Sayce cannot read, and on possibilities about the alliances of tongues concerning which we 'know next to nothing.' A method which leaves on one side the common, natural, widely-diffused beliefs about the magic virtue of herbs (beliefs which we have seen at work in Kensington and in Central Africa), to hunt for moly among stars and undeciphered Kappadokian inscriptions, seems a dubious method. We have examined it at full length because it is a specimen of an erudite, but, as we think, a mistaken way in folklore. M. Halévy's warnings against the shifting mythical theories based on sciences so new as the lore of Assyria and 'Akkadia' are by no means superfluous. 'Akkadian' is rapidly become as ready a key to all locks as 'Aryan' was a few years ago.

'KALEVALA'; OR, THE FINNISH NATIONAL EPIC.

It is difficult to account for the fact that the scientific curiosity which is just now so busy in examining all the monuments of the primitive condition of our race, should, in England at least, have almost totally neglected to popularise the 'Kalevala,' or national poem of the Finns. Besides its fresh and simple beauty of style, its worth as a storehouse of every kind of primitive folklore, being as it is the production of an *Urvolk*, a nation that has undergone no violent revolution in language or institutions—the 'Kalevala' has the peculiar interest of occupying a position between the two kinds of primitive poetry, the ballad and the epic. So much difficulty has been introduced into the study of the first developments of song, by confusing these distinct sorts of composition under the name of popular poetry, that it may be well, in writing of a poem which occupies a middle place between epic and ballad, to define what we mean by each.

The author of our old English 'Art of Poesie' begins his work with a statement which may serve as a text: 'Poesie,' says Puttenham, writing in 1589, 'is more ancient than the *artificiall* of the Greeks and Latines, coming by instinct of nature, and used by the savage and uncivill, who were before all science and civilitie. This is proved by certificate of merchants and travellers, who by late navigations have surveyed the whole world, and discovered large countries, and strange people, wild and savage, affirming that the American, the Perusine, and the very canniball, do sing, and also say, their highest and holiest matters in certain riming versicles.' Puttenham is here referring to that instinct of primitive men, which compels them in all moments of high-wrought feeling, and on all solemn occasions, to give utterance to a kind of chant.[166] Such a chant is the song of Lamech, when he had 'slain a man to his wounding.' So in the Norse sagas, Grettir and Gunnar *sing* when they have anything particular to say; and so in the *Märchen*—the primitive fairy tales of all nations—

---

[166] Talvj, *Charakteristik der Volkslieder*, p. 3.

scraps of verse are introduced where emphasis is wanted. This craving for passionate expression takes a more formal shape in the lays which, among all primitive peoples, as among the modern Greeks to-day, [167]are sung at betrothals, funerals, and departures for distant lands. These songs have been collected in Scotland by Scott and Motherwell; their Danish counterparts have been translated by Mr. Prior. In Greece, M. Fauriel and Dr. Ulrichs; in Provence, Damase Arbaud; in Italy, M. Nigra; in Servia, Talvj; in France, Gérard de Nerval—have done for their separate countries what Scott did for the Border. Professor Child, of Harvard, is publishing a beautiful critical collection of English *Volkslieder*, with all known variants from every country.

A comparison of the collections proves that among all European lands the primitive 'versicles' of the people are identical in tone, form, and incident. It is this kind of early expression of a people's life—careless, abrupt, brief, as was necessitated by the fact that they were sung to the accompaniment of the dance—that we call ballads. These are distinctly, and in every sense, popular poems, and nothing can cause greater confusion than to apply the same title, 'popular,' to early epic poetry. Ballads are short; a long ballad, as Mr. Matthew Arnold has said, creeps and halts. A true epic, on the other hand, is long, and its tone is grand, noble, and sustained. Ballads are not artistic; while the form of the epic, whether we take the hexameter or the rougher *laisse* of the French *chansons de geste*, is full of conscious and admirable art. Lastly, popular ballads deal with vague characters, acting and living in vague places; while the characters of an epic are heroes of definite station, *whose descendants are still in the land*, whose home is a recognisable place, Ithaca, or Argos. Now, though these two kinds of early poetry—the ballad, the song of the people; the epic, the song of the chiefs of the people, of the ruling race—are distinct in kind, it does not follow that they have no connection, that the nobler may not have been developed out of the materials of the lower form of expression. And the value

---

[167] Fauriel, *Chants de la Grèce moderne.*

of the 'Kalevala' is partly this, that it combines the continuity and unison of the epic with the simplicity and popularity of the ballad, and so forms a kind of link in the history of the development of poetry. This may become clearer as we proceed to explain the literary history of the Finnish national poem.

Sixty years ago, it may be said, no one was aware that Finland possessed a national poem at all. Her people—who claim affinity with the Magyars of Hungary, but are possibly a back-wave of an earlier tide of population—had remained untouched by foreign influences since their conquest by Sweden, and their somewhat lax and wholesale conversion to Christianity: events which took place gradually between the middle of the twelfth and the end of the thirteenth centuries. Under the rule of Sweden, the Finns were left to their quiet life and undisturbed imaginings, among the forests and lakes of the region which they aptly called Pohja, 'the end of things'; while their educated classes took no very keen interest in the native poetry and mythology of their race. At length the annexation of Finland by Russia, in 1809, awakened national feeling, and stimulated research into the songs and customs which were the heirlooms of the people.

It was the policy of Russia to encourage, rather than to check, this return on a distant past; and from the north of Norway to the slopes of the Altai, ardent explorers sought out the fragments of unwritten early poetry. These runes, or *Runots*, were chiefly sung by old men called *Runoias*, to beguile the weariness of the long dark winters. The custom was for two champions to engage in a contest of memory, clasping each other's hands, and reciting in turn till he whose memory first gave in slackened his hold. The 'Kalevala' contains an instance of this practice, where it is said that no one was so hardy as to clasp hands with Wäinämöinen, who is at once the Orpheus and the Prometheus of Finnish mythology. These Runoias, or rhapsodists, complain, of course, of the degeneracy of human memory; they notice how any foreign influence, in religion or politics, is destructive to the native songs of a race.[168] 'As for the lays of old time, a thousand have been scattered to the wind, a thousand buried in the snow; . . . as for those which the Munks (the Teutonic knights) swept away, and the prayer of the priest overwhelmed, a thousand tongues were not able to recount them.' In spite of the losses thus caused, and in spite of the suspicious character of the Finns, which often made the task of collection a dangerous one, enough materials remained to furnish Dr. Lönnrot, the most noted explorer, with thirty-five *Runots*, or cantos. These were published in 1835, but later research produced the fifteen cantos which make up the symmetrical fifty of the 'Kalevala.' In the task of arranging and uniting these, Dr. Lönnrot played the part traditionally ascribed to the commission of Pisistratus in relation to the 'Iliad' and 'Odyssey.' Dr. Lönnrot is said to have handled with singular fidelity the materials which now come before us as one poem, not absolutely without a certain unity and continuous thread of narrative. It is this unity (so faint compared with that of the 'Iliad' and 'Odyssey') which gives the 'Kalevala' a claim to the title of epic.

It cannot be doubted that, at whatever period the Homeric poems took shape in Greece, they were believed to record the feats of the supposed ancestors of existing families. Thus, for example, Pisistratus, as a descendant of the Nelidæ, had an interest in securing certain parts, at least, of the 'Iliad' and the 'Odyssey' from oblivion. The same family pride embellished and preserved the epic poetry of early France. There were in France but three heroic houses, or *gestes*, and three corresponding cycles of *épopées*. Now, in the 'Kalevala,' there is no trace of the influence of family feeling; it was no one's peculiar care and pride to watch over the records of the fame of this or that hero. The poem begins with a cosmogony as wild as any Indian dream of creation; and the human characters who move in the story are shadowy inhabitants of no very definite lands, whom no family

---

[168] Thus Scotland scarcely produced any ballads, properly speaking, after the Reformation. The Kirk suppressed the dances to whose motion the ballad was sung in Scotland, as in Greece, Provence, and France.

claim as their forefathers. The very want of this idea of family and aristocratic pride gives the 'Kalevala' a unique place among epics. It is emphatically an epic of the people, of that class whose life contains no element of progress, no break in continuity; which from age to age preserves, in solitude and close communion with nature, the earliest beliefs of grey antiquity. The Greek epic, on the other hand, has, as M. Preller [169] points out, 'nothing to do with natural man, but with an ideal world of heroes, with sons of the gods, with consecrated kings, heroes, elders, *a kind of specific race of men*. The people exist only as subsidiary to the great houses, as a mere background against which stand out the shining figures of heroes; as a race of beings fresh and rough from the hands of nature, with whom, and with whose concerns, the great houses and their bards have little concern.' This feeling—so universal in Greece, and in the feudal countries of mediæval Europe, that there are two kinds of men, the golden and the brazen race, as Plato would have called them—is absent, with all its results, in the 'Kalevala.'

Among the Finns we find no trace of an aristocracy; there is scarcely a mention of kings, or priests; the heroes of the poem are really popular heroes, fishers, smiths, husbandmen, 'medicine-men,' or wizards; exaggerated shadows of the people, pursuing on a heroic scale, not war, but the common daily business of primitive and peaceful men. In recording their adventures, the 'Kalevala,' like the shield of Achilles, reflects all the life of a race, the feasts, the funerals, the rites of seed-time and harvest of marriage and death, the hymn, and the magical incantation. Were this all, the epic would only have the value of an exhaustive collection of the popular ballads which, as we have seen, are a poetical record of the intenser moments in the existence of unsophisticated tribes. But the 'Kalevala' is distinguished from such a collection, by presenting the ballads as they are produced by the events of a continuous narrative, and thus it takes a distinct

---

[169] L. Preller's *Ausgewählte Aufsätze*. Greek ideas on the origin of Man. It is curious that the myth of a gold, a silver, and a copper race occurs in South America. See Brasseur de Bourbourg's *Notes on the Popol Vuh*.

131

place between the aristocratic epics of Greece, or of the Franks, and the scattered songs which have been collected in Scotland, Sweden, Denmark, Greece, and Italy.

Besides the interest of its unique position as a popular epic, the 'Kalevala' is very valuable, both for its literary beauties and for the confused mass of folklore which it contains.

Here old cosmogonies, attempts of man to represent to himself the beginning of things, are mingled with the same wild imaginings as are found everywhere in the shape of fairy-tales. We are hurried from an account of the mystic egg of creation, to a hymn like that of the Ambarval Brothers, to a strangely familiar scrap of a nursery story, to an incident which we remember as occurring in almost identical words in a Scotch ballad. We are among a people which endows everything with human characters and life, which is in familiar relations with birds, and beasts, and even with rocks and plants. Ravens and wolves and fishes of the sea, sun, moon, and stars, are kindly or churlish; drops of blood find speech, man and maid change to snake or swan and resume their forms, ships have magic powers, like the ships of the Phæacians.

Then there is the oddest confusion of every stage of religious development: we find a supreme God, delighting in righteousness; Ukko, the lord of the vault of air, who stands apart from men, and sends his son, Wäinämöinen, to be their teacher in music and agriculture.

Across this faith comes a religion of petrified abstractions like those of the Roman Pantheon. There are gods of colour, a goddess of weaving, a goddess of man's blood, besides elemental spirits of woods and waters, and the *manes* of the dead. Meanwhile, the working faith of the people is the belief in magic—generally a sign of the lower culture. It is supposed that the knowledge of certain magic words gives power over the elemental bodies which obey them; it is held that the will of a distant sorcerer can cross the lakes and plains like the breath of a fantastic frost, with power to change an enemy to ice or stone. Traces remain of the worship of animals: there is a hymn to the

132

bear; a dance like the bear-dance of the American Indians; and another hymn tells of the birth and power of the serpent. Across all, and closing all, comes a hostile account of the origin of Christianity—the end of joy and music.

How primitive was the condition of the authors of this medley of beliefs is best proved by the survival of the custom called exogamy.[170] This custom, which is not peculiar to the Finns, but is probably a universal note of early society, prohibits marriage between members of the same tribe. Consequently, the main action, such as it is, of the 'Kalevala' turns on the efforts made by the men of Kaleva to obtain brides from the hostile tribe of Pohja. [171]

Further proof of ancient origin is to be found in what is the great literary beauty of the poem—its pure spontaneity and simplicity. It is the production of an intensely imaginative race, to which song came as the most natural expression of joy and sorrow, terror or triumph—a class which lay near to nature's secret, and was not out of sympathy with the wild kin of woods and waters.

'These songs,' says the prelude, 'were found by the wayside, and gathered in the depths of the copses; blown from the branches of the forest, and culled among the plumes of the pine-trees. These lays came to me as I followed the flocks, in a land of meadows honey-sweet, and of golden hills. . . . The cold has spoken to me, and the rain has told me her runes; the winds of heaven, the waves of the sea, have spoken and sung to me; the wild birds have taught me, the music of many waters has been my master.'

---

[170] See essay on Early History of the Family.
[171] This constant struggle may be, and of course by one school of comparative mythologists will be, represented as the strife between light and darkness, the sun's rays, and the clouds of night, and so on. M. Castren has well pointed out that the struggle has really an historical meaning. Even if the myth be an elementary one, its constructors must have been in the exogamous stage of society.

The metre in which the epic is chanted resembles, to an English ear, that of Mr. Longfellow's 'Hiawatha'—there is assonance rather than rhyme; and a very musical effect is produced by the liquid character of the language, and by the frequent alliterations.

This rough outline of the main characteristics of the 'Kalevala' we shall now try to fill up with an abstract of its contents. The poem is longer than the 'Iliad,' and much of interest must necessarily be omitted; but it is only through such an abstract that any idea can be given of the sort of unity which does prevail amid the most utter discrepancy.

In the first place, what is to be understood by the word 'Kalevala'? The affix *la* signifies 'abode.' Thus, 'Tuonela' is 'the abode of Tuoni,' the god of the lower world; and as 'kaleva' means 'heroic,' 'magnificent,' 'Kalevala' is 'The Home of Heroes.' The poem is the record of the adventures of the people of Kalevala—of their strife with the men of Pohjola, the place of the world's end. We may fancy two old Runoias, or singers, clasping hands on one of the first nights of the Finnish winter, and beginning (what probably has never been accomplished) the attempt to work through the 'Kalevala' before the return of summer. They commence *ab ovo*, or, rather, before the egg. First is chanted the birth of Wäinämöinen, the benefactor and teacher of men. He is the son of Luonnotar, the daughter of Nature, who answers to the first woman of the Iroquois cosmogony. Beneath the breath and touch of wind and tide, she conceived a child; but nine ages of man passed before his birth, while the mother floated on 'the formless and the multiform waters.' Then Ukko, the supreme God, sent an eagle, which laid her eggs in the maiden's bosom, and from these eggs grew earth and sky, sun and moon, star and cloud. Then was Wäinämöinen born on the waters, and reached a barren land, and gazed on the new heavens and the new earth. There he sowed the grain that is the bread of man, chanting the hymn used at seed-time, calling on the mother earth to make the green herb spring, and on Ukko to send clouds and rain. So the corn sprang, and the golden cuckoo—which in

134

Finland plays the part of the popinjay in Scotch ballads, or of the three golden birds in Greek folksongs—came with his congratulations. In regard to the epithet 'golden,' it may be observed that gold and silver, in the Finnish epic, are lavished on the commonest objects of daily life.

This is a universal note of primitive poetry, and is not a peculiar Finnish idiom, as M. Leouzon le Duc supposes; nor, as Mr. Tozer seems to think, in his account of Romaic ballads, a trace of Oriental influence among the modern Greeks. It is common to all the ballads of Europe, as M. Ampère has pointed out, and may be observed in the 'Chanson de Roland,' and in Homer.

While the corn ripened, Wäinämöinen rested from his labours, and took the task of Orpheus. 'He sang,' says the 'Kalevala,' of the origin of things, of the mysteries hidden from babes, that none may attain to in this sad life, in the hours of these perishable days. The fame of the Runoia's singing excited jealousy in the breast of one of the men around him, of whose origin the 'Kalevala' gives no account. This man, Joukahainen, provoked him to a trial of song, boasting, like Empedocles, or like one of the old Celtic bards, that he had been all things. 'When the earth was made I was there; when space was unrolled I launched the sun on his way.' Then was Wäinämöinen wroth, and by the force of his enchantment he rooted Joukahainen to the ground, and suffered him not to go free without promising him the hand of his sister Aino. The mother was delighted; but the girl wept that she must now cover her long locks, her curls, her glory, and be the wife of 'the old imperturbable Wäinämöinen.' It is in vain that her mother offers her dainty food and rich dresses; she flees from home, and wanders till she meets three maidens bathing, and joins them, and is drowned, singing a sad song: 'Ah, never may my sister come to bathe in the sea-water, for the drops of the sea are the drops of my blood.' This wild idea occurs in the Romaic ballad, η κορη ταξιδευτρια, where a drop of blood on the lips of the drowned girl tinges all the waters of the world. To return to the fate of Aino. A swift hare runs (as in the Zulu legend of the Origin of Death) with the tale of sorrow to the maiden's mother, and from the mother's tears flow rivers of water, and therein are isles with golden hills where golden birds make melody. As for the old, the imperturbable Runoia, he loses his claim to the latter title, he is filled with sorrow, and searches through all the elements for his lost bride. At length he catches a fish which is unknown to him, who, like Atlas, 'knew the depths of all the seas.' The strange fish slips from his hands, a 'tress of hair, of drowned maiden's hair,' floats for a moment on the foam, and too late he recognises that 'there was never salmon yet that shone so fair, above the nets at sea.' His lost bride has been within his reach, and now is doubly lost to him. Suddenly the waves are cloven asunder, and the mother of Nature and of Wäinämöinen appears, to comfort her son, like Thetis from the deep. She bids him go and seek, in the land of Pohjola, a bride alien to his race. After many a wild adventure, Wäinämöinen reaches Pohjola and is kindly entreated by Loutri, the mother of the maiden of the land. But he grows homesick, and complains, almost in Dante's words, of the bitter bread of exile. Loutri will only grant him her daughter's hand on condition that he gives her a *sampo*. A sampo is a mysterious engine that grinds meal, salt, and money. In fact, it is the mill in the well-known fairy tale, 'Why the Sea is Salt.' [172]

Wäinämöinen cannot fashion this mill himself, he must seek aid at home from Ilmarinen, the smith who forged 'the iron vault of hollow heaven.' As the hero returns to Kalevala, he meets the Lady of the Rainbow, seated on the arch of the sky, weaving the golden thread. She promises to be his, if he will accomplish certain tasks, and in the course of those he wounds himself with an axe. The wound can only be healed by one who knows the mystic words that hold the secret of the birth of iron. The legend of this evil birth, how iron grew from the milk of a maiden, and

---

[172] Sampo *may* be derived from a Thibetan word, meaning 'fountain of good,' or it may possibly be connected with the Swedish *Stamp*, a hand-mill. The talisman is made of all the quaint odds and ends that the Fetichist treasures: swan's feathers, flocks of wool, and so on.

was forged by the primeval smith, Ilmarinen, to be the bane of warlike men, is communicated by Wäinämöinen to an old magician. The wizard then solemnly curses the iron, *as a living thing*, and invokes the aid of the supreme God Ukko, thus bringing together in one prayer the extremes of early religion. Then the hero is healed, and gives thanks to the Creator, 'in whose hands is the end of a matter.'

Returning to Kalevala, Wäinämöinen sends Ilmarinen to Pohjola to make the sampo, 'a mill for corn one day, for salt the next, for money the next.' The fatal treasure is concealed by Loutri, and is obviously to play the part of the fairy hoard in the 'Nibelungen Lied.'

With the eleventh canto a new hero, Ahti, or Lemminkainen, and a new cycle of adventures, is abruptly introduced. Lemminkainen is a profligate wanderer, with as many loves as Hercules. The fact that he is regarded as a form of the sea-god makes it strange that his most noted achievement, the seduction of the whole female population of his island, should correspond with a like feat of Krishna's. 'Sixteen thousand and one hundred,' says the Vishnu Purana, 'was the number of the maidens; and into so many forms did the son of Madhu multiply himself, so that every one of the damsels thought that he had wedded her in her single person.' Krishna is the sun, of course, and the maidens are the dew-drops; [173]it is to be hoped that Lemminkainen's connection with sea-water may save him from the solar hypothesis. His first regular marriage is unhappy, and he is slain in trying to capture a bride from the people of Pohjola. The black waters of the river of forgetfulness sweep him away, and his comb, which he left with his mother, bursts out bleeding—a frequent incident in Russian and other fairy tales. In many household tales, the hero, before setting out on a journey, erects a stick which will fall down when he is in distress, or death. The natives of Australia use this form of divination in actual practice, tying round the stick some of the hair of the person whose fate is

---

[173] Sir G. W. Cox's Popular Romances of the Middle Ages, p. 19.

137

to be ascertained. Then, like Demeter seeking Persephonê, the mother questions all the beings of the world, and their answers show a wonderful poetic sympathy with the silent life of Nature. 'The moon said, I have sorrows enough of my own, without thinking of thy child. My lot is hard, my days are evil. I am born to wander companionless in the night, to shine in the season of frost, to watch through the endless winter, to fade when summer comes as king.' The sun is kinder, and reveals the place of the hero's body. The mother collects the scattered limbs, the birds bring healing balm from the heights of heaven, and after a hymn to the goddess of man's blood, Lemminkainen is made sound and well, as the scattered 'fragments of no more a man' were united by the spell of Medea, like those of Osiris by Isis, or of the fair countess by the demon blacksmith in the Russian *Märchen*, or of the Carib hero mentioned by Mr. McLennan, [174]or of the ox in the South African household tale.

With the sixteenth canto we return to Wäinämöinen, who, like all epic heroes, visits the place of the dead, Tuonela. The maidens who play the part of Charon are with difficulty induced to ferry over a man bearing no mark of death by fire or sword or water. Once among the dead, Wäinämöinen refuses—being wiser than Psyche or Persephonê—to taste of drink. This 'taboo' is found in Japanese, Melanesian, and Red Indian accounts of the homes of the dead. Thus the hero is able to return and behold the stars. Arrived in the upper world, he warns men to 'beware of perverting innocence, of leading astray the pure of heart; they that do these things shall be punished eternally in the depths of Tuoni. There is a place prepared for evil-doers, a bed of stones burning, rocks of fire, worms and serpents.' This speech throws but little light on the question of how far a doctrine of rewards and punishments enters into primitive ideas of a future state. The 'Kalevala,' as we possess it, is necessarily, though faintly, tinged with Christianity; and the peculiar vices which are here threatened

---

[174] *Fortnightly Review*, 1869: 'The Worship of Plants and Animals.'

with punishment are not those which would have been most likely to occur to the early heathen singers of this *runot*.

Wäinämöinen and Ilmarinen now go together to Pohjola, but the fickle maiden of the land prefers the young forger of the sampo to his elder and imperturbable companion. Like a northern Medea, or like the Master-maid in Dr. Dasent's 'Tales from the Norse,' or like the hero of the Algonquin tale and the Samoan ballad, she aids her alien lover to accomplish the tasks assigned to him. He ploughs with a plough of gold the adder-close, or field of serpents; he bridles the wolf and the bear of the lower world, and catches the pike that swim in the waters of forgetfulness. After this, the parents cannot refuse their consent, the wedding-feast is prepared, and all the world, except the *séduisant* Lemminkainen, is bidden to the banquet. The narrative now brings in the ballads that are sung at a Finnish marriage.

First, the son-in-law enters the house of the parents of the bride, saying, 'Peace abide with you in this illustrious hall.' The mother answers, 'Peace be with you even in this lowly hut.' Then Wäinämöinen began to sing, and no man was so hardy as to clasp hands and contend with him in song. Next follow the songs of farewell, the mother telling the daughter of what she will have to endure in a strange home: 'Thy life was soft and delicate in thy father's house. Milk and butter were ready to thy hand; thou wert as a flower of the field, as a strawberry of the wood; all care was left to the pines of the forest, all wailing to the wind in the woods of barren lands. But now thou goest to another home, to an alien mother, to doors that grate strangely on their hinges.' 'My thoughts,' the maiden replies, 'are as a dark night of autumn, as a cloudy day of winter; my heart is sadder than the autumn night, more weary than the winter day.' The maid and the bridegroom are then lyrically instructed in their duties: the girl is to be long-suffering, the husband to try five years' gentle treatment before he cuts a willow wand for his wife's correction. The bridal party sets out for home, a new feast is spread, and the bridegroom congratulated on the courage he must have shown in stealing a girl from a hostile tribe.

While all is merry, the mischievous Lemminkainen sets out, an unbidden guest, for Pohjola. On his way he encounters a serpent, which he slays by the song of serpent-charming. In this 'mystic chain of verse' the serpent is not addressed as the gentle reptile, god of southern peoples, but is spoken of with all hatred and loathing: 'Black creeping thing of the low lands, monster flecked with the colours of death, thou that hast on thy skin the stain of the sterile soil, get thee forth from the path of a hero.' After slaying the serpent, Lemminkainen reaches Pohjola, kills one of his hosts, and fixes his head on one of a thousand stakes for human skulls that stood about the house, as they might round the hut of a Dyak in Borneo. He then flees to the isle of Saari, whence he is driven for his heroic profligacy, and by the hatred of the only girl whom he has *not* wronged. This is a very pretty touch of human nature.

He now meditates a new incursion into Pohjola. The mother of Pohjola (it is just worth noticing that the leadership assumed by this woman points to a state of society when the family was scarcely formed) calls to her aid 'her child the Frost;' but the frost is put to shame by a hymn of the invader's, a song against the Cold: 'The serpent was his foster-mother, the serpent with her barren breasts; the wind of the north rocked his cradle, and the ice-wind sang him to sleep, in the midst of the wild marsh-land, where the wells of the waters begin.' It is a curious instance of the animism, the vivid power of personifying all the beings and forces of nature, which marks the 'Kalevala,' that the Cold speaks to Lemminkainen in human voice, and seeks a reconciliation.

At this part of the epic there is an obvious lacuna. The story goes to Kullervo, a luckless man, who serves as shepherd to Ilmarinen. Thinking himself ill-treated by the heroic smith's wife, the shepherd changes his flock into bears and wolves, which devour their mistress. Then he returns to his own home, where he learns that his sister has been lost for many days, and is believed to be dead. Travelling in search of her he meets a girl, loves her, and all unwittingly commits an inexpiable offence. 'Then,' says the 'Kalevala,' 'came up the new dawn, and the maiden spoke, saying, "What is thy race, bold young man, and who is thy father?" Kullervo said, "I am the wretched son of Kalerva; but tell me, what is thy race, and who is thy father?" Then said the maiden, "I am the wretched daughter of Kalerva. Ah! would God that I had died, then might I have grown with the green grass, and blossomed with the flowers, and never known this sorrow." With this she sprang into the midst of the foaming waves, and found peace in Tuoni, and rest in the waters of forgetfulness.' Then there was no word for Kullervo, but the bitter moan of the brother in the terrible Scotch ballad of the *Bonny Hind*, and no rest but in death by his own sword, where grass grows never on his sister's tomb.

The epic now draws to a close. Ilmarinen seeks a new wife in Pohja, and endeavours with Wäinämöinen's help to recover the mystic sampo. On the voyage, the Runoia makes a harp out of the bones of a monstrous fish, so strange a harp that none may play it but himself. When he played, all four-footed things came about him, and the white birds dropped down 'like a storm of snow.' The maidens of the sun and the moon paused in their weaving, and the golden thread fell from their hands. The Ancient One of the sea-water listened, and the nymphs of the wells forgot to comb their loose locks with the golden combs. All men and maidens and little children wept, amid the silent joy of nature; nay, the great harper wept, and *of his tears were pearls made*.

In the war with Pohjola the heroes were victorious, but the sampo was broken in the fight, and lost in the sea, and that, perhaps, is 'why the sea is salt.' Fragments were collected, however, and Loutri, furious at the success of the heroes of Kalevala, sent against them a bear, destructive as the boar of Calydon. But Wäinämöinen despatched the monster, and the body was brought home with the bear-dance, and the hymn of the bear. 'Oh, Otso,' cry the singers, 'be not angry that we come near thee. The bear, the honey-footed bear, was born in lands between sun and moon, and he died not by men's hands, but of his own will.' The Finnish savants are probably right, who find here a trace of the beast-worship which in many lands has placed the bear among the number of the stars. Propitiation of the bear is practised by Red Indians, by the Ainos of Japan, and (in the case of the 'native bear') by Australians. The Red Indians have a myth to prove that the bear is immortal, does not die, but, after his apparent death, rises again in another body. There is no trace, however, that the Finns claimed, like the Danes, descent from the bear. The Lapps, a people of confused belief, worshipped him along with Thor, Christ, the sun, and the serpent. [175]

But another cult, an alien creed, is approaching Kalevala. There is no part of the epic more strange than the closing canto, which tells in the wildest language, and through the most exaggerated forms of savage imagination, the tale of the introduction of Christianity. Marjatta was a maiden, 'as pure as the dew is, as holy as stars are that live without stain.' As she fed her flocks, and listened to the singing of the golden cuckoo, a berry fell into her bosom. After many days she bore a child, and the people despised and rejected her, and she was thrust forth, and her babe was born in a stable, and cradled in the manger. Who should baptize the babe? The god of the wilderness refused, and Wäinämöinen would have had the young child slain. Then the infant rebuked the ancient Demigod, who fled in anger to the sea, and with his magic song he built a magic barque, and he sat therein, and took the helm in his hand. The tide bore him out to sea, and he lifted his voice and sang: 'Times go by, and suns shall rise and set, and then shall men have need of me, and shall look for the promise of my coming that I may make a new sampo, and a new harp, and bring back sunlight and moonshine, and the joy that is banished from the world.' Then he crossed the waters, and gained the limits of the sea, and the lower spaces of the sky.

Here the strange poem ends at its strangest moment, with the cry, which must have been uttered so often, but is heard here alone, of a people reluctantly deserting the gods that it has

---

[175] Mr. McLennan in the *Fortnightly Review*, February 1870.

fashioned in its own likeness, for a faith that has not sprung from its needs or fears. Yet it cherishes the hope that this tyranny shall pass over: 'they are gods, and behold they shall die, and the waves be upon them at last.'

As the 'Kalevala,' and as all relics of folklore, all *Märchen* and ballads prove, the lower mythology—the elemental beliefs of the people—do survive beneath a thin covering of Christian conformity. There are, in fact, in religion, as in society, two worlds, of which the one does not know how the other lives. The class whose literature we inherit, under whose institutions we live, at whose shrines we worship, has changed as outworn raiment its manners, its gods, its laws; has looked before and after, has hoped and forgotten, has advanced from the wilder and grosser to the purest faith. Beneath the progressive class, and beneath the waves of this troublesome world, there exists an order whose primitive form of human life has been far less changeful, a class which has put on a mere semblance of new faiths, while half-consciously retaining the remains of immemorial cults.

Obviously, as M. Fauriel has pointed out in the case of the modern Greeks, the life of such folk contains no element of progress, admits no break in continuity. Conquering armies pass and leave them still reaping the harvest of field and river; religions appear, and they are baptized by thousands, but the lower beliefs and dreads that the progressive class has outgrown remain unchanged.

Thus, to take the instance of modern Greece, the high gods of the divine race of Achilles and Agamemnon are forgotten, but the descendants of the Penestæ, the *villeins* of Thessaly, still dread the beings of the popular creed, the Nereids, the Cyclopes, and the Lamia. [176]

The last lesson we would attempt to gather from the 'Kalevala' is this: that a comparison of the *thoroughly popular* beliefs of all countries, the beliefs cherished by the non-literary classes whose ballads and fairy tales have only recently been

---

[176] M. Schmidt, *Volksleben der Neugriechen,* finds comparatively few traces of the worship of Zeus, and these mainly in proverbial expressions.

143

collected, would probably reveal a general identity, concealed by diversity of name, among the 'lesser people of the skies,' the elves, fairies, Cyclopes, giants, nereids, brownies, lamiæ. It could then be shown that some of these spirits survive among the lower beings of the mythology of what the Germans call a *cultur-volk* like the Greeks or Romans. It could also be proved that much of the narrative element in the classic epics is to be found in a popular or childish form in primitive fairy tales. The question would then come to be, Have the higher mythologies been developed, by artistic poets, out of the materials of a race which remained comparatively untouched by culture; or are the lower spirits, and the more simple and puerile forms of myth, degradations of the inventions of a cultivated class?

THE DIVINING ROD.

There is something remarkable, and not flattering to human sagacity, in the periodical resurrection of superstitions. Houses, for example, go on being 'haunted' in country districts, and no educated man notices the circumstance. Then comes a case like that of the Drummer of Tedworth, or the Cock Lane Ghost, and society is deeply moved, philosophers plunge into controversy, and he who grubs among the dusty tracts of the past finds a world of fugitive literature on forgotten bogies. Chairs move untouched by human hands, and tables walk about in lonely castles of Savoy, and no one marks them, till a day comes when the furniture of some American cottage is similarly afflicted, and then a shoddy new religion is based on the phenomenon. The latest revival among old beliefs is faith in the divining rod. 'Our liberal shepherds give it a *shorter* name,' and so do our conservative peasants, calling the 'rod of Jacob' the 'twig.' To 'work the twig' is rural English for the craft of Dousterswivel in the 'Antiquary,' and perhaps from this comes our slang expression to 'twig,' or divine, the hidden meaning of another. Recent correspondence in the newspapers has proved that, whatever may be the truth about the 'twig,' belief in its powers is still very prevalent. Respectable people are not ashamed to bear signed witness of its miraculous powers of detecting springs of water and secret mines. It is habitually used by the miners in the Mendips, as Mr. Woodward found ten years ago; and forked hazel divining rods from the Mendips are a recognised part of ethnological collections. There are two ways of investigating the facts or fancies about the rod. One is to examine it in its actual operation—a task of considerable labour, which will doubtless be undertaken by the Society for Psychical Research; the other, and easier, way is to study the appearances of the divining wand in history, and that is what we propose to do in this article.

When a superstition or belief is widely spread in Europe, as the faith in the divining rod certainly is (in Germany rods are hidden under babies' clothes when they are baptized), we naturally expect to find traces of it in ancient times and among savages all over the modern world. We have already examined, in 'The Bull-Roarer,' a very similar example. We saw that there is a magical instrument—a small fish-shaped piece of thin flat wood tied to a thong—which, when whirled in the air, produces a strange noise, a compound of roar and buzz. This instrument is sacred among the natives of Australia, where it is used to call together the men, and to frighten away the women from the religious mysteries of the males. The same instrument is employed for similar purposes in New Mexico, and in South Africa and New Zealand—parts of the world very widely distant from each other, and inhabited by very diverse races. It has also been lately discovered that the Greeks used this toy, which they called ρομβος, in the Mysteries of Dionysus, and possibly it may be identical with the *mystica vannus Iacchi* (Virgil, 'Georgics,' i. 166). The conclusion drawn by the ethnologist is that this object, called *turndun* by the Australians, is a very early savage invention, probably discovered and applied to religious purposes in various separate centres, and retained from the age of savagery in the mystic rites of Greeks and perhaps of Romans. Well, do we find anything analogous in the case of the divining rod?

Future researches may increase our knowledge, but at present little or nothing is known of the divining rod in classical ages, and not very much (though that little is significant) among uncivilised races. It is true that in all countries rods or wands, the Latin *virga*, have a magical power. Virgil obtained his mediæval repute as a wizard because his name was erroneously connected with *virgula*, the magic wand. But we do not actually know that the ancient wand of the enchantress Circe, in Homer, or the wand of Hermes, was used, like the divining rod, to indicate the whereabouts of hidden wealth or water. In the Homeric hymn to Hermes (line 529), Apollo thus describes the *caduceus*, or wand of Hermes: 'Thereafter will I give thee a lovely wand of wealth and riches, a golden wand with three leaves, which shall keep thee ever unharmed.' In later art this wand, or *caduceus*, is usually entwined with serpents; but on one vase, at least, the wand of

146

Hermes is simply the forked twig of our rustic miners and water-finders. The same form is found on an engraved Etruscan mirror. [177]

Now, was a wand of this form used in classical times to discover hidden objects of value? That wands were used by Scythians and Germans in various methods of casting lots is certain; but that is not the same thing as the working of the twig. Cicero speaks of a fabled wand by which wealth can be procured; but he says nothing of the method of its use, and possibly was only thinking of the rod of Hermes, as described in the Homeric hymn already quoted. There was a Roman play, by Varro, called 'Virgula Divina'; but it is lost, and throws no light on the subject. A passage usually quoted from Seneca has no more to do with the divining rod than with the telephone. Pliny is a writer extremely fond of marvels; yet when he describes the various modes of finding wells of water, he says nothing about the divining wand. The isolated texts from Scripture which are usually referred to clearly indicate wands of a different sort, if we except Hosea iv. 12, the passage used as motto by the author of 'Lettres qui découvrent l'illusion des Philosophes sur la Baguette' (1696). This text is translated in our Bible, 'My people ask counsel at their stocks, *and their staff declareth unto them*.' Now, we have here no reference to the search for wells and minerals, but to a form of divination for which the modern twig has ceased to be applied. In rural England people use the wand to find water, but not to give advice, or to detect thieves or murderers; but, as we shall see, the rod has been very much used for these purposes within the last three centuries.

This brings us to the moral powers of the twig; and here we find some assistance in our inquiry from the practices of uncivilised races. In 1719 John Bell was travelling across Asia; he fell in with a Russian merchant, who told him of a custom common among the Mongols. The Russian had lost certain pieces of cloth, which were stolen out of his tent. The Kutuchtu

---

[177] Preller, *Ausgewählte Aufsätze*, p. 154.

147

Lama ordered the proper steps to be taken to find out the thief. 'One of the Lamas took a bench with four feet, and after turning it in several directions, at last it pointed directly to the tent where the stolen goods were concealed. The Lama now mounted across the bench, and soon carried it, or, as was commonly believed, it carried him, to the very tent, where he ordered the damask to be produced. The demand was directly complied with; for it is vain in such cases to offer any excuse.'[178] Here we have not a wand, indeed, but a wooden object which turned in the direction, not of water or minerals, but of human guilt. A better instance is given by the Rev. H. Rowley, in his account of the Mauganja. [179]A thief had stolen some corn. The medicine-man, or sorcerer, produced two sticks, which he gave to four young men, two holding each stick. The medicine-man danced and sang a magical incantation, while a zebra-tail and a rattle were shaken over the holders of the sticks. 'After a while, the men with the sticks had spasmodic twitchings of the arms and legs; these increased nearly to convulsions. . . . According to the native idea, *it was the sticks which were possessed primarily*, and through them the men, *who could hardly hold them*. The sticks whirled and dragged the men round and round like mad, through bush and thorny shrub, and over every obstacle; nothing stopped them; their bodies were torn and bleeding. At last they came back to the assembly, whirled round again, and rushed down the path to fall panting and exhausted in the hut of one of a chief's wives. The sticks, rolling to her very feet, denounced her as a thief. She denied it; but the medicine-man answered, "The spirit has declared her guilty; the spirit never lies."' The woman, however, was acquitted, after a proxy trial by ordeal: a cock, used as her proxy, threw up the *muavi*, or ordeal-poison.

Here the points to be noted are, first, the violent movement of the sticks, which the men could hardly hold; next, the physical agitation of the men. The former point is illustrated by the confession of a civil engineer writing in the 'Times.' This

[178] Tylor, *Prim. Cult.*, ii. 156. Pinkerton, vii. 357.
[179] Universities Mission to Central Africa, p. 217. Prim. Cult,, ii. 156, 157.

gentleman had seen the rod successfully used for water; he was asked to try it himself, and he determined that it should not twist in his hands 'if an ocean rolled under his feet.' Twist it did, however, in spite of all his efforts to hold it, when he came above a concealed spring. Another example is quoted in the 'Quarterly Review,' vol. xxii. p. 374. A narrator, in whom the editor had 'implicit confidence,' mentions how, when a lady held the twig just over a hidden well, 'the twig turned so quick as to snap, breaking near her fingers.' There seems to be no indiscretion in saying, as the statement has often been printed before, that the lady spoken of in the 'Quarterly Review' was Lady Milbanke, mother of the wife of Byron. Dr. Hutton, the geologist, is quoted as a witness of her success in the search for water with the divining rod. He says that, in an experiment at Woolwich, 'the twigs twisted themselves off below her fingers, which were considerably indented by so forcibly holding the rods between them.'[180] Next, the violent excitement of the four young men of the Mauganja is paralleled by the physical experience of the lady quoted in the 'Quarterly Review.' 'A degree of agitation was visible in her face when she first made the experiment; she says this agitation was great' when she began to practise the art, or whatever we are to call it. Again, in 'Lettres qui découvrent l'illusion' (p. 93), we read that Jacques Aymar (who discovered the Lyons murderer in 1692) *se sent tout ému*—feels greatly agitated—when he comes on that of which he is in search. On page 97 of the same volume, the body of the man who holds the divining rod is described as 'violently agitated.' When Aymar entered the room where the murder, to be described later, was committed, 'his pulse rose as if he were in a burning fever, and the wand turned rapidly in his hands' ('Lettres,' p. 107). But the most singular parallel to the performance of the African wizard must be quoted from a curious pamphlet already referred to, a translation of the old French 'Verge de Jacob,' written, annotated, and published by a Mr. Thomas Welton. Mr. Welton seems to

---

[180] Quoted in 'Jacob's Rod': London, n.d., a translation of *La Verge de Jacob*, Lyon, 1693.

have been a believer in mesmerism, animal magnetism, and similar doctrines, but the coincidence of his story with that of the African sorcerer is none the less remarkable. It is a coincidence which must almost certainly be 'undesigned.' Mr. Welton's wife was what modern occult philosophers call a 'Sensitive.' In 1851, he wished her to try an experiment with the rod in a garden, and sent a maid-servant to bring 'a certain stick that stood behind the parlour door. In great terror she brought it to the garden, her hand firmly clutched on the stick, nor could she let it go . . . ' The stick was given to Mrs. Welton, 'and it drew her with very considerable force to nearly the centre of the garden, to a bed of poppies, where she stopped.' Here water was found, and the gardener, who had given up his lease as there was no well in the garden, had the lease renewed.

We have thus evidence to show (and much more might be adduced) that the belief in the divining rod, or in analogous instruments, is not confined to the European races. The superstition, or whatever we are to call it, produces the same effects of physical agitation, and the use of the rod is accompanied with similar phenomena among Mongols, English people, Frenchmen, and the natives of Central Africa. The same coincidences are found in almost all superstitious practices, and in the effects of these practices on believers. The Chinese use a form of *planchette*, which is half a divining rod—a branch of the peach tree; and 'spiritualism' is more than three-quarters of the religion of most savage tribes, a Maori *séance* being more impressive than anything the civilised Sludge can offer his credulous patrons. From these facts different people draw different inferences. Believers say that the wide distribution of their favourite mysteries is a proof that 'there is something in them.' The incredulous look on our modern 'twigs' and turning-tables and ghost stories as mere 'survivals' from the stage of savage culture, or want of culture, when the fancy of half-starved man was active and his reason uncritical.

The great authority for the modern history of the divining rod is a work published by M. Chevreuil, in Paris, in 1854. M.

Chevreuil, probably with truth, regarded the wand as much on a par with the turning-tables, which, in 1854, attracted a good deal of attention. He studied the topic historically, and his book, with a few accessible French tracts and letters of the seventeenth century, must here be our guide. A good deal of M. Chevreuil's learning, it should be said, is reproduced in Mr. Baring Gould's 'Curious Myths of the Middle Ages,' but the French author is much more exhaustive in his treatment of the topic. M. Chevreuil could find no earlier book on the twig than the 'Testament du Frère Basil Valentin,' a holy man who flourished (the twig) about 1413; but whose treatise is possibly apocryphal. According to Basil Valentin, the twig was regarded with awe by ignorant labouring men, which is still true. Paracelsus, though he has a reputation for magical daring, thought the use of the twig 'uncertain and unlawful'; and Agricola, in his 'De Re Metallica' (1546) expresses a good deal of scepticism about the use of the rod in mining. A traveller of 1554 found that the wand was *not* used—and this seems to have surprised him—in the mines of Macedonia. Most of the writers of the sixteenth century accounted for the turning of the rod by 'sympathy,' which was then as favourite an explanation of everything as evolution is to-day. In 1630 the Baron de Beau Soleil of Bohemia (his name sounds rather Bohemian) came to France with his wife, and made much use of the rod in the search for water and minerals. The Baroness wrote a little volume on the subject, afterwards reprinted in a great storehouse of this lore, 'La Physique Occulte,' of Vallemont. Kircher, a Jesuit, made experiments which came to nothing; but Gaspard Schott, a learned writer, cautiously declined to say that the Devil was always 'at the bottom of it' when the rod turned successfully. The problem of the rod was placed before our own Royal Society by Boyle, in 1666, but the Society was not more successful here than in dealing with the philosophical difficulty proposed by Charles II. In 1679 De Saint Remain, deserting the old hypothesis of secret 'sympathies,' explained the motion of the rod (supposing it to move) by the action of *corpuscules.* From this time the question became the playing ground of the Cartesian and other philosophers. The struggle was between theories of 'atoms,' magnetism, 'corpuscules,' electric effluvia, and so forth, on one side, and the immediate action of devils or of conscious imposture, on the other. The controversy, comparatively simple as long as the rod only indicated hidden water or minerals, was complicated by the revival of the savage belief that the wand could 'smell out' moral offences. As long as the twig turned over material objects, you could imagine sympathies and 'effluvia' at pleasure. But when the wand twirled over the scene of a murder, or dragged the expert after the traces of the culprit, fresh explanations were wanted. Le Brun wrote to Malebranche on July 8, 1689, to tell him that the wand only turned over what the holder had the *intention* of discovering.[181] If he were following a murderer, the wand good-naturedly refused to distract him by turning over hidden water. On the other hand, Vallemont says that when a peasant was using the wand to find water, it turned over a spot in a wood where a murdered woman was buried, and it conducted the peasant to the murderer's house. These events seem inconsistent with Le Brun's theory of *intention*. Malebranche replied, in effect, that he had only heard of the turning of the wand over water and minerals; that it then turned (if turn it did) by virtue of some such force as electricity; that, if such force existed, the wand would turn over open water. But it does not so turn; and, as physical causes are constant, it follows that the turning of the rod cannot be the result of a physical cause. The only other explanation is an intelligent cause—either the will of an impostor, or the action of a spirit. Good spirits would not meddle with such matters; therefore either the Devil or an impostor causes the motion of the rod, if it *does* move at all. This logic of Malebranche's is not agreeable to believers in the twig; but there the controversy stood, till, in 1692, Jacques Aymar, a peasant of Dauphine, by the use of the twig discovered one of the Lyons murderers.

---

[181] *Lettres sur la Baguette*, pp. 106-112.

Though the story of this singular event is pretty well known, it must here be briefly repeated. No affair can be better authenticated, and our version is abridged from the 'Relations' of 'Monsieur le Procureur du Roi, Monsieur l'Abbé de la Garde, Monsieur Panthot, Doyen des Médecins de Lyon, et Monsieur Aubert, Avocat célèbre.'

On July 5, 1692, a vintner and his wife were found dead in the cellar of their shop at Lyons. They had been killed by blows from a hedging-knife, and their money had been stolen. The culprits could not be discovered, and a neighbour took upon him to bring to Lyons a peasant out of Dauphiné, named Jacques Aymar, a man noted for his skill with the divining rod. The Lieutenant-Criminel and the Procureur du Roi took Aymar into the cellar, furnishing him with a rod of the first wood that came to hand. According to the Procureur du Roi, the rod did not move till Aymar reached the very spot where the crime had been committed. His pulse then rose, and the wand twisted rapidly. 'Guided by the wand or by some internal sensation,' Aymar now pursued the track of the assassins, entered the court of the Archbishop's palace, left the town by the bridge over the Rhone, and followed the right bank of the river. He reached a gardener's house, which he declared the men had entered, and some children confessed that three men (*whom they described*) had come into the house one Sunday morning. Aymar followed the track up the river, pointed out all the places where the men had landed, and, to make a long story short, stopped at last at the door of the prison of Beaucaire. He was admitted, looked at the prisoners, and picked out as the murderer a little hunchback (had the children described a hunchback?) who had just been brought in for a small theft. The hunchback was taken to Lyons, and he was recognised, on the way, by the people at all the stages where he had stopped. At Lyons he was examined in the usual manner, and confessed that he had been an accomplice in the crime, and had guarded the door. Aymar pursued the other culprits to the coast, followed them by sea, landed where they had landed, and only desisted from his search when they crossed the frontier. As for the hunchback, he was broken on the wheel, being condemned on his own confession. It does not appear that he was put to the torture to make him confess. If this had been done his admissions would, of course, have been as valueless as those of the victims in trials for witchcraft.

This is, in brief, the history of the famous Lyons murders. It must be added that many experiments were made with Aymar in Paris, and that they were all failures. He fell into every trap that was set for him; detected thieves who were innocent, failed to detect the guilty, and invented absurd excuses; alleging, for example, that the rod would not indicate a murderer who had confessed, or who was drunk when he committed his crime. These excuses seem to annihilate the wild contemporary theory of Chauvin and others, that the body of a murderer naturally exhales an invisible *matière meurtrière*—peculiar indestructible atoms, which may be detected by the expert with the rod. Something like the same theory, we believe, has been used to explain the pretended phenomena of haunted houses. But the wildest philosophical credulity is staggered by a *matière meurtrière* which is disengaged by the body of a sober, but not by that of an intoxicated, murderer, which survives tempests in the air, and endures for many years, but is dissipated the moment the murderer confesses. Believers in Aymar have conjectured that his real powers were destroyed by the excitements of Paris, and that he took to imposture; but this is an effort of too easy good-nature. When Vallemont defended Aymar (1693) in the book called 'La Physique Occulte,' he declared that Aymar was physically affected to an unpleasant extent by *matière meurtrière*, but was not thus agitated when he used the rod to discover minerals. We have seen that, if modern evidence can be trusted, holders of the rod are occasionally much agitated even when they are only in search of wells. The story gave rise to a prolonged controversy, and the case remains a judicial puzzle, but little elucidated by the confession of the hunchback, who may have been insane, or morbid, or vexed by constant questioning till he was weary of his life. He was only nineteen years of age.

The next use of the rod was very much like that of 'tipping' and turning tables. Experts held it (as did Le Père Ménestrier, 1694), questions were asked, and the wand answered by turning in various directions. By way of showing the inconsistency of all philosophies of the wand, it may be said that one girl found that it turned over concealed gold if she held gold in her hand, while another found that it indicated the metal so long as she did *not* carry gold with her in the quest. In the search for water, ecclesiastics were particularly fond of using the rod. The Maréchal de Boufflers dug many wells, and found no water, on the indications of a rod in the hands of the Prieur de Dorenic, near Guise. In 1700 a curé, near Toulouse, used the wand to answer questions, which, like *planchette*, it often answered wrong. The great *sourcier*, or water-finder, of the eighteenth century was one Bleton. He declared that the rod was a mere index, and that physical sensations of the searcher communicated themselves to the wand. This is the reverse of the African theory, that the stick is inspired, while the men who hold it are only influenced by the stick. On the whole, Bleton's idea seems the less absurd, but Bleton himself often failed when watched with scientific care by the incredulous. Paramelle, who wrote on methods of discovering wells, in 1856, came to the conclusion that the wand turns in the hands of certain individuals of peculiar temperament, and that it is very much a matter of chance whether there are, or are not, wells in the places where it turns.

On the whole, the evidence for the turning of the wand is a shade better than that for the magical turning of tables. If there are no phenomena of this sort at all, it is remarkable that the belief in them is so widely diffused. But if the phenomena are purely subjective, owing to the conscious or unconscious action of nervous patients, then they are precisely of the sort which the cunning medicine-man observes, and makes his profit out of, even in the earliest stages of society. Once introduced, these practices never die out among the conservative and unprogressive class of peasants; and, every now and then, they attract the curiosity of philosophers, or win the belief of the credulous among the

155

educated classes. Then comes, as we have lately seen, a revival of ancient superstition. For it were as easy to pluck the comet out of the sky by the tail, as to eradicate superstition from the mind of man.

Perhaps one good word may be said for the divining rod. Considering the chances it has enjoyed, the rod has done less mischief than might have been expected. It might very well have become, in Europe, as in Asia and Africa, a kind of ordeal, or method of searching for and trying malefactors. Men like Jacques Aymar might have played, on a larger scale, the part of Hopkins, the witch-finder. Aymar was, indeed, employed by some young men to point out, by help of the wand, the houses of ladies who had been more frail than faithful. But at the end of the seventeenth century in France, this research was not regarded with favour, and put the final touch on the discomfiture of Aymar. So far as we know, the hunchback of Lyons was the only victim of the 'twig' who ever suffered in civilised society. It is true that, in rural England, the movements of a Bible, suspended like a pendulum, have been thought to point out the guilty. But even that evidence is not held good enough to go to a jury.

HOTTENTOT MYTHOLOGY.

'What makes mythology mythological, in the true sense of the word, is what is utterly unintelligible, absurd, strange, or miraculous.' So says Mr. Max Müller in the January number of the *Nineteenth Century* for 1882. Men's attention would never have been surprised into the perpetual study and questioning of mythology if it had been intelligible and dignified, and if its report had been in accordance with the reason of civilised and cultivated races. What mythologists wish to discover is the origin of the countless disgusting, amazing, and incongruous legends which occur in the myths of all known peoples. According to Mr. Müller—

There are only two systems possible in which the irrational element in mythology can be accounted for. One school takes the irrational as a matter of fact; and if we read that Daphne fled before Phœbus, and was changed into a laurel tree, that school would say that there probably was a young lady called Aurora, like, for instance, Aurora Königsmark; that a young man called Robin, or possibly a man with red hair, pursued her, and that she hid behind a laurel tree that happened to be there. This was the theory of Euhemeros, re-established by the famous Abbé Bernier [Mr. Müller doubtless means Banier], and not quite extinct even now. According to another school, the irrational element in mythology is inevitable, and due to the influence of language on thought, so that many of the legends of gods and heroes may be rendered intelligible if only we can discover the original meaning of their proper names. The followers of this school try to show that Daphne, the laurel tree, was an old name for the dawn, and that Phoibos was one of the many names of the sun, who pursued the dawn till she vanished before his rays. Of these two schools, the former has always appealed to the mythologies of savage nations, as showing that gods and heroes were originally human beings, worshipped after their death as ancestors and as gods, while the latter has confined itself chiefly to an etymological analysis of mythological names in Greek, Latin, and Sanskrit, and

157

other languages, such as had been sufficiently studied to admit of a scientific, grammatical, and etymological treatment.

This is a long text for our remarks on Hottentot mythology; but it is necessary to prove that there are not two schools only of mythologists: that there are inquirers who neither follow the path of the Abbé Banier, nor of the philologists, but a third way, unknown to, or ignored by Mr. Müller. We certainly were quite unaware that Banier and Euhemeros were very specially concerned, as Mr. Müller thinks, with savage mythology; but it is by aid of savage myths that the school unknown to Mr. Müller examines the myths of civilised peoples like the Greeks. The disciples of Mr. Müller interpret all the absurdities of Greek myth, the gods who are beasts on occasion, the stars who were men, the men who become serpents or deer, the deities who are cannibals and parricides and adulterers, as the result of the influence of Aryan speech upon Aryan thought. Men, in Mr. Müller's opinion, had originally pure ideas about the gods, and expressed them in language which we should call figurative. The figures remained, when their meaning was lost; the names were then supposed to be gods, the *nomina* became *numina*, and out of the inextricable confusion of thought which followed, the belief in cannibal, bestial, adulterous, and incestuous gods was evolved. That is Mr. Müller's hypothesis; with him the evolution, a result of a disease of language, has been from early comparative purity to later religious abominations. Opposed to him is what may be called the school of Mr. Herbert Spencer: the modern Euhemerism, which recognises an element of historical truth in myths, as if the characters had been real characters, and which, in most gods, beholds ancestral ghosts raised to a higher power.

There remains a third system of mythical interpretation, though Mr. Müller says only two methods are possible. The method, in this third case, is to see whether the irrational features and elements of civilised Greek myth occur also in the myths of savages who speak languages quite unlike those from whose diseases Mr. Müller derives the corruption of religion. If the same features recur, are they as much in harmony with the mental habits of savages, such as Bushmen and Hottentots, as they are out of accord with the mental habits of civilised Greeks? If this question can be answered in the affirmative, then it may be provisionally assumed that the irrational elements of savage myth are the legacy of savage modes of thought, and have survived in the religion of Greece from a time when the ancestors of the Greeks were savages. But inquirers who use this method do not in the least believe that either Greek or savage gods were, for the more part, originally real men. Both Greeks and savages have worshipped the ghosts of the dead. Both Greeks and savages assign to their gods the miraculous powers of transformation and magic, which savages also attribute to their conjurers or shamans. The mantle (if he had a mantle) of the medicine-man has fallen on the god; but Zeus, or Indra, was not once a real medicine-man. A number of factors combine in the conception of Indra, or Zeus, as either god appears in Sanskrit or Greek literature, of earlier or later date. Our school does not hold anything so absurd as that Daphne was a real girl pursued by a young man. But it has been observed that, among most savage races, metamorphoses like that of Daphne not only exist in mythology, but are believed to occur very frequently in actual life. Men and women are supposed to be capable of turning into plants (as the bamboo in Sarawak), into animals, and stones, and stars, and those metamorphoses happen as contemporary events—for example, in Samoa. [182]

When Mr. Lane was living at Cairo, and translating the 'Arabian Nights,' he found that the people still believed in metamorphosis. Any day, just as in the 'Arabian Nights,' a man might find himself turned by an enchanter into a pig or a horse. Similar beliefs, not derived from language, supply the matter of the senseless incidents in Greek myths.

Savage mythology is also full of metamorphoses. Therefore the mythologists whose case we are stating, when they find identical metamorphoses in the classical mythologies, conjecture

---

[182] Turner's *Samoa*, pp, 77, 119.

that these were first invented when the ancestors of the Aryans were in the imaginative condition in which a score of rude races are to-day. This explanation they apply to many other irrational elements in mythology. They do not say, 'Something like the events narrated in these stories once occurred,' nor 'A disease of language caused the belief in such events,' but 'These stories were invented when men were capable of believing in their occurrence as a not unusual sort of incident'

Philologists attempt to explain the metamorphoses as the result of some oblivion and confusion of language. Apollo, they say, was called the 'wolf-god' (Lukeios) by accident: his name really meant the 'god of light.' A similar confusion made the 'seven shiners' into the 'seven bears.'[183] These explanations are distrusted, partly because the area to be covered by them is so vast. There is scarcely a star, tree, or beast, but it has been a man or woman once, if we believe civilised and savage myth. Two or three possible examples of myths originating in forgetfulness of the meaning of words, even if admitted, do not explain the incalculable crowd of metamorphoses. We account for these by saying that, to the savage mind, which draws no hard and fast line between man and nature, all such things are possible; possible enough, at least, to be used as incidents in story. Again, as has elsewhere been shown, the laxity of philological reasoning is often quite extraordinary; while, lastly, philologists of the highest repute flatly contradict each other about the meaning of the names and roots on which they agree in founding their theory. [184]

By way of an example of the philological method as applied to savage mythology, we choose a book in many ways admirable, Dr. Hahn's 'Tsuni Goam, the Supreme Being of the Khoi Khoi.'[185] This book is sometimes appealed to as a crushing argument against the mythologists who adopt the method we have just explained. Let us see if the blow be so very crushing.

---

[183] Cox, *Mythol. of Aryan Races, passim.*
[184] See examples in 'A Far-travelled Tale,' 'Cupid and Psyche,' and 'The Myth of Cronus.'
[185] Trübner, 1881.

160

To put the case in a nutshell, the Hottentots have commonly been described as a race which worshipped a dead chief, or conjurer—Tsui Goab his name is, meaning Wounded Knee, a not unlikely name for a savage. Dr. Hahn, on the other hand, labours to show that the Hottentots originally worshipped no dead chief, but (as a symbol of the Infinite) the Red Dawn. The meaning of the name Red Dawn, he says, was lost; the words which meant Red Dawn were erroneously supposed to mean Wounded Knee, and thus arose the adoration and the myths of a dead chief, or wizard, Tsui Goab, Wounded Knee. Clearly, if this can be proved, it is an excellent case for the philological school, an admirable example of a myth produced by forgetfulness of the meaning of words. Our own opinion is that, even if Tsui Goab originally meant Red Dawn, the being, as now conceived of by his adorers, is bedizened in the trappings of the dead medicine-man, and is worshipped just as ghosts of the dead are worshipped. Thus, whatever his origin, his myth is freely coloured by the savage fancy and by savage ideas, and we ask no more than this colouring to explain the wildest Greek myths. What truly 'primitive' religion was, we make no pretence to know. We only say that, whether Greek religion arose from a pure fountain or not, its stream had flowed through and been tinged by the soil of savage thought, before it widens into our view in historical times. But it will be shown that the logic which connects Tsui Goab with the Red Dawn is far indeed from being cogent.

Tsui Goab is thought by the Hottentots themselves to be a dead man, and it is admitted that among the Hottentots dead men are adored. 'Cairns are still objects of worship,' [186]and Tsui Goab lies beneath several cairns. Again, soothsayers are believed in (p. 24), and Tsui Goab is regarded as a deceased soothsayer. As early as 1655, a witness quoted by Hahn saw women worshipping at one of the cairns of Heitsi Eibib, another supposed ancestral being. Kolb, the old Dutch traveller, found that the Hottentots, like the Bushmen, revered the mantis insect.

---

[186] Hahn, p. 23.

This creature they called Gaunab. They also had some moon myths, practised adoration of the moon, and danced at dawn. Thunberg (1792) saw the cairn-worship, and, on asking its meaning, was told that a Hottentot lay buried there.[187] Thunberg also heard of the worship of the mantis, or grey grasshopper. In 1803 Liechtenstein noted the cairn-worship, and was told that a renowned Hottentot doctor of old times rested under the cairn. Appleyard's account of 'the name God in Khoi Khoi, or Hottentot,' deserves quoting in full:—

> Hottentot: Tsoei'koap.
> Namaqua: Tsoei'koap.
> Koranna: Tshu'koab, and the author adds: 'This is the word from which the Kafirs have probably derived their u-Tixo, a term which they have universally applied, like the Hottentots, to designate the Divine Being, since the introduction of Christianity. Its derivation is curious. It consists of two words, which together mean the "wounded knee." It is said to have been originally applied to a doctor or sorcerer of considerable notoriety and skill amongst the Hottentots or Namaquas some generations back, in consequence of his having received some injury in his knee. Having been held in high repute for extraordinary powers during life, he appeared to be invoked even after death, as one who could still relieve and protect; and hence, in process of time, he became nearest in idea to their first conceptions of God.'

Other missionaries make old Wounded Knee a good sort of being on the whole, who fights Gaunab, a bad being. Dr. Moffat heard that 'Tsui Kuap' was 'a notable warrior,' who once received a wound in the knee. Sir James Alexander [188] found that the Namaquas believed their 'great father' lay below the cairns on which they flung boughs. This great father was Heitsi Eibib, and, like other medicine-men, 'he could take many forms.' Like Tsui Goab, he died several times and rose again. Hahn gives (p. 61) a

---

[187] Ibid., p. 45.
[188] *Expedition,* i. 166.

long account of the Wounded Knee from an old chief, and a story of the battle between Tsui Goab, who 'lives in a beautiful heaven,' and Gaunab, who 'lives in a dark heaven.' As this chief had dwelt among missionaries very long, we may perhaps discount his remarks on 'heaven' as borrowed. Hahn thinks they refer to the red sky in which Tsui Goab lived, and to the black sky which was the home of Gaunab. The two characters in this crude religious dualism thus inhabit light and darkness respectively.

* * * * *

As far as we have gone, Tsui Goab, like Heitsi Eibib among the Namas, is a dead sorcerer, whose graves are worshipped, while, with a common inconsistency, he is also thought of as dwelling in the sky. Even Christians often speak of the dead with similar inconsistency. Tsui Goab's worship is intelligible enough among a people so credulous that they took Hahn himself for a conjurer (p. 81), and so given to ancestor-worship that Hahn has seen them worship their own fathers' graves, and expect help from men recently dead (pp. 112, 113). But, while the Khoi Khoi think that Tsui Goab was once a real man, we need not share their Euhemerism. More probably, like Unkulunkulu among the Zulus, Tsui Goab is an ideal, imaginary ancestral sorcerer and god. No one man requires many graves, and Tsui Goab has more than Osiris possessed in Egypt. [189]

If the Egyptians in some immeasurably distant past were once on the level of Namas and Hottentots, they would worship Osiris at as many barrows as Heitsi Eibib and Tsui Goab are adored. In later times the numerous graves of one being would require explanation, and explanations would be furnished by the myth that the body of Osiris was torn to pieces and each fragment buried in a separate tomb.

---

[189] Herodotus, ii.

Again, lame gods occur in Greek, Australian, and Brazilian creeds, and the very coincidence of Tsui Goab's lameness makes us sceptical about his claims to be a real dead man. On the other hand, when Hahn tells us that epical myths are now sung in the dances in honour of warriors lately slain (p. 103), and that similar dances and songs were performed in the past to honour Tsui Goab, this looks more as if Tsui Goab had been an actual person. Against this we must set (p. 105) the belief that Tsui Goab made the first man and woman, and was the Prometheus of the Hottentots.

* * * * *

So far Dr. Hahn has given us facts which entirely fit in with our theory that an ancestor-worshipping people, believing in metamorphosis and sorcery, adores a god who is supposed to be a deceased ancestral sorcerer with the power of magic and metamorphosis. But now Dr. Hahn offers his own explanation. According to the philological method, he will 'study the names of the persons, until we arrive at the naked root and original meanings of the words.' Starting then with Tsui Goab, whom all evidence declares to be a dead lame conjurer and warrior, Dr. Hahn avers that 'Tsui Goab, originally Tsuni Goam, was the name by which the Red Men called the Infinite.' As the Frenchman said of the derivation of *jour* from *dies*, we may hint that the Infinite thus transformed into a lame Hottentot 'bush-doctor' is *diablement changé en route*. To a dead lame sorcerer from the Infinite is a fall indeed. The process of the decline is thus described. *Tsui Goab* is composed of two roots, *tsu* and *goa*. *Goa* means 'to go on,' 'to come on.' In Khoi Khoi *goa-b* means 'the coming on one,' the dawn, and *goa-b* also means 'the knee.' Dr. Hahn next writes (making a logical leap of extraordinary width), 'it is now obvious that, //*goab* in Tsui Goab cannot be translated with knee,'—why not?—'but we have to adopt the other metaphorical meaning, the *approaching* day, *i.e.* the dawn.' Where is the necessity? In ordinary philology, we

164

should here demand a number of attested examples of *goab*, in the sense of dawn, but in Khoi Khoi we cannot expect such evidence, as there are probably no texts. Next, after arbitrarily deciding that all Khoi Khois misunderstand their own tongue (for that is what the rendering here of *goab* by 'dawn' comes to), Dr. Hahn examines *tsu*, in *Tsui. Tsu* means 'sore,' 'wounded,' 'painful,' as in 'wounded knee'—Tsui Goab. This does not help Dr Hahn, for 'wounded dawn' means nothing. But he reflects that a wound is red, *tsu* means wounded: therefore *tsu* means red, therefore Tsui Goab is the Red Dawn. Q.E.D.

This kind of reasoning is obviously fallacious. Dr. Hahn's point could only be made by bringing forward examples in which *tsu* is employed to mean red in Khoi Khoi. Of this use of the word *tsu* he does not give one single instance, though on this point his argument depends. His etymology is not strengthened by the fact that Tsui Goab has once been said to live in the red sky. A red house is not necessarily tenanted by a red man. Still less is the theory supported by the hymn which says Tsui Goab paints himself with red ochre. Most idols, from those of the Samoyeds to the Greek images of Dionysus, are and have been daubed with red. By such reasoning is Tsui Goab proved to be the Red Dawn, while his gifts of prophecy (which he shares with all soothsayers) are accounted for as attributes of dawn, of the Vedic *Saranyu.*

Turning from Tsui Goab to his old enemy Gaunab, we learn that his name is derived from //*gau*, 'to destroy,' and, according to old Hottentot ideas, 'no one was the destroyer but the night' (p. 126). There is no apparent reason why the destroyer should be the night, and the night alone, any more than why 'a lame broken knee' should be 'red' (p. 126). Besides (p. 85), Gaunab is elsewhere explained, not as the night, but as the malevolent ghost which is thought to kill people who die what we call a 'natural' death. Unburied men change into this sort of vampire, just as Elpenor, in the Odyssey, threatens, if unburied, to become mischievous. There is another Gaunab, the mantis insect, which is worshipped by Hottentots and Bushmen (p. 92). It appears

165

that the two Gaunabs are differently pronounced. However that may be, a race which worships an insect might well worship a dead medicine-man.

* * * * *

The conclusion, then, to be drawn from an examination of Hottentot mythology is merely this, that the ideas of a people will be reflected in their myths. A people which worships the dead, believes in sorcerers and in prophets, and in metamorphosis, will have for its god (if he can be called a god) a being who is looked on as a dead prophet and sorcerer. He will be worshipped with such rites as dead men receive; he will be mixed up in such battles as living men wage, and will be credited with the skill which living sorcerers claim. All these things meet in the legend of Tsui Goab, the so-called 'supreme being' of the Hottentots. His connection with the dawn is not supported by convincing argument or evidence. The relation of the dawn to the Infinite again rests on nothing but a theory of Mr. Max Müller's.[190] His adversary, though recognised as the night, is elsewhere admitted to have been, originally, a common vampire. Finally, the Hottentots, a people not much removed from savagery, have a mythology full of savage and even disgusting elements. And this is just what we expect from Hottentots. The puzzle is when we find myths as low as the story of the incest of Heitsi Eibib among the Greeks. The reason for this coincidence is that, in Dr. Hahn's words, 'the same objects and the same phenomena in nature will give rise to the same ideas, whether social or mythical, among different races of mankind,' especially when these races are in the same well-defined state of savage fancy and savage credulity.

Dr. Hahn's book has been regarded as a kind of triumph over inquirers who believe that ancestor-worship enters into myth, and that the purer element in myth is the later. But where is the triumph? Even on Dr. Hahn's own showing, ancestor-worship

---

[190] See Fetichism and the Infinite.

among the Hottentots has swamped the adoration of the Infinite. It may be said that Dr. Hahn has at least proved the adoration of the Infinite to be earlier than ancestor-worship. But it has been shown that his attempt to establish a middle stage, to demonstrate that the worshipped ancestor was really the Red Dawn, is not logical nor convincing. Even if that middle stage were established, it is a far cry from the worship of Dawn (supposed by the Australians to be a woman of bad character in a cloak of red' possum-skin) to the adoration of the Infinite. Our own argument has been successful if we have shown that there are not only two possible schools of mythological interpretation—the Euhemeristic, led by Mr. Spencer, and the Philological, led by Mr. Max Müller. We have seen that it is possible to explain the legend of Tsui Goab without either believing him to have been a real historical person (as Mr. Spencer may perhaps believe), or his myth to have been the result of a 'disease of language' as Mr. Müller supposes. We have explained the legend and worship of a supposed dead conjurer as natural to a race which believes in conjurers and worships dead men. Whether he was merely an ideal ancestor and warrior, or whether an actual man has been invested with what divine qualities Tsui Goab enjoys, it is impossible to say; but, if he ever lived, he has long been adorned with ideal qualities and virtues which he never possessed. The conception of the powerful ancestral ghost has been heightened and adorned with some novel attributes of power: the conception of the Infinite has not been degraded, by forgetfulness of language, to the estate of an ancestral ghost with a game leg.

* * * * *

If this view be correct, myth is the result of thought, far more than of a disease of language. The comparative importance of language and thought was settled long ago, in our sense, by no less a person than Pragapati, the Sanskrit Master of Life.

'Now a dispute once took place between Mind and Speech, as to which was the better of the two. Both Mind and Speech said,

"I am excellent!" Mind said, "Surely I am better than thou, for thou dost not speak anything that is not understood by me; and since thou art only an imitator of what is done by me and a follower in my wake, I am surely better than thou!" Speech said, "Surely I am better than thou, for what thou knowest I make known, I communicate." They went to appeal to Pragapati for his decision. He (Pragapati) decided in favour of Mind, saying (to Speech), "Mind is indeed better than thou, for thou art an imitator of its deeds, and a follower in its wake; and inferior, surely, is he who imitates his better's deeds, and follows in his wake."'

So saith the 'Satapatha Brahmana.' [191]

---

[191] Sacred Books of the East, xii. 130, 131,

FETICHISM AND THE INFINITE.

What is the true place of Fetichism, to use a common but unscientific term, in the history of religious evolution? Some theorists have made fetichism, that is to say, the adoration of odds and ends (with which they have confused the worship of animals, of mountains, and even of the earth), the first moment in the development of worship. Others, again, think that fetichism is 'a corruption of religion, in Africa, as elsewhere.' The latter is the opinion of Mr Max Müller, who has stated it in his 'Hibbert Lectures,' on 'The Origin and Growth of Religion, especially as illustrated by the Religions of India.' It seems probable that there is a middle position between these two extremes. Students may hold that we hardly know enough to justify us in talking about the *origin* of religion, while at the same time they may believe that Fetichism is one of the earliest traceable steps by which men climbed to higher conceptions of the supernatural. Meanwhile Mr. Max Müller supports his own theory, that fetichism is a 'parasitical growth,' a 'corruption' of religion, by arguments mainly drawn from historical study of savage creeds, and from the ancient religious documents of India.

These documents are to English investigators ignorant of Sanskrit 'a book sealed with seven seals.' The Vedas are interpreted in very different ways by different Oriental scholars. It does not yet appear to be known whether a certain word in the Vedic funeral service means 'goat' or 'soul'! Mr. Max Müller's rendering is certain to have the first claim on English readers, and therefore it is desirable to investigate the conclusions which he draws from his Vedic studies. The ordinary anthropologist must first, however, lodge a protest against the tendency to look for *primitive* matter in the Vedas. They are the elaborate hymns of a specially trained set of poets and philosophers, living in an age almost of civilisation. They can therefore contain little testimony as to what man, while still 'primitive,' thought about God, the world, and the soul. One might as well look for the first germs of religion, for *primitive* religion strictly so called, in 'Hymns

Ancient and Modern' as in the Vedas. It is chiefly, however, by way of deductions from the Vedas, that Mr. Max Müller arrives at ideas which may be briefly and broadly stated thus: he inclines to derive religion from man's sense of the Infinite, as awakened by natural objects calculated to stir that sense. Our position is, on the other hand, that the germs of the religious sense in early man are developed, not so much by the vision of the Infinite, as by the idea of Power. Early religions, in short, are selfish, not disinterested. The worshipper is not contemplative, so much as eager to gain something to his advantage. In fetiches, he ignorantly recognises something that possesses power of an abnormal sort, and the train of ideas which leads him to believe in and to treasure fetiches is one among the earliest springs of religious belief.

Mr. Müller's opinion is the very reverse: he believes that a contemplative and disinterested emotion in the presence of the Infinite, or of anything that suggests infinitude or is mistaken for the Infinite, begets human religion, while of this religion fetichism is a later corruption.

* * * * *

In treating of fetichism Mr. Müller is obliged to criticise the system of De Brosses, who introduced this rather unfortunate term to science, in an admirable work, 'Le Culte des Dieux Fetiches' (1760). We call the work 'admirable,' because, considering the contemporary state of knowledge and speculation, De Brosses's book is brilliant, original, and only now and then rash or confused. Mr. Müller says that De Brosses 'holds that all nations had to begin with fetichism, to be followed afterwards by polytheism and monotheism.' This sentence would lead some readers to suppose that De Brosses, in his speculations, was looking for the origin of religion; but, in reality, his work is a mere attempt to explain a certain element in ancient religion and mythology. De Brosses was well aware that heathen religions were a complex mass, a concretion of many materials. He admits

170

the existence of regard for the spirits of the dead as one factor, he gives Sabaeism a place as another. But what chiefly puzzles him, and what he chiefly tries to explain, is the worship of odds and ends of rubbish, and the adoration of animals, mountains, trees, the sun, and so forth. When he masses all these worships together, and proposes to call them all Fetichism (a term derived from the Portuguese word for a talisman), De Brosses is distinctly unscientific. But De Brosses is distinctly scientific when he attempts to explain the animal-worship of Egypt, and the respect paid by Greeks and Romans to shapeless stones, as survivals of older savage practices.

The position of De Brosses is this: Old mythology and religion are a tissue of many threads. Sabaeism, adoration of the dead, mythopœic fancy, have their part in the fabric. Among many African tribes, a form of theism, Islamite or Christian, or self-developed, is superimposed on a mass of earlier superstitions. Among these superstitions, is the worship of animals and plants, and the cult of rough stones and of odds and ends of matter. What is the origin of this element, so prominent in the religion of Egypt, and present, if less conspicuous, in the most ancient temples of Greece? It is the survival, answers De Brosses, of ancient practices like those of untutored peoples, as Brazilians, Samoyeds, Negroes, whom the Egyptians and Pelasgians once resembled in lack of culture.

This, briefly stated, is the hypothesis of De Brosses. If he had possessed our wider information, he would have known that, among savage races, the worships of the stars, of the dead, and of plants and animals, are interlaced by the strange metaphysical processes of wild men. He would, perhaps, have kept the supernatural element in magical stones, feathers, shells, and so on, apart from the triple thread of Sabaeism, ghost-worship, and totemism, with its later development into the regular worship of plants and animals. It must be recognised, however, that De Brosses was perfectly well aware of the confused and manifold character of early religion. He had a clear view of the truth that what the religious instinct has once grasped, it does not, as a rule, abandon, but subordinates or disguises, when it reaches higher ideas. And he avers, again and again, that men laid hold of the coarser and more material objects of worship, while they themselves were coarse and dull, and that, as civilisation advanced, they, as a rule, subordinated and disguised the ruder factors in their system. Here it is that Mr. Max Müller differs from De Brosses. He holds that the adoration of stones, feathers, shells, and (as I understand him) the worship of animals are, even among the races of Africa, a corruption of an earlier and purer religion, a 'parasitical development' of religion.

However, Mr. Max Müller himself held 'for a long time' what he calls 'De Brosses's theory of fetichism.' What made him throw the theory overboard? It was 'the fact that, while in the earliest accessible documents of religious thought we look in vain for any very clear traces of fetichism, they become more and more frequent everywhere in the later stages of religious development, and are certainly more visible in the later corruptions of the Indian religion, beginning with the Âtharvana, than in the earliest hymns of the Rig Veda.' Now, by the earliest accessible documents of religious thought, Professor Max Müller means the hymns of the Rig Veda. These hymns are composed in the most elaborate metre, by sages of old repute, who, I presume, occupied a position not unlike that of the singers and seers of Israel. They lived in an age of tolerably advanced cultivation. They had wide geographical knowledge. They had settled government. They dwelt in States. They had wealth of gold, of grain, and of domesticated animals. Among the metals, they were acquainted with that which, in most countries, has been the latest worked—they used iron poles in their chariots. How then can the hymns of the most enlightened singers of a race thus far developed be called 'the earliest religious documents'? Oldest they may be, the oldest that are accessible, but that is a very different thing. How can we possibly argue that what is absent in these hymns, is absent because it had not yet come into existence? Is it not the very office of *pii vates et Phœbo digna locuti* to purify religion, to cover up decently its rude shapes, as the unhewn stone was

172

concealed in the fane of Apollo of Delos? If the race whose noblest and oldest extant hymns were pure, exhibits traces of fetichism in its later documents, may not that as easily result from a recrudescence as from a corruption? Professor Max Müller has still, moreover, to explain how the process of corruption which introduced the same fetichistic practices among Samoyeds, Brazilians, Kaffirs, and the people of the Âtharva*n*a Veda came to be everywhere identical in its results.

Here an argument often urged against the anthropological method may be shortly disposed of. 'You examine savages,' people say, 'but how do you know that these savages were not once much more cultivated; that their whole mode of life, religion and all, is not debased and decadent from an earlier standard?' Mr. Müller glances at this argument, which, however, cannot serve his purpose. Mr. Müller has recognised that savage, or 'nomadic,' languages represent a much earlier state of language than anything that we find, for example, in the oldest Hebrew or Sanskrit texts. 'For this reason,' he says, [192]'the study of what I call *nomad* languages, as distinguished from *State* languages, becomes so instructive. We see in them what we can no longer expect to see even in the most ancient Sanskrit or Hebrew. We watch the childhood of language with all its childish freaks.' Yes, adds the anthropologist, and for this reason the study of savage religions, as distinguished from State religions, becomes so instructive. We see in them what we can no longer expect to see even in the most ancient Sanskrit or Hebrew faiths. We watch the childhood of religion with all its childish freaks. If this reasoning be sound when the Kaffir tongue is contrasted with ancient Sanskrit, it should be sound when the Kaffir faith is compared with the Vedic faith. By parity of reasoning, the religious beliefs of peoples as much less advanced than the Kaffirs as the Kaffirs are less advanced than the Vedic peoples, should be still nearer the infancy of faith, still 'nearer the beginning.'

---

[192] *Lectures on Language.* Second series, p. 41.

We have been occupied, perhaps, too long with De Brosses and our apology for De Brosses. Let us now examine, as shortly as possible, Mr. Max Müller's reasons for denying that fetichism is 'a primitive form of religion.' The negative side of his argument being thus disposed of, it will then be our business to consider (1) his psychological theory of the subjective element in religion, and (2) his account of the growth of Indian religion. The conclusion of the essay will be concerned with demonstrating that Mr. Max Müller's system assigns little or no place to the superstitious beliefs without which, in other countries than India, society could not have come into organised existence.

* * * * *

In his polemic against Fetichism, it is not always very easy to see against whom Mr. Müller is contending. It is one thing to say that fetichism is a 'primitive form of religion,' and quite another to say that it is 'the very beginning of all religion.' Occasionally he attacks the 'Comtian theory,' which, I think, is not now held by many people who study the history of man, and which I am not concerned to defend. He says that the Portuguese navigators who discovered among the negroes 'no other trace of any religious worship' except what they called the worship of *feitiços*, concluded that this was the whole of the religion of the negroes (p. 61). Mr. Müller then goes on to prove that 'no religion consists of fetichism only,' choosing his examples of higher elements in negro religion from the collections of Waitz. It is difficult to see what bearing this has on his argument. De Brosses (p. 20) shows that *he*, at least, was well aware that many negro tribes have higher conceptions of the Deity than any which are implied in fetich-worship. Even if no tribe in the world is exclusively devoted to fetiches, the argument makes no progress. Perhaps no extant tribe is in the way of using unpolished stone weapons and no others, but it does not follow that unpolished stone weapons are not primitive. It is just as easy to maintain that the purer ideas have, by this time, been reached by aid of the

174

stepping-stones of the grosser, as that the grosser are the corruption of the purer. Mr. Max Müller constantly asserts that the 'human mind advanced by small and timid steps from what is intelligible, to what is at first sight almost beyond comprehension' (p. 126). Among the objects which aided man to take these small and timid steps, he reckons rivers and trees, which excited, he says, religious awe. What he will not suppose is that the earliest small and timid steps were not unaided by such objects as the fetichist treasures—stones, shells, and so forth, which suggest no idea of infinity. Stocks he will admit, but not, if he can help it, stones, of the sort that negroes and Kanekas and other tribes use as fetiches. His reason is, that he does not see how the scraps of the fetichist can appeal to the feeling of the Infinite, which feeling is, in his theory, the basis of religion.

After maintaining (what is readily granted) that negroes have a religion composed of many elements, Mr. Müller tries to discredit the evidence about the creeds of savages, and discourses on the many minute shades of progress which exist among tribes too often lumped together as if they were all in the same condition. Here he will have all scientific students of savage life on his side. It remains true, however, that certain elements of savage practice, fetichism being one of them, are practically ubiquitous. Thus, when Mr. Müller speaks of 'the influence of public opinion' in biassing the narrative of travellers, we must not forget that the strongest evidence about savage practice is derived from the 'undesigned coincidence' of the testimonies of all sorts of men, in all ages, and all conditions of public opinion. 'Illiterate men, ignorant of the writings of each other, bring the same reports from various quarters of the globe,' wrote Millar of Glasgow. When sailors, merchants, missionaries, describe, as matters unprecedented and unheard of, such institutions as polyandry, totemism, and so forth, the evidence is so strong, because the witnesses are so astonished. They do not know that anyone but themselves has ever noticed the curious facts before their eyes. And when Mr. Müller tries to make the testimony about savage faith still more untrustworthy, by talking of the 'absence of recognised authority among savages,' do not let us forget that custom (νομος) is a recognised authority, and that the punishment of death is inflicted for transgression of certain rules. These rules, generally speaking, are of a religious nature, and the religion to which they testify is of the sort known (too vaguely) as 'fetichistic.' Let us keep steadily before our minds, when people talk of lack of evidence, that we have two of the strongest sorts of evidence in the world for the kind of religion which least suits Mr. Müller's argument—(I) the undesigned coincidences of testimony, (2) the irrefutable witness and sanction of elementary criminal law. Mr. Müller's own evidence is that much-disputed work, where 'all men see what they want to see, as in the clouds,' and where many see systematised fetichism—the Veda. [193]

The first step in Mr. Max Müller's polemic was the assertion that Fetichism is nowhere unmixed. We have seen that the fact is capable of an interpretation that will suit either side. Stages of culture overlap each other. The second step in his polemic was the effort to damage the evidence. We have seen that we have as good evidence as can be desired. In the third place he asks, What are the antecedents of fetich-worship? He appears to conceive himself to be arguing with persons (p. 127) who 'have taken for granted that every human being was miraculously endowed with the concept of what forms the predicate of every fetich, call it power, spirit, or god.' If there are reasoners so feeble, they must be left to the punishment inflicted by Mr. Müller. On the other hand, students who regard the growth of the idea of power, which is the predicate of every fetish, as a slow process, as the result of various impressions and trains of early half-conscious reasoning, cannot be disposed of by the charge that they think that 'every human being was miraculously endowed' with any concept whatever. They, at least, will agree with Mr. Max Müller that there are fetiches and fetiches, that to one reverence is assigned for one reason, to another for another. Unfortunately, it is less easy to admit that Mr. Max Müller has been happy in his choice of

---

[193] A defence of the evidence for our knowledge of savage faiths, practices, and ideas will be found in *Primitive Culture*, i. 9-11.

ancient instances. He writes (p. 99): 'Sometimes a stock or a stone was worshipped because it was a forsaken altar or an ancient place of judgment, sometimes because it marked the place of a great battle or a murder, or the burial of a king.' Here he refers to Pausanias, book i. 28, 5, and viii. 13, 3.[194] In both of these passages, Pausanias, it is true, mentions stones—in the first passage stones on which men stood οσοι δικας υπεχουσι και οι διωκοντες, in the second, barrows heaped up in honour of men who fell in battle. In neither case, however, do I find anything to show that the stones were worshipped. These stones, then, have no more to do with the argument than the milestones which certainly exist on the Dover road, but which are not the objects of superstitious reverence. No! the fetich-stones of Greece were those which occupied the holy of holies of the most ancient

---

[194] A third reference to Pausanias I have been unable to verify. There are several references to Greek fetich-stones in Theophrastus's account of the Superstitious Man. A number of Greek sacred stones named by Pausanias may be worth noticing. In Bœotia (ix. 16), the people believed that Alcmene, mother of Heracles, was changed into a stone. The Thespians worshipped, under the name of Eros, an unwrought stone, αγαλμα παλαιοτατον, 'their most ancient sacred object' (ix. 27). The people of Orchomenos 'paid extreme regard to certain stones,' said to have fallen from heaven, 'or to certain figures made of stone that descended from the sky' (ix. 38). Near Chæronea, Rhea was said to have deceived Cronus, by offering him, in place of Zeus, a stone wrapped in swaddling bands. This stone, which Cronus vomited forth after having swallowed it, was seen by Pausanias at Delphi (ix. 41). By the roadside, near the city of the Panopeans, lay the stones out of which Prometheus made men (x. 4). The stone swallowed in place of Zeus by his father lay at the exit from the Delphian temple, and was anointed (compare the action of Jacob, Gen. xxviii. 18) with oil every day. The Phocians worshipped thirty squared stones, each named after a god (vii. xxii.). '*Among all the Greeks rude stones were worshipped before the images of the gods.*' Among the Trœzenians a sacred stone lay in front of the temple, whereon the Trœzenian elders sat, and purified Orestes from the murder of his mother. In Attica there was a conical stone worshipped as Apollo (i. xliv.). Near Argos was a stone called Zeus Cappotas, on which Orestes was said to have sat down, and so recovered peace of mind. Such are examples of the sacred stones, the oldest worshipful objects, of Greece.

temples, the mysterious fanes within dark cedar or cypress groves, to which men were hardly admitted. They were the stones and blocks which bore the names of gods, Hera, or Apollo, names perhaps given, as De Brosses says, to the old fetichistic objects of worship, *after* the anthropomorphic gods entered Hellas. This, at least is the natural conclusion from the fact that the Apollo and Hera of untouched wood or stone were confessedly the *oldest.* Religion, possessing an old fetich did not run the risk of breaking the run of luck by discarding it, but wisely retained and renamed it. Mr. Max Müller says that the unhewn lump may indicate a higher power of abstraction than the worship paid to the work of Phidias; but in that case all the savage adorers of rough stones *may* be in a stage of more abstract thought than these contemporaries of Phidias who had such very hard work to make Greek thought abstract.

Mr Müller founds a very curious argument on what he calls 'the ubiquity of fetichism.' Like De Brosses, he compiles (from Pausanias) a list of the rude stones worshipped by the early Greeks. He mentions various examples of fetichistic superstitions in Rome. He detects the fetichism of popular Catholicism, and of Russian orthodoxy among the peasants. Here, he cries, in religions the history of which is known to us, fetichism is secondary, 'and why should fetiches in Africa, where we do not know the earlier development of religion, be considered as primary?' What a singular argument! According to Pausanias, this fetichism (if fetichism it is) *was* primary, in Greece. The *oldest* temples, in their holiest place, held the oldest fetich. In Rome, it is at least probable that fetichism, as in Greece, was partly a survival, partly a new growth from the primal root of human superstitions. As to Catholicism, the records of Councils, the invectives of the Church, show us that, from the beginning, the secondary religion in point of time, the religion of the Church, laboured vainly to suppress, and had in part to tolerate, the primary religion of childish superstitions. The documents are before the world. As to the Russians, the history of their conversion is pretty well known. Jaroslaf, or Vladimir, or some

178

other evangelist, had whole villages baptized in groups, and the pagan peasants naturally kept up their primary semi-savage ways of thought and worship, under the secondary varnish of orthodoxy. In all Mr. Max Müller's examples, then, fetichism turns out to be *primary* in point of time; *secondary* only, as subordinate to some later development of faith, or to some lately superimposed religion. Accepting his statement that fetichism is ubiquitous, we have the most powerful *a priori* argument that fetichism is primitive. As religions become developed they are differentiated; it only fetichism that you find the same everywhere. Thus the bow and arrow have a wide range of distribution: the musket, one not so wide; the Martini-Henry rifle, a still narrower range: it is the primitive stone weapons that are ubiquitous, that are found in the soil of England, Egypt, America, France, Greece, as in the hands of Dieyries and Admiralty Islanders. And just as rough stone knives are earlier than iron ones (though the same race often uses both), so fetichism is more primitive than higher and purer faiths, though the same race often combines fetichism and theism. No one will doubt the truth of this where weapons are concerned; but Mr. Max Müller will not look at religion in this way.

Mr. Max Müller's remarks on 'Zoolatry,' as De Brosses calls it, or animal-worship, require only the briefest comment. De Brosses, very unluckily, confused zoolatry with other superstitions under the head of Fetichism. This was unscientific; but is it scientific of Mr. Max Müller to discuss animal-worship without any reference to totemism? The worship of sacred animals is found, in every part of the globe, to be part of the sanction of the most stringent and important of all laws, the laws of marriage. It is an historical truth that the society of Ashantees, Choctaws, Australians, is actually constructed by the operation of laws which are under the sanction of various sacred plants and animals.[195] There is scarcely a race so barbarous that these laws are not traceable at work in its society, nor a people (especially an ancient

---

[195] See essays on 'Apollo and the Mouse' and 'The Early History of the Family.'

people) so cultivated that its laws and religion are not full of strange facts most easily explained as relics of totemism. Now note that actual living totemism is always combined with the rudest ideas of marriage, with almost repulsive ideas about the family. Presumably, this rudeness is earlier than culture, and therefore this form of animal-worship is one of the earliest religions that we know. The almost limitless distribution of the phenomena, their regular development, their gradual disappearance, all point to the fact that they are all very early and everywhere produced by similar causes.

Of all these facts, Mr. Max Müller only mentions one—that many races have called themselves Snakes, and he thinks they might naturally adopt the snake for ancestor, and finally for god. He quotes the remark of Diodorus that 'the snake may either have been made a god because he was figured on the banners, or may have been figured on the banners because he was a god'; to which De Brosses, with his usual sense, rejoins—'we represent saints on our banners because we revere them; we do not revere them because we represent them on our banners.'

In a discussion about origins, and about the corruption of religion, it would have been well to account for institutions and beliefs almost universally distributed. We know, what De Brosses did not, that zoolatry is inextricably blent with laws and customs which surely must be early, if not primitive, because they make the working faith of societies in which male descent and the modern family are not yet established. Anyone who wishes to show that this sort of society is a late corruption, not an early stage in evolution towards better things, has a difficult task before him, which, however, he must undertake, before he can prove zoolatry to be a corruption of religion.

As to the worship of ancestral and embodied human spirits, which (it has been so plausibly argued) is the first moment in religion, Mr. Max Müller dismisses it, here, in eleven lines and a half. An isolated but important allusion at the close of his lectures will be noticed in its place.

The end of the polemic against the primitiveness of fetichism deals with the question, 'Whence comes the supernatural predicate of the fetich?' If a negro tells us his fetich is a god, whence got he the idea of 'god'? Many obvious answers occur. Mr. Müller says, speaking of the Indians (p. 205): 'The concept of *gods* was no doubt growing up while men were assuming a more and more definite attitude towards these semi-tangible and intangible objects'—trees, rivers, hills, the sky, the sun, and so on, which he thinks suggested and developed, by aid of a kind of awe, the religious feeling of the infinite. We too would say that, among people who adore fetiches and ghosts, the concept of gods no doubt silently grew up, as men assumed a more and more definite attitude towards the tangible and intangible objects they held sacred. Again, negroes have had the idea of god imported among them by Christians and Islamites, so that, even if they did not climb (as De Brosses grants that many of them do) to purer religious ideas unaided, these ideas are now familiar to them, and may well be used by them, when they have to explain a fetich to a European. Mr. Max Müller explains the origin of religion by a term ('the Infinite ') which, he admits, the early people would not have comprehended. The negro, if he tells a white man that a fetich is a god, transposes terms in the same unscientific way. Mr. Müller asks, 'How do these people, when they have picked up their stone or their shell, pick up, at the same time, the concepts of a supernatural power, of spirit, of god, and of worship paid to some unseen being?' But who says that men picked up these ideas *at the same time?* These ideas were evolved by a long, slow, complicated process. It is not at all impossible that the idea of a kind of 'luck' attached to this or that object, was evolved by dint of meditating on a mere series of lucky accidents. Such or such a man, having found such an object, succeeded in hunting, fishing, or war. By degrees, similar objects might be believed to command success. Thus burglars carry bits of coal in their pockets, 'for luck.' This random way of connecting causes and effects which have really no inter-relation, is a common error of early reasoning. Mr. Max Müller says that 'this process of reasoning is far more in accordance with modern thought'; if so, modern thought has little to be proud of. Herodotus, however, describes the process of thought as consecrated by custom among the Egyptians. But there are many other practical ways in which the idea of supernatural power is attached to fetiches. Some fetich-stones have a superficial resemblance to other objects, and thus (on the magical system of reasoning) are thought to influence these objects. Others, again, are pointed out as worthy of regard in dreams or by the ghosts of the dead.[196] To hold these views of the origin of the supernatural predicate of fetiches is not 'to take for granted that every human being was miraculously endowed with the concept of what forms the predicate of every fetich.'

Thus we need not be convinced by Mr. Max Müller that fetichism (though it necessarily has its antecedents in the human mind) is 'a corruption of religion.' It still appears to be one of the most primitive steps towards the idea of the supernatural.

What, then, is the subjective element of religion in man? How has he become capable of conceiving of the supernatural? What outward objects first awoke that dormant faculty in his breast? Mr. Max Müller answers, that man has 'the faculty of apprehending the infinite'—that by dint of this faculty he is capable of religion, and that sensible objects, 'tangible, semi-tangible, intangible,' first roused the faculty to religious activity, at least among the natives of India. He means, however, by the 'infinite' which savages apprehend, not our metaphysical conception of the infinite, but the mere impression that there is 'something beyond.' 'Every thing of which his senses cannot

---

[196] Here I may mention a case illustrating the motives of the fetich-worshipper. My friend, Mr. J. J. Atkinson, who has for many years studied the manners of the people of New Caledonia, asked a native *why* he treasured a certain fetich-stone. The man replied that, in one of the vigils which are practised beside the corpses of deceased friends, he saw a lizard. The lizard is a totem, a worshipful animal in New Caledonia. The native put out his hand to touch it, when it disappeared and left a stone in its place. This stone he therefore held sacred in the highest degree. Here then a fetich-stone was indicated as such by a spirit in form of a lizard.

perceive a limit, is to a primitive savage or to any man in an early stage of intellectual activity *unlimited* or *infinite*? Thus, in all experience, the idea of 'a beyond' is forced on men. If Mr. Max Müller would adhere to this theory, then we should suppose him to mean (what we hold to be more or less true) that savage religion, like savage science, is merely a fanciful explanation of what lies beyond the horizon of experience. For example, if the Australians mentioned by Mr. Max Müller believe in a being who created the world, a being whom they do not worship, and to whom they pay no regard (for, indeed, he has become 'decrepit'), their theory is scientific, not religious. They have looked for the causes of things, and are no more religious (in so doing) than Newton was when he worked out his theory of gravitation. The term 'infinite' is wrongly applied, because it is a term of advanced thought used in explanation of the ideas of men who, Mr. Max Müller says, were incapable of conceiving the meaning of such a concept. Again, it is wrongly applied, because it has some modern religious associations, which are covertly and fallaciously introduced to explain the supposed emotions of early men. Thus, Mr. Müller says (p. 177)—he is giving his account of the material things that awoke the religious faculty—'the mere sight of the torrent or the stream would have been enough to call forth in the hearts of the early dwellers on the earth . . . a feeling that they were surrounded on all sides by powers invisible, infinite, or divine.' Here, if I understand Mr. Müller, 'infinite' is used in our modern sense. The question is, How did men ever come to believe in powers infinite, invisible, divine? If Mr. Müller's words mean anything, they mean that a dormant feeling that there were such existences lay in the breast of man, and was wakened into active and conscious life, by the sight of a torrent or a stream. How, to use Mr. Müller's own manner, did these people, when they saw a stream, have mentally, at the same time, 'a feeling of *infinite* powers?' If this is not the expression of a theory of 'innate religion' (a theory which Mr. Müller disclaims), it is capable of being mistaken for that doctrine by even a careful reader. The feeling of 'powers infinite, invisible, divine,' *must* be in the heart, or the mere sight of a river could not call it forth. How did the feeling get into the heart? That is the question. The ordinary anthropologist distinguishes a multitude of causes, a variety of processes, which shade into each other and gradually produce the belief in powers invisible, infinite, and divine. What tribe is unacquainted with dreams, visions, magic, the apparitions of the dead? Add to these the slow action of thought, the conjectural inferences, the guesses of crude metaphysics, the theories of isolated men of religious and speculative genius. By all these and other forces manifold, that emotion of awe in presence of the hills, the stars, the sea, is developed. Mr. Max Müller cuts the matter shorter. The early inhabitants of earth saw a river, and the 'mere sight' of the torrent called forth the feelings which (to us) seem to demand ages of the operation of causes disregarded by Mr. Müller in his account of the origin of Indian religion.

The mainspring of Mr. Müller's doctrine is his theory about 'apprehending the infinite.' Early religion, or at least that of India, was, in his view, the extension of an idea of Vastness, a disinterested emotion of awe.[197] Elsewhere, we think, early religion has been a development of ideas of Force, an interested search, not for something wide and far and hard to conceive, but for something practically *strong* for good and evil. Mr. Müller (taking no count in this place of fetiches, ghosts, dreams and magic) explains that the sense of 'wonderment' was wakened by objects only semi-tangible, trees, which are *taller* than we are, 'whose roots are beyond our reach, and which have a kind of life in them.' 'We are dealing with a quartenary, it may be a tertiary troglodyte,' says Mr. Müller. If a tertiary troglodyte was like a modern Andaman Islander, a Kaneka, a Dieyrie, would he stand and meditate in awe on the fact that a tree was taller than he, or had 'a kind of life,' 'an unknown and unknowable, yet undeniable something'?[198] Why, this is the sentiment of modern Germany,

---

[197] Much the same theory is propounded in Mr. Müller's lectures on 'The Science of Religion.'
[198] The idea is expressed in a well known parody of Wordsworth, about the tree which

and perhaps of the Indian sages of a cultivated period! A troglodyte would look for a 'possum in the tree, he would tap the trunk for honey, he would poke about in the bark after grubs, or he would worship anything odd in the branches. Is Mr. Müller not unconsciously transporting a kind of modern malady of thought into the midst of people who wanted to find a dinner, and who might worship a tree if it had a grotesque shape, that, for them, had a magical meaning, or if *boilyas* lived in its boughs, but whose practical way of dealing with the problem of its life was to burn it round the stem, chop the charred wood with stone axes, and use the bark, branches, and leaves as they happened to come handy?

Mr. Müller has a long list of semi-tangible objects 'overwhelming and overawing,' like the tree. There are mountains, where 'even a stout heart shivers before the real presence of the *infinite*'; there are rivers, those instruments of so sudden a religious awakening; there is earth. These supply the material for semi-deities. Then come sky, stars, dawn, sun, and moon: 'in these we have the germs of what, hereafter, we shall have to call by the name of deities.'

Before we can transmute, with Mr. Müller, these objects of a somewhat vague religious regard into a kind of gods, we have to adopt Noiré's philological theories, and study the effects of auxiliary verbs on the development of personification and of religion. Noiré's philological theories are still, I presume, under discussion. They are necessary, however, to Mr. Müller's doctrine of the development of the vague 'sense of the infinite' (wakened by fine old trees, and high mountains) into *devas*, and of *devas* (which means 'shining ones') into the Vedic gods. Our troglodyte ancestors, and their sweet feeling for the spiritual aspect of landscape, are thus brought into relation with the Rishis of the Vedas, the sages and poets of a pleasing civilisation. The reverence felt for such comparatively refined or remote things as

---

'Will grow ten times as tall as me
And live ten times as long.'

fire, the sun, wind, thunder, the dawn, furnished a series of stepping-stones to the Vedic theology, if theology it can be called. It is impossible to give each step in detail; the process must be studied in Mr. Müller's lectures. Nor can we discuss the later changes of faith. As to the processes which produced the fetichistic 'corruption' (that universal and everywhere identical form of decay), Mr. Müller does not afford even a hint. He only says that, when the Indians found that their old gods were mere names, 'they built out of the scattered bricks a new altar to the Unknown God'—a statement which throws no light on the parasitical development of fetichism. But his whole theory is deficient if, having called fetichism a *corruption*, he does not show how corruption arose, how it operated, and how the disease attacked all religions everywhere.

We have contested, step by step, many of Mr. Müller's propositions. If space permitted, it would be interesting to examine the actual attitude of certain contemporary savages, Bushmen and others, towards the sun. Contemporary savages may be degraded, they certainly are not primitive, but their *legends*, at least, are the oldest things they possess. The supernatural elements in their ideas about the sun are curiously unlike those which, according to Mr. Müller, entered into the development of Aryan religion.

The last remark which has to be made about Mr. Müller's scheme of the development of Aryan religion is that the religion, as explained by him, does not apparently aid the growth of society, nor work with it in any way. Let us look at a sub-barbaric society—say that of Zululand, of New Zealand, of the Iroquois League, or at a savage society like that of the Kanekas, or of those Australian tribes about whom we have very many interesting and copious accounts. If we begin with the Australians, we observe that society is based on certain laws of marriage enforced by capital punishment. These laws of marriage forbid the intermixing of persons belonging to the stock which worships this or that animal, or plant. Now this rule, as already observed, *made* the 'gentile' system (as Mr. Morgan erroneously calls it) the system which gradually reduces tribal hostility, by making tribes homogeneous. The same system (with the religious sanction of a kind of zoolatry) is in force and has worked to the same result, in Africa, Asia, America, and Australia, while a host of minute facts make it a reasonable conclusion that it prevailed in Europe. Among these facts certain peculiarities of Greek and Roman and Hindoo marriage law, Greek, Latin, and English tribal names, and a crowd of legends are the most prominent.[199] Mr. Max Müller's doctrine of the development of Indian religion (while admitting the existence of Snake or Naga tribes) takes no account of the action of this universal zoolatry on religion and society.

After marriage and after tribal institutions, look at *rank*. Is it not obvious that the religious elements (magic and necromancy) left out of his reckoning by Mr. Müller are most powerful in developing rank? Even among those democratic paupers, the Fuegians, 'the doctor-wizard of each party has much influence over his companions.' Among those other democrats, the Eskimo, a class of wizards, called Angakuts, become 'a kind of civil magistrates,' because they can cause fine weather, and can magically detect people who commit offences. Thus the germs of rank, in these cases, are sown by the magic which is fetichism in action. Try the Zulus: 'the heaven is the chief's,' he can call up clouds and storms, hence the sanction of his authority. In New Zealand, every Rangatira has a supernatural power. If he touches an article, no one else dares to appropriate it, for fear of terrible supernatural consequences. A head chief is 'tapued an inch thick, and perfectly unapproachable.' Magical power abides in and emanates from him. By this superstition, an aristocracy is formed, and property (the property, at least, of the aristocracy) is secured. Among the Red Indians, as Schoolcraft says, 'priests and jugglers are the persons that make war and have a voice in the sale of the land.' Mr. E. W. Robertson says much the same thing about early Scotland. If Odin was not a god with the gifts of a

---

[199] See Essay on 'The Early History of the Family.'

medicine-man, and did not owe his chiefship to his talent for dealing with magic, he is greatly maligned. The Irish Brehons also sanctioned legal decisions by magical devices, afterwards condemned by the Church. Among the Zulus, 'the *Itongo* (spirit) dwells with the great man; he who dreams is the chief of the village.' The chief alone can 'read in the vessel of divination.' The Kaneka chiefs are medicine-men.

Here then, in widely distant regions, in early European, American, Melanesian, African societies, we find those factors in religion which the primitive Aryans are said to have dispensed with, helping to construct society, rank, property. Is it necessary to add that the ancestral spirits still 'rule the present from the past,' and demand sacrifice, and speak to 'him who dreams,' who, therefore, is a strong force in society, if not a chief? Mr. Herbert Spencer, Mr. Tylor, M. Fustel de Coulanges, a dozen others, have made all this matter of common notoriety. As Hearne the traveller says about the Copper River Indians, 'it is almost necessary that they who rule them should profess something a little supernatural to enable them to deal with the people.' The few examples we have given show how widely, and among what untutored races, the need is felt. The rudimentary government of early peoples requires, and, by aid of dreams, necromancy, 'medicine' (*i.e.* fetiches), *tapu*, and so forth, obtains, a supernatural sanction.

Where is the supernatural sanction that consecrated the chiefs of a race which woke to the sense of the existence of infinite beings, in face of trees, rivers, the dawn, the sun, and had none of the so-called late and corrupt fetichism that does such useful social work?

To the student of other early societies, Mr. Müller's theory of the growth of Aryan religion seems to leave society without cement, and without the most necessary sanctions. One man is as good as another, before a tree, a river, a hill. The savage organisers of other societies found out fetiches and ghosts that were 'respecters of persons.' Zoolatry is intertwisted with the earliest and most widespread law of prohibited degrees. How did

188

the Hindoos dispense with the aid of these superstitions? Well, they did not quite dispense with them. Mr. Max Müller remarks, almost on his last page (376), that 'in India also . . . the thoughts and feelings about those whom death had separated from us for a time, supplied some of the earliest and most important elements of religion.' If this was the case, surely the presence of those elements and their influence should have been indicated along with the remarks about the awfulness of trees and the suggestiveness of rivers. Is nothing said about the spirits of the dead and their cult in the Vedas? Much is said, of course. But, were it otherwise, then other elements of savage religion may also have been neglected there, and it will be impossible to argue that fetichism did not exist because it is not mentioned. It will also be impossible to admit that the 'Hibbert Lectures' give more than a one-sided account of the Origin of Indian Religion.

The perusal of Mr. Max Müller's book deeply impresses one with the necessity of studying early religions and early societies simultaneously. If it be true that early Indian religion lacked precisely those superstitions, so childish, so grotesque, and yet so useful, which we find at work in contemporary tribes, and which we read of in history, the discovery is even more remarkable and important than the author of the 'Hibbert Lectures' seems to suppose. It is scarcely necessary to repeat that the negative evidence of the Vedas, the religious utterances of sages, made in a time of what we might call 'heroic culture,' can never disprove the existence of superstitions which, if current in the former experience of the race, the hymnists, as Barth observes, would intentionally ignore. Our object has been to defend the 'primitiveness of fetichism.' By this we do not mean to express any opinion as to whether fetichism (in the strictest sense of the word) was or was not earlier than totemism, than the worship of the dead, or than the involuntary sense of awe and terror with which certain vast phenomena may have affected the earliest men. We only claim for the powerful and ubiquitous practices of fetichism a place *among* the early elements of religion, and insist that what is so universal has not yet been shown to be 'a corruption' of something older and purer.

One remark of Mr. Max Müller's fortifies these opinions. If fetichism be indeed one of the earliest factors of faith in the supernatural; if it be, in its rudest forms, most powerful in proportion to other elements of faith among the least cultivated races (and *that* Mr. Müller will probably allow)—among what class of cultivated peoples will it longest hold its ground? Clearly, among the least cultivated, among the fishermen, the shepherds of lonely districts, the peasants of outlying lands—in short, among the *people*. Neglected by sacred poets in the culminating period of purity in religion, it will linger among the superstitions of the rustics. There is no real break in the continuity of peasant life; the modern folklore is (in many points) the savage ritual. Now Mr. Müller, when he was minimising the existence of fetichism in the Rig Veda (the oldest collection of hymns), admitted its existence in the Âtharvana (p. 60).[200] On p. 151, we read 'the Atharva-veda-Sanhita is a later collection, containing, besides a large number of Rig Veda verses, *some curious relics of popular poetry connected with charms, imprecations, and other superstitious usages.*' The italics are mine, and are meant to emphasise this fact:—When we leave the sages, the Rishis, and look at what is *popular*, look at what that class believed which of savage practice has everywhere retained so much, we are at once among the charms and the fetishes! This is precisely what one would have expected. If the history of religion and of mythology is to be unravelled, we must examine what the unprogressive classes in Europe have in common with Australians, and Bushmen, and Andaman Islanders. It is the function of the people to retain in folklore these elements of religion, which it is the high duty of the sage and the poet to purify away in the fire of refining thought. It is for this very reason that *ritual* has (though Mr. Max Müller curiously says that it seems not to possess) an immense scientific interest. Ritual holds on, with the

---

[200] Bergaigne's *La Religion Védique* may be consulted for Vedic Fetichism.

tenacity of superstition, to all that has ever been practised. Yet, when Mr. Müller wants to know about *origins*, about actual ancient *practice*, he deliberately turns to that 'great collection of ancient poetry' (the Rig Veda) 'which has no special reference to sacrificial acts,' not to the Brahmanas which are full of ritual.

To sum up briefly:—(1) Mr. Müller's arguments against the evidence for, and the primitiveness of, fetichism seem to demonstrate the opposite of that which he intends them to prove. (2) His own evidence for *primitive* practice is chosen from the documents of a *cultivated* society. (3) His theory deprives that society of the very influences which have elsewhere helped the Tribe, the Family, Rank, and Priesthoods to grow up, and to form the backbone of social existence.

THE EARLY HISTORY OF THE FAMILY.

What are the original forms of the human family? Did man begin by being monogamous or polygamous, but, in either case, the master of his own home and the assured central point of his family relations? Or were the unions of the sexes originally shifting and precarious, so that the wisest child was not expected to know his own father, and family ties were reckoned through the mother alone? Again (setting aside the question of what was 'primitive' and 'original'), did the needs and barbarous habits of early men lead to a scarcity of women, and hence to polyandry (that is, the marriage of one woman to several men), with the consequent uncertainty about male parentage? Once more, admitting that these loose and strange relations of the sexes do prevail, or have prevailed, among savages, is there any reason to suppose that the stronger races, the Aryan and Semitic stocks, ever passed through this stage of savage customs? These are the main questions debated between what we may call the 'historical' and the 'anthropological' students of ancient customs.

When Sir Henry Maine observed, in 1861, that it was difficult to say what society of men had *not been*, originally, based on the patriarchal family, he went, of course, outside the domain of history. What occurred in the very origin of human society is a question perhaps quite inscrutable. Certainly, history cannot furnish the answer. Here the anthropologist and physiologist come in with their methods, and even those, we think, can throw but an uncertain light on the very 'origin' of institutions, and on strictly primitive man.

For the purposes of this discussion, we shall here re-state the chief points at issue between the adherents of Sir Henry Maine and of Mr. M'Lennan, between historical and anthropological inquirers.

I. Did man *originally* live in the patriarchal family, or did he live in more or less modified promiscuity, with uncertainty of blood-ties, and especially of male parentage?

2. Did circumstances and customs at some time compel or induce man (whatever his *original* condition) to resort to practices which made paternity uncertain, and so caused kinship to be reckoned through women?

3. Granting that some races have been thus reduced to matriarchal forms of the family—that is, to forms in which the woman is the permanent recognised centre—is there any reason to suppose that the stronger peoples, like the Aryans and the Semites, ever passed through a stage of culture in which female, not male, kinship was chiefly recognised, probably as a result of polyandry, of many husbands to one wife?

On this third question, it will be necessary to produce much evidence of very different sorts: evidence which, at best, can perhaps only warrant an inference, or presumption, in favour of one or the other opinion. For the moment, the impartial examination of testimony is more important and practicable than the establishment of any theory.

(I.) Did man *originally* live in the patriarchal family, the male being master of his female mate or mates, and of his children? On this first point Sir Henry Maine, in his new volume, [201]may be said to come as near proving his case as the nature and matter of the question will permit. Bachofen, M'Lennan, and Morgan, all started from a hypothetical state of more or less modified sexual promiscuity. Bachofen's evidence (which may be referred to later) was based on a great mass of legends, myths, and travellers' tales, chiefly about early Aryan practices. He discovered *Hetärismus*, as he called it, or promiscuity, among Lydians, Etruscans, Persians, Thracians, Cyrenian nomads, Egyptians, Scythians, Troglodytes, Nasamones, and so forth. Mr. M'Lennan's view is, perhaps, less absolutely stated than Sir Henry Maine supposes. M'Lennan says [202] 'that there has been a stage in the development of the human races, when there was no such appropriation of women to particular men; when, in short, marriage, *as it exists among civilised nations,*

---

[201] Early Law and Custom.
[202] Studies in Ancient History, p. 127.

was not practised. Marriage, *in this sense*, was yet undreamt of.' Mr. M'Lennan adds (pp. 130, 131), 'as among other gregarious animals, the unions of the sexes were probably, in the earliest times, loose, transitory, and, *in some degree*, promiscuous.'

Sir Henry Maine opposes to Mr. M'Lennan's theory the statement of Mr. Darwin: 'From all we know of the passions of all male quadrupeds, promiscuous intercourse in a state of Nature is highly improbable.'[203] On this first question, let us grant to Sir Henry Maine, to Mr. Darwin, and to common sense that if the very earliest men were extremely animal in character, their unions while they lasted were probably monogamous or polygamous. The sexual jealousy of the male would secure that result, as it does among many other animals. Let the first point, then, be scored to Sir Henry Maine: let it be granted that if man was created perfect, he lived in the monogamous family before the Fall: and that, if he was evolved as an animal, the unchecked animal instincts would make for monogamy or patriarchal polygamy in the strictly primitive family.

(2.) Did circumstances and customs ever or anywhere compel or induce man (whatever his original condition) to resort to practices which made paternity uncertain, and so caused the absence of the patriarchal family, kinship being reckoned through women? If this question be answered in the affirmative, and if the sphere of action of the various causes be made wide enough, it will not matter much to Mr. M'Lennan's theory whether the strictly primitive family was patriarchal or not. If there occurred a fall from the primitive family, and if that fall was extremely general, affecting even the Aryan race, Mr. M'Lennan's adherents will be amply satisfied. Their object is to show that the family, even in the Aryan race, was developed through a stage of loose savage connections. If that can be shown, they do not care much about primitive man properly so called. Sir Henry Maine admits, as a matter of fact, that among certain races, in certain districts, circumstances have overridden the sexual jealousy which secures

---

[203] *Descent of Man,* ii. 362.

the recognition of male parentage. Where women have been few, and where poverty has been great, jealousy has been suppressed, even in the Venice of the eighteenth century. Sir H. Maine says, 'The usage' (that of polyandry—many husbands to a single wife) 'seems to me one which circumstances overpowering morality and decency might at any time call into existence. It is known to have arisen in the native Indian army.' The question now is, what are the circumstances that overpower morality and decency, and so produce polyandry, with its necessary consequences, when it is a recognised institution—the absence of the patriarchal family, and the recognition of kinship through women? Any circumstances which cause great scarcity of women will conduce to those results. Mr. M'Lennan's opinion was, that the chief cause of scarcity of women has been the custom of female infanticide—of killing little girls as *bouches inutiles*. Sir Henry Maine admits that 'the cause assigned by M'Lennan is a *vera causa*—it is capable of producing the effects.'[204] Mr. M'Lennan collected a very large mass of testimony to prove the wide existence of this cause of paucity of women. Till that evidence is published, I can only say that it was sufficient, in Mr. M'Lennan's opinion, to demonstrate the wide prevalence of the factor which is the mainspring of his whole system.[205] How frightfully female

---

[204] Early Law and Custom, p. 210.

[205] Here I would like to point out that Mr. M'Lennan's theory was not so hard and fast as his manner (that of a very assured believer in his own ideas) may lead some inquirers to suppose. Sir Henry Maine writes, that both Mr. Morgan and Mr. M'Lennan 'seem to me to think that human society went everywhere through the same series of changes, and Mr. M'Lennan, at any rate, expresses himself as if all those stages could be clearly discriminated from one another, and the close of one and the commencement of another announced with the distinctness of the clock-bell telling the end of the hour.' On the other hand, I remember Mr. M'Lennan's saying that, in his opinion, 'all manner of arrangements probably went on simultaneously in different places.' In *Studies in Ancient History*, p. 127, he expressly guards against the tendency 'to assume that the progress of the various races of men from savagery has been a uniform progress: that all the stages which any of them has gone through have been passed in their order by all.' Still more to the point is his remark on polyandry among the very early Greeks and other Aryans; 'it is quite consistent

infanticide has prevailed in India, everyone may read in the official reports of Col. M'Pherson, and other English authorities. Mr. Fison's 'Kamilaroi and Kurnai' contains some notable, though not to my mind convincing, arguments on the other side. Sir Henry Maine adduces another cause of paucity of women: the wanderings of our race, and expeditions across sea.[206] This cause would not, however, be important enough to alter forms of kinship, where the invaders (like the early English in Britain) found a population which they could conquer and whose women they could appropriate.

Apart from any probable inferences that may be drawn from the presumed practice of female infanticide, actual ascertained facts prove that many races do not now live, or that recently they did not live, in the patriarchal or modern family. They live, or did live, in polyandrous associations. The Thibetans, the Nairs, the early inhabitants of Britain (according to Cæsar), and many other races, [207]as well as the inhabitants of the Marquesas Islands, and the Iroquois (according to Lafitau), practise, or have practised, polyandry.

We now approach the third and really important problem— (3.) Is there any reason to suppose that the stronger peoples, like the Aryans and the Semites, ever passed through a stage of culture in which female, not male, kinship was chiefly recognised, probably as a result of polyandry?

Now the nature of the evidence which affords a presumption that Aryans have all passed through Australian institutions such as polyandry, is of extremely varied character. Much of it may undoubtedly be explained away. But such strength as the evidence has (which we do not wish to exaggerate) is derived from its convergence to one point—namely, the anterior existence of

---

with my view that in all these quarters (Persia, Sparta, Troy, Lycia, Attica, Crete, &c.) monandry, and even the *patria potestas*, may have prevailed at points
[206] Early Law and Custom, p. 212.
[207] Studies in Ancient History, pp. 140-147.

polyandry and the matriarchal family among Aryans before and after the dawn of real history.

For the sake of distinctness we may here number the heads of the evidence bearing on this question. We have—

1. The evidence of inference from the form of capture in bridal ceremonies.

2. The evidence from exogamy: the law which forbids marriage between persons of the same family name.

3. The evidence from totemism—that is, the derivation of the family name and crest or badge, from some natural object, plant or animal.[208] Persons bearing the name may not intermarry, nor, as a rule, may they eat the object from which they derive their family name and from which they claim to be descended.

4. The evidence from the *gens* of Rome, or γενος of ancient Greece, in connection with Totemism.

5. The evidence from myth and legend.

6. The evidence from direct historical statements as to the prevalence of the matriarchal family, and inheritance through the maternal line.

To take these various testimonies in their order, let us begin with

(I.) The form of capture in bridal ceremonies. That this form survived in Sparta, Crete, in Hindoo law, in the traditions of Ireland, in the popular rustic customs of Wales, is not denied.

If we hold, with Mr. M'Lennan, that scarcity of women (produced by female infanticide or otherwise) is the cause of the habit of capturing wives, we may see, in survivals of this ceremony of capture among Aryans, a proof of early scarcity of women, and of probable polyandry. But an opponent may argue, like Mr. J. A. Farrer in 'Primitive Manners,' that the ceremony of capture is mainly a concession to maiden modesty among early races. Here one may observe that the girls of savage tribes are notoriously profligate and immodest about illicit connections. Only honourable marriage brings a blush to the cheek of these young

---

[208] *Totem* is the word generally given by travellers and interpreters for the family crests of the Red Indians. *Cf.* p. 105.

persons. This is odd, but, in the present state of the question, we cannot lean on the evidence of the ceremony of capture. We cannot demonstrate that it is derived from a time when paucity of women made capture of brides necessary. Thus 'honours are easy' in this first deal.

(2.) The next indication is very curious, and requires much more prolonged discussion. The custom of *Exogamy* was first noted and named by Mr. M'Lennan. Exogamy is the prohibition of marriage within the supposed blood-kinship, as denoted by the family name. Such marriage, among many backward races, is reckoned incestuous, and is punishable by death. Certain peculiarities in connection with the family name have to be noted later. Now, Sir Henry Maine admits that exogamy, as thus defined, exists among the Hindoos. 'A Hindoo may not marry a woman belonging to the same *gotra*, all members of the *gotra* being theoretically supposed to have descended from the same ancestor.' The same rule prevails in China. 'There are in China large bodies of related clansmen, each generally bearing the same clan-name. They are exogamous; no man will marry a woman having the same clan-name with himself.' It is admitted by Sir Henry Maine that this wide prohibition of marriage was the early Aryan rule, while advancing civilisation has gradually permitted marriage within limits once forbidden. The Greek Church now (according to Mr. M'Lennan), and the Catholic Church in the past, forbade intermarriages 'as far as relationship could be known.' The Hindoo rule appears to go still farther, and to prohibit marriage as far as the common *gotra* name seems merely to indicate relationship.

As to the ancient Romans, Plutarch says: Formerly they did not marry women connected with them by blood, any more than they now marry aunts or sisters. It was long before they would even intermarry with cousins.' Plutarch also remarks that, in times past, Romans did not marry συγγενίδας, and if we may render this 'women of the same *gens*,' the exogamous prohibition in Rome was as complete as among the Hindoos. I do not quite gather from Sir Henry Maine's account of the Slavonic house

198

communities (pp. 254, 255) whether they dislike *all* kindred marriages, or only marriage within the 'greater blood'—that is, within the kinship on the male side. He says: 'The South Slavonians bring their wives into the group, in which they are socially organised, from a considerable distance outside. . . . Every marriage which requires an ecclesiastical dispensation is regarded as disreputable.'

On the whole, wide prohibitions of marriage are archaic: the widest are savage; the narrowest are modern and civilised. Thus the Hindoo prohibition is old, barbarous, and wide. 'The barbarous Aryan,' says Sir Henry Maine, 'is generally exogamous. He has a most extensive table of prohibited degrees.' Thus exogamy seems to be a survival of barbarism. The question for us is, Can we call exogamy a survival from a period when (owing to scarcity of women and polyandry) clear ideas of kinship were impossible? If this can be proved, exogamous Aryans either passed through polyandrous institutions, or borrowed a savage custom derived from a period when ideas of kinship were obscure.

If we only knew the origin of the prohibition to marry within the family name all would be plain sailing. At present several theories of the origin of exogamy are before the world. Mr. Morgan, the author of 'Ancient Society,' inclines to trace the prohibition to a great early physiological discovery, acted on by primitive men by virtue of a *contrat social.* Early man discovered that children of unsound constitutions were born of nearly related parents. Mr. Morgan says: 'Primitive men very early discovered the evils of close interbreeding.' Elsewhere Mr. Morgan writes: 'Intermarriage in the *gens* was prohibited, to secure the benefits of marrying out with unrelated persons.' This arrangement was 'a product of high intelligence,' and Mr. Morgan calls it a 'reform.'

Let us examine this very curious theory. First: Mr. Morgan supposes early man to have made a discovery (the evils of the marriage of near kin) which evades modern physiological science. Modern science has not determined that the marriages of kinsfolk are pernicious. Is it credible that savages should discover a fact which puzzles science? It may be replied that modern care, nursing, and medical art save children of near marriages from results which were pernicious to the children of early man. Secondly: Mr. Morgan supposes that barbarous man (so notoriously reckless of the morrow as he is), not only made the discovery of the evils of interbreeding, but acted on it with promptitude and self-denial. Thirdly: Mr. Morgan seems to require, for the enforcement of the exogamous law, a *contrat social.* The larger communities meet, and divide themselves into smaller groups, within which wedlock is forbidden. This 'social pact' is like a return to the ideas of Rousseau. Fourthly: The hypothesis credits early men with knowledge and discrimination of near degrees of kin, which they might well possess if they lived in patriarchal families. But it represents that they did not act on their knowledge. Instead of prohibiting marriage between parents and children, cousins, nephews and aunts, uncles and nieces, they prohibited marriage within the limit of the name of the kin. This is still the Hindoo rule, and, if the Romans really might not at one time marry within the *gens,* it was the Roman rule. Now observe, this rule fails to effect the very purpose for which *ex hypothesi* it was instituted. Where the family name goes by the male side, marriages between cousins are permitted, as in India and China. These are the very marriages which some theorists now denounce as pernicious. But, if the family name goes by the female side, marriages between half-brothers and half-sisters are permitted, as in ancient Athens and among the Hebrews of Abraham's time. Once more, the exogamous prohibition excludes, in China, America, Africa, Australia, persons who are in no way akin (according to our ideas) from intermarriage. Thus Mr. Doolittle writes: [209]'Males and females of the same surname will never intermarry in China. Cousins who have not the same ancestral surname may intermarry. Though the ancestors of persons of the same surname have not known each other for

---

[209] Domestic Manners of the Chinese, i. 99.

thousands of years, they may not intermarry.' The Hindoo *gotra* rule produces the same effects.

For all these reasons, and because of the improbability of the physiological discovery, and of the moral 'reform' which enforced it; and again, because the law is not of the sort which people acquainted with near degrees of kinship would make; and once more, because the law fails to effect its presumed purpose, while it does attain ends at which it does not aim—we cannot accept Mr. Morgan's suggestion as to the origin of exogamy. Mr. M'Lennan did not live to publish a subtle theory of the origin of exogamy, which he had elaborated. In 'Studies in Ancient History,' he hazarded a conjecture based on female infanticide:—

'We believe the restrictions on marriage to be connected with the practice in early times of female infanticide, which, rendering women scarce, led at once to polyandry within the tribe, and the capturing of women from without. . . . Hence the cruel custom which, leaving the primitive human hordes with very few young women of their own, occasionally with none, and in any case seriously disturbing the balance of the sexes within the hordes, forces them to prey upon one another for wives. Usage, induced by necessity, would in time establish a prejudice among the tribes observing it, a prejudice strong as a principle of religion—as every prejudice relating to marriage is apt to be—against marrying women of their own stock.'

Mr. M'Lennan describes his own hypothesis as 'a suggestion thrown out at what it was worth.'[210] In his later years, as we have said, he developed a very subtle and ingenious theory of the origin of exogamy, still connecting it with scarcity of women, but making use of various supposed stages and processes in the development of the law. That speculation remains unpublished. To myself, the suggestion given in 'Studies in Ancient History' seems inadequate. I find it difficult to conceive that the frequent habit of stealing women should indispose men to marry the native women they had at hand. That this indisposition should grow

---

[210] *Fortnightly Review*, June 1, 1877.

into a positive law, and the infringement of the law be regarded as a capital offence, seems still more inconceivable. My own impression is, that exogamy may be connected with some early superstition or idea of which we have lost the touch, and which we can no longer explain.

Thus far, the consideration of exogamy has thrown no clear light on the main question—the question whether the customs of civilised races contain relics of female kinship. On Sir Henry Maine's theory of exogamy, that Aryan custom is unconnected with female kinship, polyandry, and scarcity of women. On Mr. M'Lennan's theory, exogamy is the result of scarcity of women, and implies polyandry and female kinship. But neither theory has seemed satisfactory. Yet we need not despair of extracting some evidence from exogamy, and that evidence, on the whole, is in favour of Mr. M'Lennan's general hypothesis. (I.) The exogamous prohibition must have first come into force *when kinship was only reckoned on one side of the family.* This is obvious, whether we suppose it to have arisen in a society which reckoned by male or by female kinship. In the former case, the law only prohibits marriage with persons of the father's, in the second case with persons of the mother's, family name, and these only it recognises as kindred. (2.) Our second point is much more important. The exogamous prohibition must first have come into force *when kinship was so little understood that it could best be denoted by the family name.* This would be self-evident, if we could suppose the prohibition to be intended to prevent marriages of relations. Had the authors of the prohibition been acquainted with the nature of near kinships, they would simply (as we do) have forbidden marriage between persons in those degrees. The very nature of the prohibition, on the other hand, shows that kinship was understood in a manner all unlike our modern system. The limit of kindred was everywhere the family name: a limit which excludes many real kinsfolk and includes many who are not kinsfolk at all. In Australia especially, and in America, India, and Africa, to a slighter extent, that definition of kindred by the family name actually includes alligators, smoke, paddy melons, rain, crayfish, sardines, and what you please.[211] Will anyone assert, then, that people among whom the exogamous prohibition arose were organised on the system of the patriarchal family, which permits the nature of kinship to be readily understood at a glance? Is it not plain that the exogamous prohibition (confessedly Aryan) must have arisen in a stage of culture when ideas of kindred were confused, included kinship with animals and plants, and were to us almost, if not quite, unintelligible? It is even possible, as Mr. M'Lennan says, [212]'that the prejudice against marrying women of the same group may have been established *before the facts of blood relationship had made any deep impression on the human mind.*' How the exogamous prohibition tends to confirm this view will next be set forth in our consideration of *Totemism.*

The Evidence from Totemism.—Totemism is the name for the custom by which a stock (scattered through many local tribes) claims descent from and kindred with some plant, animal, or other natural object. This object, of which the effigy is sometimes worn as a badge or crest, members of the stock refuse to eat. As a general rule, marriage is prohibited between members of the stock—between all, that is, who claim descent from the same object and wear the same badge. The exogamous limit, therefore, is denoted by the stock-name and crest, and kinship is kinship in the wolf, bear, potato, or whatever other object is recognised as the original ancestor. Finally, as a general rule, the stock-name is derived through the mother, and where it is derived through the father there are proofs that the custom is comparatively modern. It will be acknowledged that this sort of kindred, which is traced to a beast, bird, or tree, which is recognised in every person bearing the same stock-name, which is counted through females, and which governs marriage customs, is not the sort of kindred which would naturally arise among people regulated on the patriarchal or monandrous family system.

---

[211] *Kamilaroi and Kurnai.* Natives call these objects their kin, 'of one flesh' with them.
[212] *Studies,* p. 11.

Totemism, however, is a widespread institution prevailing all over the north of the American continent, also in Peru (according to Garcilasso de la Vega); in Guiana (the negroes have brought it from the African Gold Coast, where it is in full force, as it also is among the Bechuanas); in India among Hos, Garos, Kassos, and Oraons; in the South Sea Islands, where it has left strong traces in Mangaia; in Siberia, and especially in the great island continent of Australia. The Semitic evidences for totemism (animal-worship, exogamy, descent claimed through females) are given by Professor Robertson Smith, in the 'Journal of Philology,' ix. 17, 'Animal Worship and Animal Tribes among the Arabs, and in the Old Testament.' Many other examples of totemism might be adduced (especially from Egypt), but we must restrict ourselves to the following questions:—

(1.) What light is thrown on the original form of the family by totemism? (2.) Where we find survivals of totemism among civilised races, may we conclude that these races (through scarcity of women) had once been organised on other than the patriarchal model?

As to the first question, we must remember that the origin and determining causes of totemism are still unknown. Mr. M'Lennan's theory of the origin of totemism has never been published. It may be said without indiscretion that Mr. M'Lennan thought totemism arose at a period when ideas of kinship scarcely existed at all. 'Men only thought of marking one off from another,' as Garcilasso de la Vega says: the totem was but a badge worn by all the persons who found themselves existing in close relations; perhaps in the same cave or set of caves. People united by contiguity, and by the blind sentiment of kinship not yet brought into explicit consciousness, might mark themselves by a badge, and might thence derive a name, and, later, might invent a myth of their descent from the object which the badge represented. I do not know whether it has been observed that the totems are, as a rule, objects which may be easily drawn or tattooed, and still more easily indicated in gesture-language. Some interesting facts will be found in the 'First Annual Report

204

of the Bureau of Ethnology,' p. 458 (Washington, 1881). Here we read how the 'Crow' tribe is indicated in sign-language by 'the hands held out on each side, striking the air in the manner of flying.' The Bunaks (another bird tribe) are indicated by an imitation of the cry of the bird. In mentioning the Snakes, the hand imitates the crawling motion of the serpent, and the fingers pointed up behind the ear denote the Wolves. Plainly names of the totem sort are well suited to the convenience of savages, who converse much in gesture-language. Above all, the very nature of totemism shows that it took its present shape at a time when men, animals, and plants were conceived of as physically akin; when names were handed on through the female line; when exogamy was the rule of marriage, and when the family theoretically included all persons bearing the same family name, that is, all who claimed kindred with the same plant, animal, or object, whether the persons are really akin or not. These ideas and customs are not the ideas natural to men organised in the patriarchal family.

The second question now arises: Can we infer from survivals of totemism among Aryans that these Aryans had once been organised on the full totemistic principle, probably with polyandry, and certainly with female descent? Where totemism now exists in full force, there we find exogamy and derivation of the family name through women, the latter custom indicating uncertainty of male parentage in the past. Are we to believe that the same institutions have existed wherever we find survivals of totemism? If this be granted, and if the supposed survivals of totemism among Aryans be accepted as genuine, then the Aryans have distinctly come through a period of kinship reckoned through women, with all that such an institution implies. For indications that the Aryans of Greece and India have passed through the stage of totemism, the reader may be referred to Mr. M'Lennan's 'Worship of Plants and Animals' ('Fortnightly Review,' 1869, 1870). The evidence there adduced is not all of the same value, and the papers are only a hasty rough sketch based on the first testimonies that came to hand. Probably the most important 'survival' of totemism in Greek legend is the body of stories about the amours of Zeus in animal form. Various noble houses traced their origin to Zeus or Apollo, who, as a bull, tortoise, serpent, swan, or ant, had seduced the mother of the race. The mother of the Arcadians became a she-bear, like the mother of the bear stock of the Iroquois. As we know plenty of races all over the world who trace their descent from serpents, tortoises, swans, and so forth, it is a fair hypothesis that the ancestors of the Greeks once believed in the same fables. In later times the swan, serpent, ant, or tortoise was explained as an *avatar* of Zeus. The process by which an anthropomorphic god or hero succeeds to the exploits of animals, of theriomorphic gods and heroes, is the most common in mythology, and is illustrated by actual practice in modern India. When the Brahmins convert a pig-worshipping tribe of aboriginals, they tell their proselytes that the pig was an avatar of Vishnu. The same process is found active where the Japanese have influenced the savage Ainos, and persuaded them that their bear- or dog-father was a manifestation of a deity. We know from Plutarch ('Theseus') that, in addition to families claiming descent from divine animals, one Athenian γένος, the Ioxidæ, revered an ancestral plant, the asparagus. A vaguer indication of totemism may perhaps be detected in the ancient theriomorphic statues of Greek gods, as the Ram-Zeus and the Horse-headed Demeter, and in the various animals and plants which were sacred to each god and represented as his companions.

The hints of totemism among the ancient Irish are interesting. One hero, Conaire, was the son of a bird, and before his birth his father (the bird) told the woman (his mother) that the child must never eat the flesh of fowls. 'Thy son shall be named Conaire, and that son shall not kill birds.'[213] The hero Cuchullain, being named after the dog, might not eat the flesh of the dog, and came by his ruin after transgressing this totemistic taboo. Races named after animals were common in ancient Ireland. The red-deer and the wolves were tribes dwelling near

---

[213] O'Curry, *Manners of Ancient Irish*, l. ccclxx., quoting Trin. Coll. Dublin MS.

Ossory, and Professor Rhys, from the frequency of dog names, inclines to believe in a dog totem in Erin. According to the ancient Irish 'Wonders of Eri,' in the 'Book of Glendaloch,' 'the descendants of the wolf are in Ossory,' and they could still transform themselves into wolves.[214] As to our Anglo-Saxon ancestors, there is little evidence beyond the fact that the patronymic names of many of the early settlements of Billings, Arlings, and the rest, are undeniably derived from animals and plants. The manner in which those names are scattered locally is precisely like what results in America, Africa, and Australia from the totemistic organisation.[215] In Italy the ancient custom by which animals were the leaders of the *Ver sacrum* or armed migration is well known. The Piceni had for their familiar animal or totem (if we may call it so) a woodpecker; the Hirpini were like the 'descendants of the wolf' in Ossory, and practised a wolf-dance in which they imitated the actions of the animal.[216]

Such is a summary of the evidence which shows that Aryans had once been totemists, therefore savages, and therefore, again, had probably been in a stage when women were scarce and each woman had many husbands.

Evidence from the Gens or γένος.—There is no more puzzling topic in the history of the ancient world than the origin and nature of the community called by the Romans the *gens*, and by the Greeks the γένος. To the present writer it seems that no existing community of men, neither totem kin, nor clan, nor house community, nor *gotra*, precisely answers to the *gens* or the γένος. Our information about these forms of society is slight and confused. The most essential thing to notice for the moment

---

[214] See also Elton's *Origins of English History*, pp. 299-301.
[215] Kemble's *Saxons in England*, p. 258. *Politics of Aristotle*, Bolland and Lang, p. 99.
[216] Mr. Grant Allen kindly supplied me some time ago with a list of animal and vegetable names preserved in the titles of ancient English village settlements. Among them are: ash, birch, bear (as among the Iroquois), oak, buck, fir, fern, sun, wolf, thorn, goat, horse, salmon (the trout is a totem in America), swan (familiar in Australia), and others.

is the fact that both in Greece and Rome the γένος and *gens* were extremely ancient, so ancient that the γένος was decaying in Greece when history begins, while in Rome we can distinctly see the rapid decadence and dissolution of the *gens*. In the Laws of the Twelve Tables, the *gens* is a powerful and respected corporation. In the time of Cicero the nature of the *gens* is a matter but dimly understood. Tacitus begins to be confused about the gentile nomenclature. In the Empire gentile law fades away. In Greece, especially at Athens, the early political reforms transferred power from the γένος to a purely local organisation, the Deme. The Greek of historical times did not announce his γένος in his name (as the Romans always did), but gave his own name, that of his father, and that of his deme. Thus we may infer that in Greek and Roman society the γένος and *gens* were dying, not growing, organisations. In very early times it is probable that foreign *gentes* were adopted *en bloc* into the Roman Commonwealth. Very probably, too, a great family, on entering the Roman bond, may have assumed, by a fiction, the character and name of a *gens*. But that Roman society in historical times, or that Greek society, could evolve a new *gens* or γένος in a normal natural way, seems excessively improbable.

Keeping in mind the antique and 'obsolescent' character of the *gens* and γένος, let us examine the theories of the origin of these associations. The Romans themselves knew very little about the matter. Cicero quotes the dictum of Scævola the Pontifex, according to which the *gens* consisted of *all persons of the same gentile name* who were not in any way disqualified.[217] Thus, in America, or Australia, or Africa, all persons bearing the same totem name belong to that totem kin. Festus defines members of a *gens* as persons of the same stock and same family name. Varro says (in illustration of the relationships of words and cases) 'Ab Æmilio homines orti Æmilii sunt gentiles.' The two former

---

[217] 'Gentiles sunt qui inter se eodem nomine sunt. Qui ab ingeniis oriundi sunt. Quorum majorum nemo servitutem servivit. Qui capite non sunt deminuti.'

definitions answer to the conception of a totem kin, which is united by its family name and belief in identity of origin. Varro adds the element, in the Roman *gens*, of common descent from one male ancestor. Such was the conception of the *gens* in historical times. It was in its way an association of kinsfolk, real or supposed. According to the Laws of the Twelve Tables the gentiles inherited the property of an intestate man without agnates, and had the custody of lunatics in the same circumstances. The *gens* had its own *sacellum* or chapel, and its own *sacra* or religious rites. The whole *gens* occasionally went into mourning when one of its members was unfortunate. It would be interesting if it could be shown that the *sacra* were usually examples of ancestor-worship, but the faint indications on the subject scarcely permit us to assert this.

On the whole, Sir Henry Maine strongly clings to the belief that the *gens* commonly had 'a real core of agnatic consanguinity from the very first.' But he justly recognises the principle of imitation, which induces men to copy any fashionable institution. Whatever the real origin of the *gens*, many *gentes* were probably copies based on the fiction of common ancestry.

On Sir Henry Maine's system, then, the *gens* rather proves the constant existence of recognised male descents among the peoples where it exists.

The opposite theory of the *gens* is that to which Mr. M'Lennan inclined. 'The composition and organisation of Greek and Roman tribes and commonwealths cannot well be explained except on the hypothesis that they resulted from the joint operation, in early times, of exogamy, and the system of kinship through females only.'[218] 'The *gens*', he adds, 'was composed of all the persons in the tribe bearing the same name and accounted of the same stock. Were the *gentes* really of different stocks, as their names would imply and as the people believed? If so, how came clans of different stocks to be united in the same tribe? . . . How came a variety of such groups, of different stocks, to

---

[218] Studies in Ancient History, p. 212.

coalesce in a local tribe?' These questions, Mr. M'Lennan thought, could not be answered on the patriarchal hypothesis. His own theory, or rather his theory as understood by the present writer, may be stated thus. In the earliest times there were homogeneous groups, which became, totem kin. Let us say that, in a certain district, there were groups called woodpeckers, wolves, bears, suns, swine, each with its own little territory. These groups were exogamous, and derived the name through the mother. Thus, in course of time, when sun men married a wolf girl, and her children were wolves, there would be wolves in the territory of the suns, and thus each stock would be scattered through all the localities, just as we see in Australia and America. Let us suppose that (as certainly is occurring in Australia and America) paternal descent comes to be recognised in custom. This change will not surprise Sir Henry Maine, who admits that a system of male may alter, under stress of circumstances, to a system of female descents. In course of time, and as knowledge and common sense advance, the old superstition of descent from a woodpecker, a bear, a wolf, the sun, or what not, becomes untenable. A human name is assumed by the group which had called itself the woodpeckers or the wolves, or perhaps by a local tribe in which several of these stocks are included. Then a fictitious human ancestor is adopted, and perhaps even adored. Thus the wolves might call themselves Claudii, from their chief's name, and, giving up belief in descent from a wolf, might look back to a fancied ancestor named Claudius. The result of these changes will be that an exogamous totem kin, with female descent, has become a *gens*, with male kinship, and only the faintest trace of exogamy. An example of somewhat similar processes must have occurred in the Highland clans after the introduction of Christianity, when the chief's Christian name became the patronymic of the people who claimed kinship with him and owned his sway.

Are there any traces at all of totemism in what we know of the Roman *gentes?* Certainly the traces are very slight; perhaps they are only visible to the eye of the intrepid anthropologist. I give them for what they are worth, merely observing that they do tally, as far as they go, with the totemistic theory. The reader interested in the subject may consult the learned Streinnius's 'De Gentibus Romanis,' p. 104 (Aldus, Venice, 1591).

Among well-known savage totems none is more familiar than the sun. Men claim descent from the sun, call themselves by his name, and wear his effigy as a badge.[219] Were there suns in Rome? The Aurelian *gens* is thus described on the authority of Festus Pompeius:—'The Aurelii were of Sabine descent. The Aurelii were so named from the sun (*aurum, urere*, the burning thing), because a place was set apart for them in which to pay adoration to the sun.' Here, at least, is an odd coincidence. Among other gentile names, the Fabii, Cornelii, Papirii, Pinarii, Cassii, are possibly connected with plants; while wild etymology may associate Porcii, Aquilii, and Valerii with swine and eagles. Pliny ('H. N.' xviii. 3) gives a fantastic explanation of the vegetable names of Roman *gentes*. We must remember that vegetable names are very common in American, Indian, African, and Australian totem kin. Of sun names the Natchez and the Incas of Peru are familiar examples. Turning from Rome to Greece, we find the γένος less regarded and more decadent than the *gens*. Yet, according to Grote (iii. 54) the *γένος* had—(1) *sacra*, 'in honour of the same god, supposed to be the primitive ancestor.' (2) A common burial-place. (3) Certain rights of succession to property. (4) Obligations of mutual help and defence. (5) Mutual rights and obligations to intermarry in certain cases. (6) Occasionally possession of common property.

Traces of the totem among the Greek γένη are, naturally, few. Almost all the known γένη bore patronymics derived from personal names. But it is not without significance that the Attic demes often adopted the names of obsolescent γένη, and that those names were, as Mr. Grote says, often 'derived from the plants and shrubs which grew in their neighbourhood.' We have already seen that at least one Attic γένος, the Ioxidæ, revered the plant from which they derived their lineage. One thing is certain,

---

[219] *Fortnightly Review,* October 1869: 'Archæologia Americana,' ii. 113.

the totem names, and a common explanation of the totem names in Australia, correspond with the names and Mr. Grote's explanation of the names of the Attic demes. 'One origin of family names,' says Sir George Grey (ii. 228), 'frequently ascribed by the natives, is that they were derived from some vegetable or animal being common in the district which the family inhabited.' Some writers attempt to show that the Attic γενος was once exogamous and counted kin on the mother's side, by quoting the custom which permitted a man to marry his half-sister, the child of his father but not of his mother. They infer that this permission is a survival from the time when a man's *father's* children were not reckoned as his kindred, and when kinship was counted through mothers. Sir Henry Maine (p. 105) prefers M. Fustel De Coulanges' theory, that the marriage of half-brothers and sisters on the father's side was intended to save the portion of the girl to the family estate. Proof of this may be adduced from examination of all the recorded cases of such marriages in Athens. But the reason thus suggested would have equally justified marriage between brothers and sisters on both sides, and this was reckoned incest. A well-known line in Aristophanes shows how intense was Athenian feeling about the impiety of relations with a sister uterine.

On the whole, the evidence which we have adduced tends to establish some links between the ancient γενος and *gens*, and the totem kindreds of savages. The indications are not strong, but they all point in one direction. Considering the high civilisation of Rome and Greece at the very dawn of history—considering the strong natural bent of these peoples toward refinement—it is almost remarkable that even the slight testimonies we have been considering should have survived.

(5.) On the evidence from myth and legend we propose to lay little stress. But, as legends were not invented by anthropologists to prove a point, it is odd that the traditions of Athens, as preserved by Varro, speak of a time when names were derived from the mother, and when promiscuity prevailed. Marriage itself was instituted by Cecrops, the serpent, just as the lizard, in Australia, is credited with this useful invention.[220] Similar legends among non-Aryan races, Chinese and Egyptian, are very common.

(6.) There remains the evidence of actual fact and custom among Aryan peoples. The Lycians, according to Herodotus, 'have this peculiar custom, *wherein they resemble no other men*, they derive their names from their mothers, and not from their fathers, and through mothers reckon their kin.' Status also was derived through the mothers.[221] The old writer's opinion that the custom (so common in Australia, America, and Africa) was unique, is itself a proof of his good faith. Bachofen (p. 390) remarks that several Lycian inscriptions give the names of mothers only. Polybius attributes (assigning a fantastic reason) the same custom of counting kin through mothers to the Locrians. [222]The British and Irish custom of deriving descents through women is well known, [223]and a story is told to account for the practice. The pedigrees of the British kings show that most did not succeed to their fathers, and the various records of early Celtic morals go to prove that no other system of kinship than the maternal would have possessed any value, so uncertain was fatherhood. These are but hints of the prevalence of institutions which survived among Teutonic races in the importance attached to the relationship of a man's sister's son. Though no longer his legal heir, the sister's son was almost closer than any other kinsman.

We have now summarised and indicated the nature of the evidence which, on the whole, inclines us to the belief of Mr. M'Lennan rather than of Sir Henry Maine. The point to which all the testimony adduced converges, the explanation which most readily solves all the difficulties, is the explanation of Mr. M'Lennan. The Aryan races have very generally passed through the stage of scarcity of women, polyandry, absence of recognised

---

[220] Suidas, 3102.
[221] Herod., i. 173.
[222] Cf. Bachofen, p. 309.
[223] Compare the *Irish Nennius*, p. 127.

male kinship, and recognition of kinship through women. What Sir Henry Maine admits as the exception, we are inclined to regard as having, in a very remote past, been the rule. No one kind of evidence—neither traces of marriage by capture, of exogamy, of totemism, of tradition, of noted fact among Lycians and Picts and Irish—would alone suffice to guide our opinion in this direction. But the cumulative force of the testimony strikes us as not inconsiderable, and it must be remembered that the testimony has not yet been assiduously collected.

Let us end by showing how this discussion illustrates the method of Folklore. We have found anomalies among Aryans. We have seen the *gens* an odd, decaying institution. We have seen Greek families claim descent from various animals, said to be Zeus in disguise. We have found them tracing kinship and deriving names from the mother. We have found stocks with animal and vegetable names. We have found half-brothers and sisters marrying. We have noted prohibition to marry anyone of the same family name. All these institutions are odd, anomalous, decaying things among Aryans, and the more civilised the Aryans the more they decay. All of them are living, active things among savages, and, far from being anomalous, are in precise harmony with savage notions of the world. Surely, then, where they seem decaying and anomalous, as among Aryans, these customs and laws are mouldering relics of ideas and practices natural and inevitable among savages.

THE ART OF SAVAGES. [224]

'Avoid Coleridge, he is *useless*,' says Mr. Ruskin. Why should the poetry of Coleridge be useful? The question may interest the critic, but we are only concerned with Mr. Ruskin here, for one reason. His disparagement of Coleridge as 'useless' is a survival of the belief that art should be 'useful.' This is the savage's view of art. He imitates nature, in dance, song, or in plastic art, for a definite practical purpose. His dances are magical dances, his images are made for a magical purpose, his songs are incantations. Thus the theory that art is a disinterested expression of the imitative faculty is scarcely warranted by the little we know of art's beginnings. We shall adopt, provisionally, the hypothesis that the earliest art with which we are acquainted is that of savages contemporary or extinct. Some philosophers may tell us that all known savages are only degraded descendants of early civilised men who have, unluckily and inexplicably, left no relics of their civilisation. But we shall argue on the opposite theory, that the art of Australians, for example, is really earlier in kind, more backward, nearer the rude beginnings of things, than the art of people who have attained to some skill in pottery, like the New Caledonians. These, again, are much more backward, in a state really much earlier, than the old races of Mexico and Peru; while they, in turn, show but a few traces of advance towards the art of Egypt; and the art of Egypt, at least after the times of the Ancient Empire, is scarcely advancing in the direction of the flawless art of Greece. We shall be able to show how savage art, as of the Australians, develops into barbarous art, as of the New Zealanders; while the arts of strange civilisations, like those of Peru and Mexico, advance one step further; and how, again, in the early art of Greece, in the Greek art of ages prior to Pericles, there are remains of barbaric forms which are gradually softened into

---

[224] The illustrations in this article are for the most part copied, by permission of Messrs. Cassell & Co., from the *Magazine of Art*, in which the essay appeared.

beauty. But there are necessarily breaks and solutions of continuity in the path of progress.

One of the oldest problems has already risen before us in connection with the question stated—is art the gratification of the imitative faculty? Now, among the lowest, the most untutored, the worst equipped savages of contemporary races, art is rather decorative on the whole than imitative. The patterns on Australian shields and clubs, the scars which they raise on their own flesh by way of tattooing, are very rarely imitations of any objects in nature. The Australians, like the Red Indians, like many African and some aboriginal Indian races, Peruvians, and others, distinguish their families by the names of various plants and animals, from which each family boasts its descent. Thus you have a family called Kangaroos, descended, as they fancy, from the kangaroo; another from the cockatoo, another from the black snake, and so forth. Now, in many quarters of the globe, this custom and this superstition, combined with the imitative faculty in man, has produced a form of art representing the objects from which the families claim descent. This art is a sort of rude heraldry—probably the origin of heraldry. Thus, if a Red Indian (say a Delaware) is of the family of the Turtle, he blazons a turtle on his shield or coat, probably tattoos or paints his breast with a figure of a turtle, and always has a turtle, *reversed*, designed on the pillar above his grave when he dies, just as, in our mediæval chronicles, the leopards of an English king are reversed on his scutcheon opposite the record of his death. But the Australians, to the best of my knowledge, though they are much governed by belief in descent from animals, do not usually blazon their crest on their flesh, nor on the trees near the place where the dead are buried. They have not arrived at this pitch of imitative art, though they have invented or inherited a kind of runes which they notch on sticks, and in which they convey to each other secret messages. The natives of the Upper Darling, however, do carve their family crests on their shields. In place of using imitative art, the Murri are said, I am not quite sure with what truth, to indicate the distinction of families by arrangements of patterns, lines and dots, tattooed on the breast and arms, and carved on the bark of trees near places of burial. In any case, the absence of the rude imitative art of heraldry among a race which possesses all the social conditions that produce this art is a fact worth noticing, and itself proves that the native art of one of the most backward races we know is not essentially imitative.

Anyone who will look through a collection of Australian weapons and utensils will be brought to this conclusion. The shields and the clubs are elaborately worked, but almost always without any representation of plants, animals, or the human figure. As a rule the decorations take the simple shape of the 'herring-bone' pattern, or such other patterns as can be produced without the aid of spirals, or curves, or circles. There is a natural and necessary cause of this choice of decoration. The Australians, working on hard wood, with tools made of flint, or broken glass, or sharp shell, cannot easily produce any curved lines. Everyone who, when a boy, carved his name on the bark of a tree, remembers the difficulty he had with S and G, while he got on easily with letters like M and A, which consist of straight or inclined lines. The savage artist has the same difficulty with his rude tools in producing anything like satisfactory curves or spirals. We engrave above (Fig. 1) a shield on which an Australian has succeeded, with obvious difficulty, in producing concentric ovals of irregular shape. It may be that the artist would have produced perfect circles if he could. His failure is exactly like that of a youthful carver of inscriptions coming to grief over his G's and S's. Here, however (Fig. 2), we have three shields which, like the ancient Celtic pipkin (the tallest of the three figures in Fig. 3), show the earliest known form of savage

217

decorative art—the forms which survive under the names of 'chevron' and 'herring-bone.' These can be scratched on clay with the nails, or a sharp stick, and this primeval way of decorating pottery made without the wheel survives, with other relics of savage art, in the western isles of Scotland. The Australian had not even learned to make rude clay pipkins, but he decorated his shields as the old Celts and modern old Scotch women decorated their clay pots, with the herring-bone arrangement of incised lines. In the matter of colour the Australians prefer white clay and red ochre, which they rub into the chinks in the woodwork of their shields. When they are determined on an ambush, they paint themselves all over with white, justly conceiving that their sudden apparition in this guise will strike terror into the boldest hearts. But arrangements in black and white of this sort scarcely deserve the name of even rudimentary art.

The Australians sometimes introduce crude decorative attempts at designing the human figure, as in the pointed shield opposite (Fig. 2, *a*), which, with the other Australian designs, are from Mr. Brough Smyth's 'Aborigines of Victoria.' But these ambitious efforts usually end in failure. Though the Australians chiefly confine themselves to decorative art, there are numbers of wall-paintings, so to speak, in the caves of the country which prove that they, like the Bushmen, could design the human figure in action when they pleased. Their usual preference for the employment of patterns appears to me to be the result of the nature of their materials. In modern art our mechanical advantages and facilities are so great that we are always carrying the method and manner of one art over the frontier of another. Our poetry aims at producing the effects of music; our prose at producing the effects of poetry. Our sculpture tries to vie with painting in the representation of action, or with lace-making in the production of reticulated surfaces, and so forth. But the savage, in his art, has sense enough to confine himself to the sort of work for which his materials are fitted. Set him in the bush with no implements and materials but a bit of broken shell and a lump of hard wood, and he confines himself to decorative scratches. Place the black in the large cave which Pundjel, the Australian Zeus, inhabited when on earth (as Zeus inhabited the cave in Crete), and give the black plenty of red and white ochre and charcoal, and he will paint the human figure in action on the rocky walls. Later, we will return to the cave-paintings of the Australians and the Bushmen in South Africa. At present we must trace purely decorative art a little further. But we must remember that there was once a race apparently in much the same social condition as the Australians, but far more advanced and ingenious in art. The earliest men of the European Continent, about whom we know much, the men whose bones and whose weapons are found beneath the gravel-drift, the men who were contemporary with the rhinoceros, mammoth, and cave-bear, were not further advanced in material civilisation than the Australians. They used weapons of bone, of unpolished stone, and probably of hard wood. But the remnants of their art, the scraps of mammoth or reindeer bone in our museums, prove that they had a most spirited style of sketching from the life. In a collection of drawings on bone (probably designed with a flint or a shell), drawings by palæolithic man, in the British Museum, I have only observed one purely decorative attempt. Even in this the decoration resembles an effort to use the outlines of foliage for ornamental purposes. In almost all the other cases the palæolithic artist has not decorated his bits of bone in the usual savage manner, but has treated his bone as an artist treats his sketch-book, and has scratched outlines of beasts and fishes with his sharp shell as an artist uses his point. These ancient bones, in short, are the sketch-books of European savages, whose untaught skill was far greater than that of the Australians, or even of the Eskimo. When brought into contact with Europeans, the Australian and Eskimo very quickly, even without regular teaching, learn to draw with some spirit and skill. In the Australian stele, or grave-pillar, which we have engraved (Fig. 4), the shapeless figures below the men and animals are the dead, and the *boilyas* or ghosts. Observe the patterns in the interstices. The artist had lived with Europeans. In their original conditions, however, the Australians have not attained to such free, artist-like, and unhampered use of their rude materials as the mysterious European artists who drew the mammoth that walked abroad amongst them.

We have engraved one solitary Australian attempt at drawing curved lines. The New Zealanders, a race far more highly endowed, and, when Europeans arrived amongst them, already far more civilised than the Australians, had, like the Australians, no metal implements. But their stone weapons were harder and keener, and with these they engraved the various spirals and coils on hard wood, of which we give examples here. It is sometimes said that New Zealand culture and art have filtered from some Asiatic source, and that in the coils and spirals designed, as in our engravings, on the face of the Maori chief, or on his wooden furniture, there may be found debased Asiatic influences.[225] This

---

[225] Part of the pattern (Fig. 5, *b*) recurs on the New Zealand Bull-roarer, engraved in the essay on the Bull-roarer.

is one of the questions which we can hardly deal with here. Perhaps its solution requires more of knowledge, anthropological and linguistic, than is at present within the reach of any student. Assuredly the races of the earth have wandered far, and have been wonderfully intermixed, and have left the traces of their passage here and there on sculptured stones, and in the keeping of the ghosts that haunt ancient grave-steads. But when two pieces of artistic work, one civilised, one savage, resemble each other, it is always dangerous to suppose that the resemblance bears witness to relationship or contact between the races, or to influences imported by one from the other. New Zealand work may be Asiatic in origin, and debased by the effect of centuries of lower civilisation and ruder implements. Or Asiatic ornament may be a form of art improved out of ruder forms, like those to which the New Zealanders have already attained. One is sometimes almost tempted to regard the favourite Maori spiral as an imitation of the form, not unlike that of a bishop's crozier at the top, taken by the great native ferns. Examples of resemblance, to be accounted for by the development of a crude early idea, may be traced most easily in the early pottery of Greece. No one says that the Greeks borrowed from the civilised people of America. Only a few enthusiasts say that the civilised peoples of America, especially the Peruvians, are Aryan by race. Yet the remains of Peruvian palaces are often by no means dissimilar in style from the 'Pelasgic' and 'Cyclopean' buildings of gigantic stones which remain on such ancient Hellenic sites as Argos and Mycenæ. The probability is that men living in similar social conditions, and using similar implements, have unconsciously and unintentionally arrived at like results.

Few people who are interested in the question can afford to visit Peru and Mycenæ and study the architecture for themselves. But anyone who is interested in the strange identity of the human mind everywhere, and in the necessary forms of early art, can go to the British Museum and examine the American and early Greek pottery. Compare the Greek key pattern and the wave pattern on Greek and Mexican vases, and compare the bird-faces, or human faces very like those of birds, with the similar faces on the clay pots which Dr. Schliemann dug up at Troy. The latter are engraved in his book on Troy. Compare the so-called 'cuttle-fish' from a Peruvian jar with the same figure on the early Greek vases, most of which are to be found in the last of the classical vase-rooms upstairs. Once more, compare the little clay 'whorls' of the Mexican and Peruvian room with those which Dr. Schliemann found so numerous at Hissarlik. The conviction becomes irresistible that all these objects, in shape, in purpose, in character of decoration, are the same, because the mind and the materials of men, in their early stages of civilisation especially, are the same everywhere. You might introduce old Greek bits of clay-work, figures or vases, into a Peruvian collection, or might foist Mexican objects among the clay treasures of Hissarlik, and the wisest archæologist would be deceived. The Greek fret pattern especially seems to be one of the earliest that men learnt to draw. The *svastika*, as it is called, the cross with lines at right angles to each limb, is found everywhere—in India, Greece, Scotland, Peru—as a natural bit of ornament. The allegorising fancy of the Indians gave it a mystic meaning, and the learned have built I know not what worlds of religious theories on this 'pre-Christian cross,' which is probably a piece of hasty decorative work, with no original mystic meaning at all.[226] Ornaments of this sort were transferred from wood or bone to clay, almost as soon as people learned that early art, the potter's, to which the Australians have not attained, though it was familiar to the not distant people of New Caledonia. The style of spirals and curves, again, once acquired (as it was by the New Zealanders), became the favourite of some races, especially of the Celtic. Any one who will study either the ornaments of Mycenæ, or those of any old Scotch or Irish collection, will readily recognise in that art the development of a system of ornament like that of the Maoris. Classical Greece, on the other hand, followed more in the track of the ancient system of straight and slanted lines, and we do not find in the later Greek art that love of interlacing coils and spirals which is so remarkable among the Celts, and which is very manifest in the ornaments of the Mycænean hoards—that is, perhaps, of the ancient Greek heroic age. The causes of these differences in the development of ornament, the causes that made Celtic genius follow one track, and pursue to its æsthetic limits one early *motif,* while classical art went on a severer line, it is, perhaps, impossible at present to ascertain. But it is plain enough that later art has done little more than develop ideas of ornament already familiar to untutored races.

---

[226] See Schliemann's *Troja,* wherein is much learning and fancy about the Aryan Svastika.

It has been shown that the art which aims at decoration is better adapted to both the purposes and materials of savages than the art which aims at representation. As a rule, the materials of the lower savages are their own bodies (which they naturally desire to make beautiful for ever by tattooing), and the hard substances of which they fashion their tools and weapons. These hard substances, when worked on with cutting instruments of stone or shell, are most easily adorned with straight cut lines, and spirals are therefore found to be, on the whole, a comparatively late form of ornament.

We have now to discuss the efforts of the savage to represent. Here, again, we have to consider the purpose which animates him, and the materials which are at his service. His pictures have a practical purpose, and do not spring from what we are apt, perhaps too hastily, to consider the innate love of imitation for its own sake. In modern art, in modern times, no doubt the desire to imitate nature, by painting or sculpture, has become almost an innate impulse, an in-born instinct. But there must be some 'reason why' for this; and it does not seem at all unlikely that we inherit the love, the disinterested love, of imitative art from very remote ancestors, whose habits of imitation had a direct, interested, and practical purpose. The member of Parliament who mimics the crowing of a cock during debate, or the street boy who beguiles his leisure by barking like a dog, has a disinterested pleasure in the exercise of his skill; but advanced thinkers seem pretty well agreed that the first men who imitated the voices of dogs, and cocks, and other animals, did not do so merely for fun, but with the practical purpose of indicating to their companions the approach of these creatures. Such were the rude beginnings of human language: and whether that theory be correct or not, there are certainly practical reasons which impel the savage to attempt imitative art. I doubt if there are many savage races which do not use representative art for the purposes of writing—that is, to communicate information to persons whom they cannot reach by the voice, and to assist the memory, which, in a savage, is perhaps not very strong. To take examples. A savage man meets a savage maid. She does not speak his language, nor he hers. How are they to know whether, according to the marriage laws of their race, they are lawful mates for each other? This important question is settled by an inspection of their tattooed marks. If a Thlinkeet man of the Swan stock meets an Iroquois maid of the Swan stock they cannot speak to each other, and the 'gesture language' is cumbrous. But if both are tattooed with the swan, then the man knows that this daughter of the swan is not for him. He could no more marry her than Helen of Troy could have married Castor, the tamer of horses. Both are children of the Swan, as were Helen and Castor, and must regard each other as brother and sister. The case of the Thlinkeet man and the Iroquois maid is extremely unlikely to occur; but I give it as an example of the practical use among savages, of representative art.

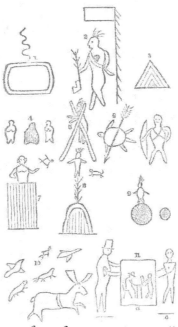

Among the uses of art for conveying intelligence we notice that even the Australians have what the Greeks would have called the σκυταλη, a staff on which inscriptions, legible to the Aborigines, are engraven. I believe, however, that the Australian σκυταλη is not usually marked with picture-writing, but with notches—even more difficult to decipher. As an example of Red Indian picture-writing we publish a scroll from Kohl's book on the natives of North America. This rude work of art, though the reader may think little of it, is really a document as important in its way as the Chaldæan clay tablets inscribed with the record of the Deluge. The coarsely-drawn figures recall, to the artist's mind, much of the myth of Manabozho, the Prometheus and the Deucalion, the Cain and the Noah of the dwellers by the great lake. Manabozho was a great chief, who had two wives that quarrelled. The two stumpy half-figures (4) represent the wives; the mound between them is the displeasure of Manabozho. Further on (5) you see him caught up between two trees—an unpleasant fix, from which the wolves and squirrels refused to

227

extricate him. The kind of pyramid with a figure at top (8) is a mountain, on which when the flood came, Manabozho placed his grandmother to be out of the water's way. The somewhat similar object is Manabozho himself, on the top of his mountain. The animals you next behold (10) were sent out by Manabozho to ascertain how the deluge was faring, and to carry messages to his grandmother. This scroll was drawn, probably on birch bark, by a Red Man of literary attainments, who gave it to Kohl (in its lower right-hand corner (11) he has pictured the event), that he might never forget the story of the Manabozhian deluge. The Red Indians have always, as far as European knowledge goes, been in the habit of using this picture-writing for the purpose of retaining their legends, poems, and incantations. It is unnecessary to say that the picture-writing of Mexico and the hieroglyphics of ancient Egypt are derived from the same savage processes. I must observe that the hasty indications of the figure used in picture-writing are by no means to be regarded as measures of the Red Men's skill in art. They can draw much better than the artist who recorded the Manabozhian legend, when they please.

In addition to picture-writing, Religion has fostered savage representative art. If a man worships a lizard or a bear, he finds it convenient to have an amulet or idol representing a bear or a lizard. If one adores a lizard or a bear, one is likely to think that prayer and acts of worship addressed to an image of the animal will please the animal himself, and make him propitious. Thus the art of making little portable figures of various worshipful beings is fostered, and the craft of working in wood or ivory is born. As a rule, the savage is satisfied with excessively rude representations of his gods. Objects of this kind—rude hewn blocks of stone and wood—were the most sacred effigies of the gods in Greece, and were kept in the dimmest recesses of the temple. No Demeter wrought by the craft of Phidias would have appeared so holy to the Phigalians as the strange old figure of the goddess with the head of a mare. The earliest Greek sacred sculptures that remain are scarcely, if at all, more advanced in art than the idols of the naked Admiralty Islanders. But this is anticipating; in the meantime it may be said that among the sources of savage representative art are the need of something like writing, and ideas suggested by nascent religion.

The singular wall-picture (Fig. 9) from a cave in South Africa, which we copy from the 'Cape Monthly Magazine,' probably represents a magical ceremony. Bushmen are tempting a great water animal—a rhinoceros, or something of that sort—to run across the land, for the purpose of producing rain. The connection of ideas is scarcely apparent to civilised minds, but it is not more indistinct than the connection between carrying a bit of the rope with which a man has been hanged and success at cards—a common French superstition. The Bushman cave-pictures, like those of Australia, are painted in black, red, and white. Savages, like the Assyrians and the early Greeks, and like children, draw animals much better than the human figure. The Bushman dog in our little engraving (Fig. 7) is all alive—almost as full of life as the dog which accompanies the centaur Chiron, in that beautiful vase in the British Museum which represents the fostering of Achilles. The Bushman wall-paintings, like those of Australia, seem to prove that savage art is capable of considerable freedom, when supplied with fitting materials. Men seem to draw better when they have pigments and a flat surface of rock to work upon, than when they are scratching on hard wood with a sharp edge of a broken shell. Though the thing has little to do with art, it may be worth mentioning, as a matter of curiosity, that the labyrinthine Australian caves are decorated, here and there, with the mark of a red hand. The same mysterious, or at least unexplained, red hand is impressed on the walls of the ruined palaces and temples of Yucatan—the work of a vanished people.

There is one singular fact in the history of savage art which reminds us that savages, like civilised men, have various degrees of culture and various artistic capacities. The oldest inhabitants of Europe who have left any traces of their lives and handiwork must have been savages. Their tools and weapons were not even formed of polished stone, but of rough-hewn flint. The people who used tools of this sort must necessarily have enjoyed but a scanty mechanical equipment, and the life they lived in caves from which they had to drive the cave-bear, and among snows where they stalked the reindeer and the mammoth, must have been very rough. These earliest known Europeans, 'palæolithic men,' as they called, from their use of the ancient unpolished stone weapons, appear to have inhabited the countries now known as France and England, before the great Age of Ice. This makes their date one of incalculable antiquity; they are removed from us by a 'dark backward and abysm of time.' The whole Age of Ice, the dateless period of the polishers of stone weapons, the arrival of men using weapons of bronze, the time which sufficed to change the climate and fauna and flora of Western Europe, lie between us and palæolithic man. Yet in him we must recognise a skill more akin to the spirit of modern art than is found in any other savage race. Palæolithic man, like other savages, decorated his weapons; but, as I have already said, he did not usually decorate them in the common savage manner with ornamental patterns. He scratched on bits of bone spirited representations of all the animals whose remains are found mixed with his own. He designed the large-headed horse of that period, and science inclines to believe that he drew the breed correctly. His sketches of the mammoth, the reindeer, the bear, and of many fishes, may be seen in the British Museum, or engraved in such works as

230

Professor Boyd Dawkins's 'Early Man in Britain.' The object from which our next illustration (Fig. 12) was engraved represents a deer, and was a knife-handle. Eyes at all trained in art can readily observe the wonderful spirit and freedom of these ancient sketches. They are the rapid characteristic work of true artists who know instinctively what to select and what to sacrifice.

Some learned men, Mr. Boyd Dawkins among them, believe that the Eskimo, that stunted hunting and fishing race of the Western Arctic circle, are descendants of the palæolithic sketchers, and retain their artistic qualities. Other inquirers, with Mr. Geikie and Dr. Wilson, do not believe in this pedigree of the Eskimo. I speak not with authority, but the submission of ignorance, and as one who has no right to an opinion about these deep matters of geology and ethnology. But to me, Mr. Geikie's arguments appear distinctly the more convincing, and I cannot think it demonstrated that the Eskimo are descended from our old palæolithic artists. But if Mr. Boyd Dawkins is right, if the Eskimo derive their lineage from the artists of the Dordogne, then the Eskimo are sadly degenerated. In Mr. Dawkins's 'Early Man' is an Eskimo drawing of a reindeer hunt, and a palæolithic sketch of a reindeer; these (by permission of the author and Messrs. Macmillan) we reproduce. Look at the vigour and life of the ancient drawing—the feathering hair on the deer's breast, his head, his horns, the very grasses at his feet, are touched with the graver of a true artist (Fig. 14). The design is like a hasty memorandum of Leech's. Then compare the stiff formality of the modern Eskimo drawing (Fig. 13). It is rather like a record, a piece of picture-writing, than a free sketch, a rapid representation of what is most characteristic in nature. Clearly, if the Eskimo come from palæolithic man, they are a degenerate race as far as art is concerned. Yet, as may be seen in Dr. Rink's books, the Eskimo show considerable skill when they have become acquainted with European methods and models, and they have at any rate a greater natural gift for design than the Red Indians, of whose sacred art the Thunderbird brooding over page 298 is a fair example. The Red Men believe in big birds which produce thunder. Quahteaht, the Adam of Vancouver's Island, married one, and this (Fig. 11) is she.

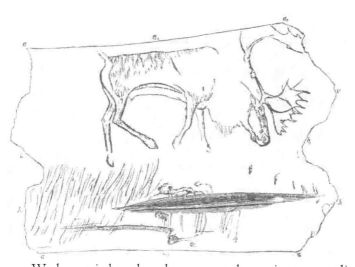

We have tried to show how savage decorative art supplied the first ideas of patterns which were developed in various ways by the decorative art of advancing civilisation. The same progress might be detected in representative art. Books, like the guide-book to ancient Greece which Pausanias wrote before the glory had quite departed, prove that the Greek temples were museums in which the development of art might be clearly traced. Furthest back in the series of images of gods came things like that large stone which was given to Cronus when he wished to swallow his infant child Zeus, and which he afterwards vomited up with his living progeny. This fetich-stone was preserved at Delphi. Next came wild bulks of beast-headed gods, like the horse-headed Demeter of Phigalia, and it seems possible enough that there was an Artemis with the head of a she-bear. Gradually the bestial characteristics dropped, and there appeared such rude anthropomorphic images of Apollo—more like South Sea idols than the archer prince—as are now preserved in Athens. Next we have the stage of semi-savage realism, which is represented by the metopes of Selinus in Sicily, now in the British Museum, and by not a few gems and pieces of gold work. Greek temples have fallen, and the statues of the gods exist only in scattered fragments. But in the representative collection of casts belonging to the Cambridge Archæological Museum, one may trace the career of Greek art backwards from Phidias to the rude idol.

'Savage realism' is the result of a desire to represent an object as it is known to be, and not as it appears. Thus Catlin, among the Red Indians, found that the people refused to be drawn in profile. They knew they had two eyes, and in profile they seemed only to have one. Look at the Selinus marbles, and you will observe that figures, of which the body is seen in profile, have the full face turned to the spectator. Again, the savage knows that an animal has two sides; both, he thinks, should be represented, but he cannot foreshorten, and he finds the profile view easiest to draw. To satisfy his need of realism he draws a beast's head full-face, and gives to the one head two bodies drawn in profile. Examples of this are frequent in very archaic Greek gems and gold work, and Mr. A. S. Murray suggests (as I understand him) that the attitude of the two famous lions, which guarded vainly Agamemnon's gate at Mycenæ, is derived from the archaic double-bodied and single-headed beast of savage realism. Very good examples of these oddities may be found in the 'Journal of the Hellenic Society,' 1881, pl. xv. Here are double-bodied and single headed birds, monsters, and sphinxes. We engrave (Fig. 15) three Greek gems from the islands as examples of savagery in early Greek art. In the oblong gem the archers are rather below the Red Indian standard of design. The hunter figured in the first gem is almost up to the Bushman mark. In his dress ethnologists will recognise an arrangement now common among the natives of New Caledonia. In the third gem the woman between two swans may be Leda, or she may represent Leto in Delos. Observe the amazing rudeness of the design, and note the modern waist and crinoline. The artists who engraved these gems on hard stone had, of necessity, much better tools than any savages possess, but their art was truly savage. To discover how Greek art climbed in a couple of centuries from this coarse and childish work to the grace of the Ægina marbles, and thence to the absolute freedom and perfect unapproachable beauty of the work of Phidias, is one of the most singular problems in the

234

history of art. Greece learned something, no doubt, from her early knowledge of the arts the priests of Assyria and Egypt had elaborated in the valleys of the Euphrates and the Nile. That might account for a swift progress from savage to formal and hieratic art; but whence sprang the inspiration which led her so swiftly on to art that is perfectly free, natural, and god-like? It is a mystery of race, and of a divine gift. 'The heavenly gods have given it to mortals.'